Data Quality for
the Information Age

For a complete listing of the *Artech House Computer Science* library
turn to the back of this book.

Data Quality for
the Information Age

Thomas C. Redman

Artech House
Boston • London

Library of Congress Cataloging-in-Publication Data
Redman, Thomas C.
  Data Quality for the information age / Thomas C. Redman.
    p.   cm.
  Includes bibliographical references and index.
  ISBN 0-89006-883-6 (alk. paper)
    1. Business—Data processing—Management.   2. Database management—
  Quality control.   3. Database design.   I. Title.
  HF5548.2.R3265   1996
  658'.05—dc21   96-37205
                                                                           CIP

British Library Cataloguing in Publication Data
Redman, Thomas C.
  Data quality for the information age
  1. Databases   2. Database management   3. Quality assurance   4. Quality control
  I. Title
  005.7'4

  ISBN 0-89006-883-6

Cover design by Jennifer Makower

© 1996 ARTECH HOUSE, INC.
685 Canton Street
Norwood, MA 02062

International Standard Book Number: 0-89006-883-6
Library of Congress Catalog Card Number: 96-37205

10 9 8 7 6 5 4 3 2 1

Chapters 7–13 are revisions of material previously published in *Data Quality: Management and Technology*

For Nancy

Contents

Acknowledgments

There is a Chinese proverb that says, "A journey of a thousand miles begins with a single step." Over the last several years, we have taken the first several steps in understanding what data are, how to manage them as business assets, and how to improve their quality. This book synthesizes the work (ideas, methods, case studies) of many people with whom I have had the pleasure of taking these first steps. I will attempt to name all of them (the critical reader will already recognize omissions as a data quality problem).

First, it was my pride and pleasure to lead the (virtual) Data Quality Laboratory at AT&T Bell Labs (now AT&T Laboratories) for many years. An eclectic, suspicious bunch, this group of men and women helped nurture the idea of applying modern approaches of quality technology and management to data and information through its infancy. They went down any number of paths, rejecting those directions that did not bear fruit and aggressively pursuing those that did. Members included Pramila Agarwala, Sig Amster, Ben Ang, Roman Antosik, Colleen Bernhard, Steve Borbash, Sandra Boyles, Marty Brilliant, Errol Caby, Cheryl Cirigliano, Pat Dean, Susan Derus, Chris Fox, Bob Gottdenker, Gersony Hildebrand, Young Huh, Pat Janenko, Yeona Jang,

Jose Joseph, F. Ron Keller, Arnold Lent, Anany Levitin, David Lubinsky, Steve Michaele, Blake Patterson, Bob Pautke, Morteza Shohrati, Gary Ulrich, Al Watkins, Ken Weiss, and Jingsheng Zheng. Many of their contributions are cited herein. Caby, Lent, Levitin, and Pautke in particular have invested considerable portions of their careers in data quality and had considerable impact on the direction of the field.

The Data Quality Lab's charter was *not* to develop the ideas of data quality. Rather, it was to help AT&T units and AT&T business partners improve and derive a business advantage. So the Data Quality Lab had the benefit of demanding, leading-edge customers, eager not just for ideas, but for their application to critical business issues. The real world can be a demanding laboratory and lots of ideas failed to pass muster. Leading-edge customers included Pat Baker, Carolyn Bekampis, Becky Bennett, Jim Colleran, Richard Drummond, Dennis Flentje (Telstra), Brian Fuller (Telstra), Sandra Fuller, and Lionel Galway (Rand Corporation—actually, Lionel became my customer after I left AT&T).

Other leading-edge customers included Tom Gardner, Rich Goldberg, Joe Gorini (now at AMP, Inc.—Joe was a customer at AT&T and also after both of us left AT&T), Bob Kotch (now at SIM Associates), Darrell Link, Kathy Marsico, Monica Mehan, Kerin Montgomery, Bob Pautke, Grant Salmon (Telstra), Phil Scanlan, June Slonim, Carol Spears, Larry Theleman, John Tomka, Anita True, Lynne Wickens (Telstra), and Scott Williamson. Baker, Bennett, Flentje, both Fullers, Gorini, Pautke, Salmon, Tomka, and Williamson have been especially influential. The success stories of customers in AT&T's Access Management organization and Telstra (the telephone giant of Australia) are retold here.

The Data Quality Lab also benefited from supportive management. I thank Luis Boza, Ed Fuchs, Jeff Hooper, Arun Netravali, Bill Scheerer, Norm Shaer, Stu Tartarone, and Ralph Wyndrum, Jr. I spent my last year at AT&T in the Chief Information Office and thank Mike Parfett and Ron Ponder for their support, also.

Personally, I've enjoyed the camaraderie and counsel of the best people in the world. Though not directly involved in data quality, they've asked the hard questions, suggested ideas, and looked for novel applications. I include Mary Allen, Tom Bean, Rich Bennett, Michele Carey, Mahmoud Daneshmand, Art Deacon, Phil DiPiazza, Patty Donohue, Paul Gandel (at Ohio University), Blan Godfrey (at the Juran Institute), Ellen Herrick, Gary Kochman, Andrew Reibman, Kathy Schierman, Greg Shaw, Rick Urso, and Randall Willie in this group. Alan Rose at Intertext Publications helped me learn to write a better book.

A group in Cambridge, Massachusetts, led by Stuart Madnick and Richard Wang of MIT and Diane Strong of Worcester Tech has been actively engaged in data quality research and we have shared ideas from time to time. A student can now pursue graduate work in data quality, and a journal devoted specifically to the subject has appeared. Similarly, a number of vendors provide tools to clean up poor data.

It is important to acknowledge that the data quality journey has been lit up by the true greats of Quality Management, especially W. Edwards Deming, Joseph Juran, and Walter Shewhart.

Finally, and most importantly, I wish to thank my family for their continued support and encouragement. My in-laws, Bud and Sue Balkin, have been terrific. So have my parents, Charlie and Joan Redman. My dad can be especially critical of ill-formed ideas. He is also masterful at adapting good ones to work in real-life circumstances.

If there is a slice of the real world that provides the best test of new ideas, it is home life. Something as mundane as getting phone messages to and from teenagers can provide a brutal test of data quality, and my family has endured (and caused) dozens of such tests. So here's to Jenn, Andy, and Greg.

And to Nancy, my wife and soulmate of 20 years, may we continue our adventures.

Foreword

A few months ago, I participated in a focus group of senior executives and quality leaders from many top international companies. One of the questions was about the most pressing challenges in quality facing their organizations today. The response from the group was almost unanimous: information quality. Global, national, and even local enterprises are driven by information. In the past few years, many companies have discovered how critical this information is to the success of their businesses. And yet, few companies have effective ways of managing the quality of this information, which is so important to their competitiveness.

Recently I watched as two passengers discovered someone already in their seats in a completely full airplane. Their boarding passes indicated the same seats as the two other passengers. The flight attendant checked both sets of boarding passes, shook her head sadly, and apologized to the two passengers. They had to get off and wait for a flight the next day. As our plane landed in New York, the flight attendant found out that the two seated passengers were on the wrong plane! They were ticketed to Washington. She confided to me that she did not even check the flight number. "Our ticketing is so frequently messed up, I didn't even think about seeing if they were on the right flight."

Several months ago, the headline stories in all the newspapers in a major eastern city were about the death of a well-loved journalist. While being treated for cancer at one of the most highly regarded hospitals, she had been given the wrong dose of medicine—four times what she should have received. The massive overdose killed her.

On the evening of January 27, 1986, there was a three-hour teleconference among managers and engineers that focused on the performance of a critical part in low temperatures. The conclusion was that there was no evidence from the data about a temperature effect. On the next morning, the space shuttle, Challenger, exploded in a huge burst of flame in front of the horrified eyes of millions of watchers around the world. After a long and thorough investigation, the presidential commission noted that a mistake in the analysis of the thermal-distress data led to failure to understand the relationship between o-ring failure and temperature.

These three examples, and thousands more like them—ranging from the merely irritating to life-and-death mistakes—all have a common cause: the failure to manage information quality. Many organizations, even those with outstanding quality management systems in many areas, have no systematic approach to information quality management.

Sometimes the correct data are not collected. The right answer is impossible, because the company doesn't have the necessary data, much less the correct information. In other cases, the data are available, but no one has "tortured the data until these data confessed." But somehow they have failed to act. They did not close the feedback loop. They knew what to do, but they didn't do it.

In many cases, the problem is somewhere in between. We fail to analyze the data we have. The analysis is lacking; key information is lost. At times we add errors to the data, to our analysis, and to our presentation. Other times we have everything we need, just not when or where we need it.

Fortunately, managing information quality is not fundamentally different from managing the quality of manufactured goods or services. The first step is to clearly define the dimensions of information quality. After we clearly understand these dimensions for a particular situation, we can discover which dimensions are important to our customers. We can then start to measure this quality.

These measurements will often lead to stunning discoveries of major opportunities to improve customer service, retention, and loyalty, or to opportunities for huge cost savings. Years ago I was involved in a large project to improve the delivery of private-line telecommunications services to customers. With the split up of the Bell System, the process of taking the orders, scheduling the installation, and delivering the service had become hopelessly complex. The process often took over 90 days, and even then many customers did not feel they received the service they had requested. A team was chartered to redesign the system. They soon found one major root cause: the order-entry process. There were so many errors in this key step that everything else was a nightmare. The customers were repeatedly called back for further information, wrong equipment was assembled, and the installers had incomplete information.

The team fixed the order-entry process and within a few months the installation time was only a few days and over 60% fewer people were needed in the process. And this was long before the word re-engineering was coined!

The basic approach to managing information quality is familiar to any one who has been involved in managing quality of either goods or services. One of the true pioneers in this area has been the author of this book, Tom Redman. His first book, *Data Quality: Management and Technology*, introduced the subject of managing an enterprise's data resource to many readers. Tom carefully defined the major dimensions of quality, explained many of the sources of variation, and discussed how data quality can be measured. But more importantly, he introduced the ideas of process management to data quality.

None of these ideas of quality management is new to experienced quality professionals, but the application of these methods to data and information is. Many leading organizations cannot even answer simple questions about data quality, such as the accuracy of their critical databases, the completeness of the database (e.g., what percent of their customers are captured), how much of their marketing budget is wasted due to data errors, how long it takes to capture recent translations, or how long it takes to answer a basic service question from a key customer. These companies are just not managing their data resources at all. In *Data Quality*, Tom described an overall data quality program. This program provided a step-by-step means for creating the quality requirements, for measuring performance, for data edits, and for database cleanups.

A few years later, Tom again advanced the state of the art in his *Sloan Management Review* article, "Opinion: Improve Data Quality for Competitive Advantage." Here he defined a model data policy and introduced the idea of treating data as a major corporate asset. His discussion of process management provided a clear guide on how to get started in managing data quality. He also provided guidance on how to design processes to make them less error prone.

In this book, Tom again advances the state of the art. We are quickly learning a great deal about managing data quality. In every company where Tom or others have worked in this area, the examples and horror stories flow like water: hospitals with errors in over 80% of medical records, retail companies with 30% errors in inventory records, international companies with 20% waste in marketing due to errors in mailing lists, millions in uncollected bills due to lost records, unrecorded shipments, and incomplete orders.

Many of the ideas and methods described in this book sound simple at first. We all know we should know the users of the information systems and their needs before defining quality, but how many organizations actually do know? We all know that information quality has many different dimensions, but have we actually done the hard work of defining them for our particular situation? We know we have to measure something before we have any chance of managing it, but do we have the necessary measurements of information quality in our organization? We also know the importance of prevention in managing quality, but do we even know the possible error sources in our information systems, much less have the quality systems in place to eliminate or minimize these errors?

For information quality, as for any other aspect of management, we must set clear goals and objectives. We must also design working quality control plans and quality improvement plans. In this book, Tom Redman gives us the concepts and methods to do this. He has made a significant contribution to quality management. He has given us the tools to get started and the means to manage a critical part of our enterprises.

Dr. A. Blanton Godfrey
Chairman and CEO
Juran Institute, Inc.

Preface

Only four types of organizations need to worry about data quality:

- those that care about their customers,
- those that care about profit and loss,
- those that care about their employees, and
- those that care about their futures.

The following example illustrates this claim in a personal way. I ask the reader to recall the last two or three times something similar happened to him or her.

The example involves our woes in checking into a hotel. It was late and my wife, Nancy, and I were exhausted. We finally found the hotel and stumbled to the front desk. My wife gave our name and the clerk typed on her keyboard. "I'm sorry," she said, "but I have no record of your reservation." In addition, she informed us, "We have no more rooms." So began a frustrating experience for us and the clerk. It also turned out to be costly for the hotel chain.

At the root of our checking-in problem was a piece of incorrect data. Somewhere, somehow, the simple fact that we had guaranteed our reservation got lost. It could be that a reservations clerk made a typing mistake, an application program erred, or a database failed momentarily.

My wife, who is very diligent about such things, informed the clerk that she was sure that she had guaranteed the room. "No," the clerk told her, "the travel agent must have made a mistake." Now Nancy, who is normally calm at such times, is also a travel agent and it was she who made these reservations. It took a few anxious moments, but she found our confirmation certificate and presented it to the clerk. I am sure the reader knows what happened next. The clerk called her supervisor, who also told my wife that "the travel agent made a mistake," and she (my wife) explained the situation again. Eventually, another phone call was placed, to headquarters I suppose, and our reservation was found. The hotel then gave us our room free for two nights to "pay for the inconvenience." All told, it took about an hour to check in.

Let's total up the consequences to the hotel:

- First, they lost a customer. My wife and I were livid. The free stay did not compensate for the inconvenience, and we will never stay with that hotel chain again.

- Second, they lost the revenue for two nights' stay (about $200). This may not seem like a lot of money, but it is 100% of potential revenue.

- Third, the clerk, a bright and eager college student, was just as frustrated as we were. Her job satisfaction was lowered.

- Fourth, my wife will steer her clients to other hotel chains whenever she has a chance. She books about 1,000 nights of hotels per year and she estimates this will cost the chain about 50 nights, say $5,000 of revenue, per year. I've told a couple of people and she has told everyone in her agency (about 10 agents), but it's hard to estimate the consequence.

This example is a small, but typical, illustration of the impact of poor data. A tiny error destroyed customer satisfaction, lost both short- and long-term revenue, and lowered employee morale. Perhaps the hotel chain does not care about such things, but I suspect it does.

Almost everyone I tell this story to can recount similar incidents. Most had not thought about poor data quality as the root cause, but quickly made the connection. Unfortunately, the evidence is clear that such incidents happen all the time. And business customers are treated no better than consumers.

It doesn't have to be this way. This book is intended for enterprises that desire to succeed in the Information Age. The only prerequisite is an open mind to consider improving data quality as a means to improve customer satisfaction, employee satisfaction, the bottom line, and their future.

But no "silver bullets" are presented here. While those who make improvements are sure to benefit, making those improvements requires hard work. Virtually everyone touches data in some way or another. Operations, including customer service, manufacturing, and so forth, create huge amounts of new data each day, data processing and information managers store and manipulate them, and virtually everyone uses them. Data created as part of a simple sales transaction one day may wind up as a key figure in a report used by the board of directors the next. Because data are so highly dynamic, it is difficult to "assign data quality" to any one group. Rather, a number of groups, including the organization's most senior leaders, those who manage processes that create and/or use data, and information professionals all must contribute.

This book is structured to meet the needs of three audiences:

- Part I aims to address the needs of those who will lead the improvement program. Hopefully senior management will provide this leadership, but businesses need leaders at all levels. Anyone can apply the lessons presented here within his or her sphere of influence. Chapter 1 makes the case that poor data quality is pervasive and costly. It builds on the anecdote presented above. Chapters 2, 3, and 4 present the key ideas leaders need to start and manage an improvement program. Issues of strategy, policy, assignment of responsibility, program management, and the like are addressed. Chapters 5 and 6 present case studies from AT&T and Telstra, the telecommunications giant in Australia. The first example shows the intimate relationships between data quality and re-engineering, and the second shows how improving data quality helps improve competitive position. These case studies illustrate the points of Chapters 1–4.

- Part II aims to address the needs of process owners who are faced with the daunting task of actually measuring data quality levels, deciding what improvements to make, making them, and sustaining the improvements. Chapter 7 is an overview of process management. Chapters 8–11 discuss statistical quality control and other techniques for applying process management to information chains, the horizontal threads by which data are created, stored, processed, and used.

- Part III aims to address the needs of information professionals and those who desire a deeper understanding of what data are, how they differ from more traditional assets, their life cycle, and quality dimensions. Parts II and III are updates of the chapters from *Data Quality:*

Management and Technology that received the best feedback. The discussion, in Chapter 12, of differences between data and other assets, is of particular importance.

- Part IV is a summary.

As a practical matter, those desiring to improve have two choices:

- They can improve data they have already collected and stored in their databases. There are any number of ways to go about doing this—I lump them into what I call the "clean-up" approach.

- They can improve processes that create new data. I call this the "process approach" to data quality.

Each approach has its place, but I am very much a process bigot for several reasons. First, it works. Improvements of an order of magnitude or more can be made and good things happen as a result. Second, the results are sustainable. Once needed improvements are made, good data are the result on an ongoing basis. And enterprises create huge amounts of new data each day. In contrast, clean-up activities, even when they work, have no impact on the quality of data to be gathered tomorrow. Third, the process approach costs considerably less to implement.

In this regard, a dirty database is very much like an unclean lake. If you need clean water, you can filter the lake. This works, although it is expensive, time-consuming, and never ends (and doesn't make the lake any more fit for fish). It is far better to find and eliminate the sources of pollution upstream. This takes a bit longer, but is less expensive and the results last (the fish like it too!).

Enterprises that already have a strong customer and process focus will find the techniques and underlying philosophy presented here readily applicable. Enterprises without such a focus will have a much more difficult time—but their need is greater!

Part I: For Leaders

Chapter 1

Why Care About Data Quality?

"I'm sorry Mr. Smith, but according to our records, you're dead."
—A customer service representative,
with any organization, any day

1.1 Introduction

In this chapter, we explain why data quality is or should be important to almost all organizations. The case for improving data quality involves three parts.

1. Poor data quality is pervasive. We gave a single example in the preface. In this chapter we show just how typical that example is and estimate current quality levels. Poor data quality is a plague to which no industry is immune—nor is government or academia.

2. Poor data quality is costly. It lowers customer satisfaction, adds expense, and makes it more difficult to run a business and pursue tactical improvements such as data warehouses and re-engineering.

Poor data quality hurts employee job satisfaction and breeds organizational mistrust. It makes it more difficult, and in some cases impossible, to pursue the enterprise's most important, long-term strategies.

3. Data quality can be improved and the impacts noted above mitigated. Indeed, it seems that improved data quality can be a source of competitive advantage.

We consider each in turn.

1.2   Poor Data Quality Is Pervasive

Most people tend not to think much about data quality. Indeed, there is a natural human reaction to think that "if it's in the computer, it must be right." But this intuition is just plain wrong. Three streams of evidence support the claim that poor data quality is pervasive. These are personal experience, newspaper and other popular accounts, and careful studies. It is usually not a good idea to place too much weight on personal experiences. They're included here to encourage the reader to expand his or her intuition about data quality by catalyzing recollection of similar situations in which he or she was personally involved. Once they think about it, most people will recall similar incidents.

Indeed, most people can recall several recent incidents. In addition to the hotel check-in story, I was personally impacted by at least four other instances of poor data quality in the past 12 months.

-   A company that read x-rays for a hospital sent an unpaid bill to a collection agency, which in turn sent me a collection notice. When I checked my files, I found that my insurance company had paid the bill. It took hours for me and the x-ray firm to straighten this out.

-   The bank that lent me the money for the last car I bought sent me a notice reminding me that I hadn't satisfied their insurance requirement. My address and the car model and year were wrong on the notice. I followed up and was not surprised to learn that they had incorrectly entered my insurance information into their computer. I can only hope that they properly credit my payment each month.

-   My alma mater sent me a letter urging me "as a letterman, to contribute to the Athletic Department." I'm always flattered when people ask me for money, but I am not a letterman.

- I received a check from a telecommunications company thanking me for signing up. I checked. I had not signed up and, luckily, in the chaos of telecommunications marketing, I had not been "slammed." In addition, the check they sent was addressed incorrectly. But it cleared.

These incidents come from the travel, health care, financial services, academic, and telecommunications fields. As I noted, similar situations have impacted almost everyone. My favorite example involves the student who worked for a division of taxation in another country. His rebate check was addressed "To The Estate Of. . . ." He took it to his bank, but it refused to cash the check. Evidently there are rules that prohibit dead people from cashing checks.

The second stream of evidence is the incidents reported by others. Many such accounts have appeared in newspapers and trade magazines. Data quality issues occur in many areas, including the medical profession [1], credit-reporting industry [2], financial services [3], scanning data [4], economic data [5], billing [6], and even publication of lottery numbers [7]. One unfortunate example involved a negative sign (–) being dropped, turning a $1.3B loss into a $1.3B gain, making an error of $2.6B [3]. *Datamation* [8] noted that poor data quality was among the most difficult problems to solve in implementing data warehouses.

There is a temptation to dismiss the data quality problem as consisting only of a series of anecdotes. But the anecdotes are just too numerous and involve every segment of the economy. A good summary article appeared in the *Wall Street Journal* [9]. The *WSJ* article cited a study by MIT researchers in which over half of 50 companies surveyed reported that their data were less than 95% accurate. *Computerworld* [10] and *InformationWeek* [11] conducted surveys of large businesses and concluded that the majority of businesses are plagued by data quality problems.

The incidents and surveys noted are supplemented by a number of carefully conducted and controlled studies [12–19]. These confirm the general thrust of the personal examples and trade accounts. Indeed, poor data quality appears the norm rather than the exception.

Estimating actual quality levels is difficult. Error rates between 1% and 75% are reported. It should be noted that there are at least two different ways of counting errors—at the so-called "record" and "field" levels. When counted at the field level, the error rate is the number of erred records divided by the total number of records. At the record level, a record is counted as erred if any field is in error and the error rate is the number of erred records divided by the total number of records. Obviously record-level error rates are higher than field-level error rates (see Figure 1.1). The field-level measurement is more basic, but for

	field 1	field 2	field 3	field 4	field 5
record 1					
record 2			X		
record 3		X		X	
record 4					
record 5					
record 6	X				
record 7					
record 8					
record 9				X	
record 10	X				

Figure 1.1   In this example, there are 10 records with five fields each. Fields marked with an **X** are in error. There are six errors in the 50 fields, so the field error rate is 6/50 = 12%. Five records have at least one error, so the record error rate is 5/10 = 50%.

some purposes the record-level measurement is more appropriate. Counted at the field level, the error rate for a typical database on which data quality is not being actively addressed is between 1% and 5%. For individual fields within the database, the error rates vary considerably. Error rates from .5% to 30% are not atypical.

Now, let's consider the impact.

1.3   Poor Data Quality Impacts Business Success

1.3.1   Poor Data Quality Lowers Customer Satisfaction

Poor data quality makes it much more difficult to satisfy customers. Many problems involve situations where the data are ancillary to the product or service provided. Billing is a good example. All customers expect to be billed properly. And they aren't very forgiving of billing errors. In fact, many customers assume that billing is "the easy part" and if "they can't get my bill correct, how can I expect them to fill my order properly?" You can't earn a customer's trust when the bill is wrong. And so it is with many other data errors. In a significant number of the incidents related in Section 1.2, data are only a fractional component of the product supplied or service performed. My experience checking into the hotel and the data details of my car loan are two more examples. In such cases, poor data quality is a customer *dissatisfier.* You can't delight the customer, but you certainly can't turn him or her off.

Of course, in many situations data are the essence of the product or service, not an ancillary component such as the bill. This is certainly the case in credit reporting, financial services, and publication of lottery numbers. If customers expect correct bills, they positively demand that these data be correct.

In many of our examples, the customer has been a consumer. The satisfaction of business customers is also impacted. In particular, the quality movement has encouraged companies to view its key customers and suppliers as partners. The mistrust that poor data quality breeds is even greater among partners and can sour otherwise good working relationships. Further, the failings of one may impact the customer's view of the other. The car company that sold me my last car and the company that financed it are partners, and the finance company's incompetence colors my opinion of the car company. Building on customer satisfaction is the long-term business strategy of customer intimacy [20]. Companies that pursue the discipline of customer intimacy must know more about their customers—who they are, where they live, what their problems are, what they want, what their past purchases were, and so forth. This can involve hundreds or thousands of individual pieces of data. But you simply can't build an intimate relationship when the data are wrong. One of my neighbors recently reported that he had received an exciting offer to become a customer of a leading company that is pursuing a strategy of customer intimacy. The offer discounted prices substantially. There were only two problems. First, he was already a customer. And second, they sent their offer to the wrong address (the post office managed to deliver the offer anyway). "How," he asked, "can I work with a company that doesn't even know where I live?"

It is essential that companies that wish to satisfy their customers in the short run or pursue a business strategy of customer intimacy create and sustain extremely high levels of data quality.

1.3.2 Poor Data Quality Leads to High and Unnecessary Costs

In the early 1980s, American business made its first response to the Japanese quality levels: "Well, of course, you can have higher quality. It just costs a lot more." Recent years have proven this statement false. It is almost always less costly to produce a product or service correctly the first time and minimize the costs associated with rework, warranty, repair, and so forth. This principle seems to hold in practically every industry group.

High and unnecessary costs are characteristic of poor data quality as well. We can see such costs in each of the examples above. The immediate costs in the "hotel story" exceed any revenue that could be expected. Immediate costs in the "medical example" are even greater as percentage of revenue. In some cases, of course, the immediate costs are fairly minor. Despite my frustration with the bank, their only immediate costs were the costs of sending me letters, the time it took to correct their records, and the time their clerk spent with me on the phone. The newspaper that occasionally publishes an incorrect lottery number only loses a few subscribers (those holding tickets they later learned to be winners and those who were embarrassed when trying to cash losers).

In large organizations, most of the cost of poor data quality is effectively hidden by the accounting system. Responding to customer complaints is just part of customer service. Inspecting and correcting erred data, passed from one organization to the next, is usually not measured, as the organization receiving bad data simply views checking and correcting them as part of the job, without realizing the total cost to the enterprise. Regarding billing, most companies have the equivalent of an accounts receivable organization, whose job it is to ensure that bills received are correct, make any changes needed, and render payment. Two-thirds or more of the cost of this operation may stem directly from poor bills. Billing departments are impacted from both sides. On the one hand, they must haggle with unhappy customers over the bills they rendered. On the other hand, they receive incorrect data from (say) Order Entry and Shipping, so they must find and correct such errors as well. And neither is captured by most accounting systems.

Poor data quality adds expense in at least two other ways: First, it leads the organization to have more data than it needs—for example, I once visited a large manufacturer that had two redundant and discrepant databases, each owned by a different department. Each department knew that it would be best to have only one database for the entire facility, but neither trusted the other's data. So they each developed and maintained their own database. Unfortunately, neither was particularly adept at creating good data, so both databases were poor. Second, poor data quality makes it more expensive to adopt new technologies. The *Datamation* article [8] estimates that up to 50% of the cost in implementing a data warehouse is due to poor data quality.

It is difficult to estimate the total cost due to poor data quality at the organizational level. I know of three careful studies of the cost of rework, not including the costs of customer dissatisfaction and other costs. All are proprietary, so any details that might reveal where they were conducted are not presented. The results are as follows.

- Study 1: The direct cost to one organization to accommodate errors in data it received from a second organization was 6% of its total budget.

- Study 2: The estimated cost to one company of poor customer data was 6–14% of its revenue.

- Study 3: The estimated cost due to poor data associated with one major operation in a third company was 3–6% of revenue.

A good, although I believe conservative, rule of thumb is that without an active data quality program in place, the cost of poor data quality to a medium to large size enterprise is 10% of revenue.

1.3.3   Poor Data Quality Lowers Job Satisfaction and Breeds Organizational Mistrust

Poor data quality lowers job satisfaction. Customer service representatives and others on the front line who must deal with customers who are angry, upset, and confused are especially impacted. Customer service representatives have some of the most demanding jobs in most companies and it is unfair to add the impact of poor data to their load. But most companies, such as the hotel chain, do just that.

Just as customers mistrust companies that cannot get simple data correct, so too do internal organizations learn to mistrust one another. Two good examples were noted in Section 1.3.2. The first involved Billing and Order Entry. It is inconceivable that the Billing Department thinks highly of Order Entry. The second was the manufacturing facility with two overlapping databases, each owned and operated by a separate organization. It's hard to imagine that these two organizations will ever work together productively.

1.3.4   Poor Data Quality Impacts Decision Making

Poor data quality makes it difficult to run the business, day to day [21]. The comments of one executive, frustrated by inaccurate data, illustrate this point very well. "In our corporation, each unit makes P/L commitments to the chair. In the fall, we get agreements on those commitments for the following year. Then we develop and implement plans to meet those commitments. And early each month, we get summaries of the previous month's and year-to-date progress toward those commitments. So if we're not on target, say, in February, I can adjust my strategy to meet my commitment. But I don't really get January results in early February—for example, I simply don't know what my true expenses are. Instead, I get an estimate or forecast. Let's suppose the January forecasts show I'm on track. January actuals trickle in for many months. Not until July, do I close the books on January. Sometimes in July I'll receive a real January expense that is nowhere near the forecast. Now I'm way off track in meeting commitments, and, since half the year is gone, I have virtually no chance of adjusting my strategy in any significant way. Of course, I may get lucky. The February actuals, which I finally close in August, may make up the difference. And I may even exceed my commitment. But even when I'm lucky, this is no way to run a business." Decision making, by its very nature, involves risk. At the very least, poor data increase that risk.

Recent advances in database technology, the so-called "data warehouses," together with powerful "data-mining" software, promise to bring the power of modern information technology (IT) to decision making. Data warehouses and data mining will allow decision makers to routinely analyze data in new and clever ways to better understand customer needs, reduce costs, and find new sources of value. While we cannot be certain what the impact of poor data quality in such situations will be, the signs are not good. One tenet of modern quality management is that you shouldn't automate a poor quality process. So, implementation of data warehouses with current data quality levels is, at best, very risky.

1.3.5   Poor Data Quality Impedes Re-engineering

Re-engineering is one of the most popular techniques available to business leaders to completely rebuild business processes, enabling heretofore unheard of levels of productivity and customer satisfaction. Any number of good books describe the basic methods [22, 23]. And re-engineering has produced some spectacular successes. But a very high fraction of re-engineering projects fail. Projects fail for many reasons. The Gartner Group [24] reported that poor data quality is one of the most important reasons for projects to fail. This makes perfect sense. In many re-engineering projects the whole point is to get the right data in the right place at the right time so someone can do something for a customer. But if the data that arrive in the right place at the right time are themselves wrong, the operation simply will not serve the customer.

While Mike Hammer, the "father of re-engineering," does not specifically mention data quality, it is interesting that a majority of the cases cited in *The Re-engineering Revolution* [25] involve data quality in one way or another.

1.3.6 Poor Data Quality Hinders Long-Term Business Strategy

Companies that wish to be excellent are almost required to have very high data quality. Treacy and Weirsma, in their landmark book, *The Discipline of Market Leaders* [20], describe the three strategies that their research suggests are associated with excellence. All require outstanding data. Companies pursuing a strategy of customer intimacy require high-quality customer data so they can gain insights into the customer's next need. If they are pursuing a strategy of operational excellence, they can't afford the costs associated with poor data. Companies that pursue a strategy of product excellence depend on data in more subtle ways. More and more of the value of their product is in data and information. Poor data quality compromises this source of value.

I wish to build on the theme of data and information as new sources of value a bit further. Futurists argue that the Information Age has reached maturity [26–29]. They point to the penetration of computing and telecommunications capabilities, the declining numbers of people employed in agriculture and manufacturing, and the similarities in the progress of the Agrarian and Industrial Ages. They use chains such as this:

DATA——->INFORMATION——->KNOWLEDGE——->WISDOM

and note that progressively greater insights (and sources of value) are obtained higher up the chain. While I personally think the futurists are a bit optimistic (but I hope I'm wrong) about our progress, their point underscores the need for high-quality data. Ultimately, information (and knowledge, etc.) is derived from data. So high-quality information can only come from high-quality data. Those who desire to work up this chain must first ensure that the data are of high enough quality.

1.3.7 Data Fill the White Space on the Organization Chart

Enterprises reorganize continually. They have to. The landscape changes so quickly and responding requires different alignments. Corporations reorganize to better interface with customers, promote core competencies, and respond to competitive pressures. New forms, such as self-managed work teams and networked organizations, and old forms in new guises (matrix management) are being invented, tried, and incorporated or discarded. The data structures are much more stable. However, even when it reorganizes, the enterprise does not immediately change its data about customers, inventory levels, and so forth.

1.3.8   The Enabling Role of Information Technology

IT has been spectacularly successful in automating many operations. And the technology continues to advance in a seemingly infinite number of directions. But the advances of IT have and will continue to exacerbate the impact of poor data quality. First, technology makes data available to more people. Those who are unfamiliar with what the data mean or how they were produced are especially prone to misunderstanding and are easily victimized by bad data. This is exacerbated by the natural human tendency to assume that "if it's in the computer, it must be right." These problems can grow as data warehouses are implemented. And the Internet offers the possibility of expanding such problems to a truly global scale. IT organizations often reflect the impact of poor data in a microcosm. Such organizations often bear the added costs to clean up bad data. Their reputations may suffer when the data are poor. Just as it is natural to assume that computerized data are correct, so too is it natural to blame the IT organization when data are poor. These problems are only going to get worse unless aggressive steps to improve data quality are taken.

1.4   Data Quality Can Be a Unique Source of Competitive Advantage

Those who have improved data quality have been able to mitigate many of these impacts and obtain a measurable source of sustainable advantage [6, 11, 19, 30]. Two case studies are presented in Chapters 5 and 6. The possibilities go far beyond simply eliminating the negatives. Why not:

- Focus on customer data to improve customer interactions and create a source of advantage?
- Reduce costs due to poor data quality and use the resultant high-quality data to find new sources of savings?
- Use data to build a sense of community and continuity into the entire enterprise?
- Define streamlined decision-making processes that push decision making down?

- Use improved data quality to suggest opportunities to re-engineer? As presented in Chapter 5, this is just what AT&T Access Financial Assurance organization did.

- Empower the strategy by making data quality improvement the first (and essential) step to achieving customer intimacy, operational efficiency, or product leadership?

- Create the basis for a smarter company by focusing first on data, the root of all information and knowledge?

Data are a wonderful means to create a sustainable advantage. They (data) are a unique asset and their advantage lies in that uniqueness (we'll explore this uniqueness in detail in Chapter 12). Consider customer data. Clearly, customer data are a virtual treasure chest—rich with insights into customers' behavior and individual needs. And the data values are highly dynamic. They renew themselves with each transaction. Each time a customer buys something, uses your service, or even calls to complain, the data asset grows. The marginal cost of obtaining that data is literally nothing, since it is a necessary part of operations. Using data does not consume them—they are reusable to an unlimited degree. Data are probably the only asset that is uniquely owned by a company. The competition simply cannot match your data, since they have not had the same transactions with the customer that you did. In contrast, the people asset grows in knowledge and experience rather slowly, and putting someone on one project means he or she can't work on another. The competition can purchase the same technology you do, observe and respond to your marketing efforts, and take apart and reverse engineer your products. They can hire your employees, benchmark your processes (*especially if they are good!*), and read about your strategy in the trade literature. Obviously, you can't ignore advanced technology; clever marketing; brilliant strategy; and superior products, processes, and employees. But it is difficult to create advantages using these assets and even more difficult to sustain them. Why not use your data?

1.5 Summary

Poor data quality is seen to be an almost universal problem, impacting all segments of the economy: companies, governments, and academia and their customers. Numerous examples and studies confirm this conclusion. There is a considerable range of error rates, although 1–5% appears to be typical. The associated costs are enormous. We estimate that the immediate cost stemming from the 1–5% error rate is about 10% of revenue. Customers and employees are impacted through poor service, billing, and inconvenience. Poor data quality also hinders decision making and makes it more difficult to take advantage of new technologies. Finally, companies cannot pursue their most important strategies in the face of poor data. We now turn our attention to what to do about it.

REFERENCES

[1]   Kolata, G., "New Frontier in Research: Mining Patterns from Data," *New York Times,* August 9, 1994, pp. A19–21.

[2]   "TRW Sued Over Credit Reports," *Asbury Park Press,* July 12, 1991, p. D7.

[3]   "Accountant Blamed by Fidelity," *Asbury Park Press,* January 5, 1995, p. C10.

[4]   Garry, M., "How's Your Scan Data?" *Progressive Grocer,* October 1992, pp. 83–90.

[5]   Hershey, R. D., "US Is Considering a Large Overhaul of Economic Data," *New York Times,* January 16, 1995, pp. A1 and D3.

[6]   Redman, T. C., "Opinion: Improve Data Quality for Competitive Advantage," *Sloan Management Review,* Vol. 36, No. 2, Winter 1995, pp. 99–107.

[7]   Tuers, R. J., "Sorry, Wrong Numbers," *Asbury Park Press,* November 19, 1995, p. C3.

[8]   Celko, J., "Don't Warehouse Dirty Data," *Datamation,* October 15, 1995, pp. 42–52.

[9]   Bulkeley, W. M., "Databases Are Plagued by a Reign of Error," *Wall Street Journal,* May 26, 1992, p. B.6.

[10]   Knight, B., "The Data Pollution Problem," *Computerworld,* September 28, 1992, pp. 81–84.

[11]   Wilson, L., "The Devil in Your Data," *InformationWeek,* August 1992, pp. 48–54.

[12]   Ballou, D. P., and G. K. Tayi, "Methodology for Allocating Resources for Data Quality Enhancements," *Communications of the ACM,* Vol. 32, 1989, pp. 320–329.

[13] Johnson, J. R., R. A. Leitch, and J. Neter, "Characteristics of Errors in Accounts Receivables and Inventory Audits," *Accounting Review*, Vol. 56, 1981, pp. 270–293.

[14] Laudon, K. C., "Data Quality and Due Process in Large Interorganizational Record Systems," *Communications of the ACM*, Vol. 29, 1986, pp. 4–18.

[15] Morey, R. C., "Estimating and Improving Quality of Information in an MIS," *Communications of the ACM*, Vol. 25, 1982, pp. 337–342.

[16] O'Neill, E. T., and D. Vizine-Goetz, "Quality Control in On-line Databases," in M. E. Williams (ed.), *Annual Review of Information, Science, and Technology*, Vol. 23, 1988, pp. 125–156.

[17] Liepens, G. E., R. S. Garfinkel, and A. S. Kunnathur, "Error Localization for Erroneous Data: A Survey," *TIMS/Studies in Management Science*, Vol. 19, 1982, pp. 205–219.

[18] Sly, K. J., and A. Robbin, "Federal Statistical Policies and Programs: How Good Are the Numbers?" in M. E. Williams (ed.), *Annual Review of Information, Science, and Technology*, Vol. 25, 1990, pp. 3–54.

[19] Barstow, R., "Centel Bashes Database Errors," *Telephony*, Vol. 28, January 1991, pp. 36–39.

[20] Treacy, M., and F. Wiersema, *The Discipline of Market Leaders,* Reading, MA: Addison-Wesley, 1995.

[21] Nayer, M., "Achieving Information Integrity: A Strategic Imperative," *Information Systems Management*, Vol. 10, No. 2, pp. 51–58.

[22] Davenport, T. H., *Process Innovation Reengineering Work through Information Technology*, Boston, MA: Harvard Business School Press, 1993.

[23] Hammer, M., and J. Champy, *Reengineering the Corporation: A Manifesto for Business Revolution*, New York: HarperCollins, 1993.

[24] Light, M., "Data Pollution Can Choke Business Process Reengineering," *Inside Gartner Group This Week*, Vol. 23, April 1993, pp. 5–6.

[25] Hammer, M., and S. Stanton, *The Reengineering Revolution*, New York: HarperCollins, 1995.

[26] Davis, S., and B. Davidson, *2020 Vision*, New York: Simon & Schuster, 1991.

[27] Tapscott, D., *The Digital Economy: Promise and Peril in the Age of Networked Intelligence*, New York: McGraw-Hill, 1996.

[28] Davis, S., and J. Botkin, *The Monster Under the Bed,* New York: Simon & Schuster, 1994.

[29] Drucker, P., *The New Realities*, New York: Harper & Row, 1989.

[30] Fuller, B. J., and T. C. Redman, "Data Quality: Lessons Learned at Telecom Australia," *Proc. QUALCON 94,* November 13–16, 1994, Melbourne, Australia, pp. 379–386.

Chapter **2**

Strategies for Improving Data Accuracy

"The river Rhine, it is well known
Doth wash your city of Cologne
But tell me, nymphs! what power divine
Shall henceforth wash the river Rhine?"
                                        —Coleridge

2.1   Introduction

The task facing an enterprise desiring to improve its data quality can be daunting. Even relatively small enterprises may have enormous quantities of data spread over several databases owned by different organizations and employing different technologies. And vendors promise that new technologies, such as data warehouses, object-oriented databases, and fourth-generation tools will greatly increase the quantity of data available and enable a whole new class of decision-support processes.

In Part I of this book we explain how, faced with such a daunting task, an enterprise can develop and implement an overall data quality program. Good data quality plans satisfy the following criteria.

1. They should focus on the most important data. Here "most important" means those data that are most critical to the enterprise's business strategies.

2. They should be "customer-driven." This means data should meet the needs of users or customers. Here a "customer" may be a real (paying) customer or an internal customer. Even though customers may not always be able to articulate clear objectives, the data quality program should be customer-driven.

3. The gains should be sustainable. Nothing is less satisfying than completing a two-year data clean-up only to find, six months later, that the major data quality issues have returned and, consequently, the business is now a year behind in its plans to implement a major strategy.

4. The plan should clearly define management responsibilities, both for actual improvements and for overall program administration.

Thus, a good data quality program will consist of four interrelated components.

- Clear business direction, objectives, and goals.
- Management infrastructure that properly assigns responsibilities for data and ensures that those responsible have the tools needed to succeed.

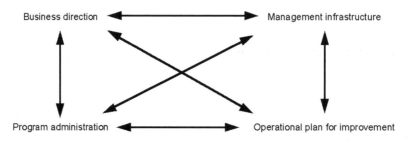

Figure 2.1   A good data quality program consists of four interrelated components.

- An operational plan for improvement. Essentially this plan specifies which improvement methods are to be applied to which data.

- Program administration.

As Figure 2.1 depicts, the four components are interrelated. For example, business strategy dictates which data are to be improved and the operational plan dictates how to make the improvements. We began in Chapter 1 with a discussion of business considerations motivating the need for improved data. We continue, in this chapter, with the operational plan. We start with needed background about data, data quality, and improvement options. We then show how to employ these options in three situations.

- The "one database" case in which the focus is on a single database. This situation is one that smaller enterprises or individual departments within larger enterprises find most relevant.

- The "two database" case in which data in two databases overlap and quality issues such as inconsistency between the two databases arise. Obviously this situation may be extended to any number of overlapping databases and this situation is the one that many large enterprises will find most relevant.

- Migrating data from any number of databases to a data warehouse. This situation is relevant to those considering data warehouses.

2.2 Background

2.2.1 Quality, Data, and Data Quality

We'll discuss what data are, model their life cycle, and define their quality dimensions in detail in Part III. Here we provide a brief sketch of the few points most important to leaders of enterprises.

First, while there are many definitions of quality, we will use the following operational definition here: A datum or collection of data X is of *higher (or better) quality* than a datum or collection of data Y if X meets customer needs better than Y. Note that the operational definition implies that data quality is inherently subjective. The customer or customers are the final arbiters of quality. Their needs continually evolve and they are not always able to articulate their needs clearly. And two customers may have needs that conflict.

In general though, there are certain things that all customers seem to want from data.

- They want the data to be relevant for their use.
- They want the data to be correct and they want a minimum of inconsistencies. They want the most up-to-date data possible.
- They want to get or see the data in ways that are best suited to their applications.
- They want easy access to needed data.
- They want their data to be secure and private.

It is convenient to group quality dimensions into four categories: those, such as relevancy, that concern the *data model* or aspect of reality that the data capture; those, such as accuracy, that concern *data values*; those that involve *data presentation*; and those that involve the performance of *information technology* (IT) used to store, move, and manage the data. Note the distinction among quality requirements such as accuracy, relevancy, and currency, which pertain to the data per se, and requirements such as privacy and security, which pertain to information technology used to store and manage the data. Our concern here is with those dimensions that pertain to the data themselves. Most enterprises pay far greater attention to the IT than they do to the data, so customers may not be able to distinguish quality dimensions associated with IT from those associated with data. We'll discuss the specific dimensions of data quality in detail in Chapter 13.

A fifth category of data quality requirements is those at the enterprise level. For example, enterprises may require a certain amount of data redundancy for security or backup. A greater or lesser amount is indicative of an enterprise-level data quality issue. The next important point involves the flow of data into the enterprise, among organizations that create and use data, and back out of the enterprise. Indeed, data are incredibly dynamic. Many, if not all, transactions with customers and many internal operations create new data values. And the new data wind their way throughout the enterprise. Data created by Order Entry are passed to Shipping, which uses those data and adds some of its own. Then the data are passed to Billing and Marketing, each of which has its own uses of the data it receives and adds more. This sequence can continue almost indefinitely. For example, Marketing may "sell" the data to a clearinghouse, which "sells" the data to a host of other organizations. We call data and information flows, such as the one noted above, "information chains."[1] Properly managed, they are akin to the "value chains" favored by Michael Porter [1]. Tom Davenport [2] (though he does not use the term "information chain") argues that managing such chains and the information culture is a Chief Information Officer's primary function.

The implications are as follows: First, a view of data as "the stuff stored in a database" is naive. Managing data and their quality is not akin to database management nor, since they generally have little influence on sources, are managers of databases equipped to make many sustainable improvements. Second, data must be managed "horizontally" as a series of hand-offs, manipulations, and creations of new data. Finally, business processes that create new data, themselves steps in the information chains, are of critical importance to data quality improvement. Third, newer data tend to be more interesting and valuable than older data. For example, customers who recently made a purchase are more likely to make a subsequent purchase than those who haven't purchased anything in two years. An enterprise is more likely to market to recent purchasers, so their data are more interesting and valuable.

That said, important data can also have enormously long lifetimes. For example, a person's DATE-OF-BIRTH and BIRTHPLACE are determined at birth. Such data are historical facts and (almost) never change. Many historical facts become uninteresting after a short time. The grade you earned in sixth grade math class probably is such an example. But importantly, it is often difficult to predict whether data will be useful in the future. So there is a tendency in most enterprises to hold onto them.

Over the years any number of approaches to improving data quality have been developed and employed in various situations. In subsequent sections we review the main features of major approaches, cite their advantages and disadvantages, and note when their use is appropriate. The essence of crafting an appropriate operational plan lies in developing a detailed understanding of the situation at hand, dividing the overall problem into small pieces, and using the most appropriate approach to address each piece.

We should note that organizations can adopt a laissez faire approach—that is, do no more than the enterprise is already doing. This approach is usually not the same as doing nothing at all. Most enterprises, as discussed in Chapter 1, deal with incorrect data all the time—when customers call to complain, when shipments don't arrive when they should, when bills they receive are incorrect. Current quality levels and associated costs are the baseline against which other approaches should be measured.

---

1.   We also use the term "data-creating process" to denote the portion(s) of an information chain in which data are created.

The field of quality management recognizes three basic approaches to achieving quality [3–6].

- Inspection and rework. Here products are inspected for conformance to standards and rejected items are discarded or reworked until they pass inspection. As applied to data, this approach is called *error detection and correction* or *database clean-up*.
- Process control and improvement. The goal in this approach is to identify and eliminate root causes of errors.
- Process design. The focus is on making the process less error prone at the design stage.

In practice, most quality programs employ all approaches to some extent. Higher quality levels and lower total costs are obtained with the more advanced methods. We examine each of these basic approaches, as applied to data, in turn.

2.2.2   Choice 1: Error Detection and Correction

First, we consider error detection and correction. Interestingly, the laissez faire approach is a form of error detection and correction. Customers and others detect the errors and the enterprise tries to correct them, often while in contact with the customer. As noted, error rates and total costs are the highest.

There are several other methods to detect and correct errors. The simplest and most basic method is to *compare data values with their real-world counterparts*. An employer can, for example, survey employees each year to verify their work locations and home addresses. And if employees take the survey seriously, such a procedure can work well. But comparing data to their real-world counterparts is expensive and time-consuming. It can be embarrassing if the technique must be applied repeatedly. And, of course, comparing data to the real world does not help prevent further errors. It is often appropriate to apply this technique on a sample basis. Done carefully, it can yield precise estimates of error rates at low cost. This is especially valuable in determining where a new data quality program should be focused and, later, in verifying improvements.

A second approach to error detection and correction involves comparing records from two or more databases. This method is sometimes called *database bashing*. Instead of taking the time and expense to compare records to their real-world counterparts, records of interest in the database are compared to their counterparts in the second database. The procedure is easily extended to many databases. Data that agree are assumed to be correct. Those data that do not agree are flagged for further investigation and correction.

The principal advantage of database bashing is that it is fairly easy to manage and one-time costs are often reasonable. It does a decent (but far from perfect) job in detecting errors when two or more overlapping and independent databases are available. Correcting errors may be more difficult (this difficulty also plagues data editing, discussed in the following text). Having identified that two records disagree, it is much harder to determine the correct value (bear in mind that both may be wrong). If one value is obviously wrong (missing or out-of-range), one can assume the other value to be correct, although this is risky. Survey practitioners sometimes use a method called imputation [7–11], but this process is generally not acceptable for business purposes. Often, it is best to check flagged fields with their real-world counterparts to determine the correct value.

Aside from difficulties in making corrections, database bashing has four principal disadvantages: First, the assumption that data that agree are correct is not usually warranted. Second, the data used to match up records may themselves be erred, making the required matching difficult. Third, database bashing does not prevent future errors. Finally, it is easy to get into the habit of employing database bashing on an ongoing basis. For example, an Accounts Payable Department may find that a significant fraction of the bills it receives are erred. As a result, it may build a parallel database to generate "predicted bills," which are then compared with supplier bills. This is database bashing in an insidious, expensive, and dangerous form.

Data edits are computerized routines, which verify whether data values and/or their representations satisfy predetermined constraints. Such constraints are sometimes called business rules [12] and they can be very simple or quite sophisticated, involving:

- A single data field. For example, "the data values must be an element of the domain {0,1,2, . . . ,10}.
- More than one field. For example, "the ZIP CODE and AREA CODE must not conflict." In this example, ZIP CODE = 90210 (California) and AREA CODE = 908 (New Jersey) would raise a flag.
- Probability. For example, the combination SEX = FEMALE and HEIGHT = 78 inches is an unlikely one and might be flagged.

Data edits may be applied to an entire database or as a screen or filter within a process or information chain. In the latter case, they can be used to control and improve process performance or to make a process less error prone. In these situations, they fall into the second or third major category of approach to quality improvement and are discussed in those contexts in Sections 2.2.3 and 2.2.4.

As applied to a database clean-up, the first step is to define the edits. This can be an exciting task. As the number of fields grows, the number of possible edits grows exponentially (for a full discussion, see [13–16]), so it takes a lot of effort to develop a good set. These are then applied to the database and possible discrepancies are flagged for further investigation and correction. Sophisticated edits often give good clues about which data must be corrected. For example, consider the combination ZIP CODE = 70760, AREA CODE = 908, STATE = NJ. As AREA CODE and STATE do not conflict, and ZIP CODE conflicts with both, one might conclude that ZIP CODE is the erred field. Further, a simple transposition of the first two digits in ZIP CODE would yield ZIP CODE = 07760, a valid New Jersey zip, and the conflict is eliminated.

Database clean-ups using data edits have two advantages. First, in many cases they do help eliminate inconsistencies. Second, they are usually easier and less costly to implement than database bashing. In many cases, the edits may be developed at the same time the data requirements are developed [17].

This approach also has several distinct disadvantages. First, and most importantly, like other methods of error detection and correction, it does not yield sustainable improvements. Second, data edits promise *integrity*, or conformance to business rules. But data integrity does *not* guarantee data accuracy. In the example above, there is absolutely no proof that the ZIP CODE was the erred field, that the correction was proper, or that the other fields were correct. Finally, it is tempting to employ data clean-ups based on editing on an ongoing basis; but, like database bashing, this is dangerous and expensive.

To summarize the discussion about error detection and correction, the basic idea is to compare data to something, flag discrepancies, and make corrections. There are many sources of comparison. The real world, other data, and business rules are all legitimate sources. Correcting errors is usually more difficult. Such methods should not be the mainstay of a data quality program, because they do not prevent future errors. They are especially ineffective on data that are created or changed rapidly. And these data are usually the most critical. It is especially important that error detection and correction not be employed on an ongoing basis, as they are too expensive and give a false sense of security that data are accurate. But these methods may play important niche roles in the data quality overall program. Used once and properly focused, database bashing and clean-ups using edits are often appropriate for data that have long lifetimes and do not change. BIRTHDATE is a good example. Similarly comparing data to the real world is occasionally appropriate. Table 2.1 presents a summary of pros and cons of these methods and those discussed in the next two sections.

Method	Improvement		Total Cost		When Appropriate
	Short-term	Long-term	Short-term	Long-term	
Laissez faire	Low	Low	High	High	Unimportant data
Compare to real world, one time	High	Low	High	High	To estimate current quality levels—certain critical business problems
Compare to real world, ongoing	High	High	High	Very High	Never
Database bashing, one time	Medium	Low	Medium	High	On data that are replaced slowly, when a second DB is available
Database bashing, ongoing	Medium	Medium	Medium	Very High	Never
Clean-up using edits, one time	Medium	Low	Medium	High	On data that are replaced slowly
Clean-ups using edits, ongoing	Medium	Medium	Medium	High	Never
Process control and improvement	Medium	High	Medium	Low	On all data that are created and/or replaced at high rates
Process design to make error proof	Medium	High	Medium	Very Low	Every time a process or information chain is designed, re-engineered

Table 2.1 A summary of the main methods to improve data quality, the expected benefits in terms of quality improvement, total cost, and when each method should be used. Here "total cost" refers to the cost of using the method PLUS the cost of errors that are not corrected.

2.2.3   Process Control and Improvement

As noted repeatedly above, the principal problem with methods of quality improvement based on error detection and correction is that they don't prevent future errors. So if a process is creating or replacing 1,000 new or existing records each day, each record has 20 fields, and the process's field-level error rate is 2% (not bad), then roughly 400 new errors are produced each day. And that number of errors will be produced indefinitely. At the end of a year, there will be over 140,000 errors. Not all will be of great consequence, but the clean-up task will again be enormous. Methods of process management recognize this. Ultimately, they seek to identify root causes of errors, eliminate those causes to lower the error rate, and ensure that gains are sustained.

The following example illustrates how process management typically works. Consider a hypothetical "billing information chain," consisting of Customer Service, Order Entry, Shipping, and Billing departments. What often happens is that the four organizations require different data to do their jobs. Customer Service is concerned with the sale, Order Entry is concerned with getting the order entered into the computer, and Shipping with getting the order shipped. None cares too much about Billing. In attempting to understand why it has so many problems, Billing determines that STOCK NUMBER is the most frequently erred field. Upon investigation, it learns that Shipping changes many STOCK NUMBERS because it (Shipping) thinks Order Entry has entered them incorrectly. Order Entry, for its part, is simply following the manual.

No one organization need be at fault. But the gaps between organizations lead to an information chain with broken links. Experience shows such problems can be resolved and the error rate for STOCK NUMBER dramatically reduced by managing the information chain horizontally, as a series of hand-offs among the four organizations. Further, a chain or process manager can put in simple controls to ensure the problem doesn't return.

Part II of this book is a full description of how to apply process management to information chains and processes that create data. Edits and data tracking are the principal means to make the required measurements of process performance. Applied within a process or information chain, edits may screen certain types of errors before they are committed to the database. If identified quickly, errors can be corrected before they do any damage. For example, an Order Entry clerk may be given the opportunity to rekey a customer's order. This helps make the process less error prone (see Section 2.2.4). To improve the process, a log of failed edits, whether corrected or not, is made, studied to determine patterns of errors, and the root causes systematically eliminated.[2] Data tracking extends the concept much further and is discussed in full detail in Chapter 11.

By now there is no doubt that quality improvement based on process management leads to higher quality levels, improved customer satisfaction, and

---

2.   One important, but subtle point in quality management involves the distinction between measurement and how the measurement is used. Edits, as discussed, can be used to make corrections, to improve a process, and to design a less error-prone process. Many organizations use edits, but only to make corrections. This is unfortunate, because so little extra effort is required to make significant process improvements.

lower total cost. This has been shown in industry after industry. Process management is only beginning to be employed on the creation of data and information, and the early results suggest it will be just as effective here. It is especially effective for data that are created or replaced at high rates.

While the results are almost always good, some investment is required. The most difficult problem is often in getting people who are not familiar with modern methods of quality management to try them. And many people think that process management has become passé, preferring the breakthrough gains that re-engineering enables. For processes that are nowhere near meeting customer requirements, this may be true. But re-engineering is a risky and time-consuming venture, and re-engineered processes still must be managed.

2.2.4   Process Design

Process design focuses on making processes less error prone. Unfortunately there is relatively little systematic research or experience in this area. But a few good ideas have been developed. First, data edits may be designed into new processes and database management systems. They help avoid some rather simple mistakes and don't cost much to implement. One problem is that people can be very creative at bypassing the edits. They quickly learn that certain codes (such as "Not Applicable") will pass the edit and enter it even when they know it is not correct.

Second, design the process measurement capability needed to control and improve the process into the process as well. Third, use IT to minimize activities that people don't do well such as transcription, data entry, format changes, and so forth. Bar-code readers can, for example, make some processes less error prone. Fourth, processes can often be simplified to minimize hand-offs. This minimizes transcriptions and format changes and helps make the process less error prone. And finally, properly placing management responsibility can help. Deming [18] gives an example of an enterprise that minimized data quality problems with purchase orders by moving management accountability from Purchasing to the requesting organization. We provide a more complete list and discussion in Chapter 14. In general, when designing new processes and information chains, it is a good idea to incorporate as many of these ideas as possible.

2.3   Which Data to Improve?

The discussion above makes clear what results should be expected from each improvement method. See Table 2.1. We now turn our attention to properly applying these methods. First, we consider which data to improve, as even a single database may contain all sorts of data, created by any number of processes and used for any number of purposes. It is rarely practical to improve all data at once.

There are a number of considerations in determining those data to pursue first and they can be applied in almost any sequence. The objective is to develop an agreed-upon priority-order listing of data to improve. One consideration is importance to the enterprise's overall business strategy. Thus, an enterprise that is pursuing a strategy of customer intimacy should focus its efforts first on customer data. Similarly, an enterprise pursuing a strategy of operational efficiency may wish to consider logistics data. At the organizational level, it is usually evident which data are the most important. Sales, no matter what the enterprise, needs good customer data. And Billing needs good sales and pricing data.

"Customer" and "logistics" data may still be too large to pursue. So a second consideration is association with known business problems [19]. Thus, the enterprise pursuing customer relations may already know that "late/missed appointments with customers" is a dissatisfier. Two data issues—"incorrect street address" and "incorrect contact number"—contribute to the overall problem. These are good data items to improve. Conversely, solutions to many business problems may require lots of data. The set of data selected for improvement should not be so narrowly focused as to impede solution to the larger problem.

A third consideration is the current error rates and requirements. All things being equal, those fields with the largest gap between current and required error rates should be pursued first. As noted above, it is often possible to get good estimates by checking a sample of records against its real-world counterparts. And sometimes informal estimates can be obtained through conversations with customer service representatives, those who work on the loading dock, and others close to the action whose jobs are complicated by poor data quality.

Economics, the cost of poor data quality, is another consideration. Data about a large customer are more important than data about a small customer. Similarly, errors in some fields are almost inconsequential, while errors in others, such as name and address, are enormously expensive. It is worth noting that developing consensus on those data to improve can be extremely difficult. And due to the breadth of information chains, one unhappy organization can spoil otherwise solid improvement efforts. Therefore, despite the difficulties, getting consensus is extremely important. The so-called "nominal group technique" is often a useful way to do so [20].

2.4   Improving Data Accuracy for One Database

We now turn our attention to developing the operational plan for improvement. In this section, we assume that the data to be improved reside in a single database. We'll consider more complex situations in the next sections.

The essence of the operational plan is to apply the best method of improvement to the data selected for improvement. From Section 2.2, the following are evident.

- If the rates of new data creation and data replacement are high, a method of process control and improvement is needed. Together, we call the rate of data creation and the rate of data replacement the *turnover parameters.*

- If the turnover parameters are low, a method of error detection and correction is appropriate.

- Independent of the turnover parameters, any new process design or re-engineering should strive to make the new process as error free as possible.

It is likely that some of the selected data fall into each of the first two categories. Thus, if a number of customer-related fields have been selected, DATE-OF-BIRTH should be cleaned up and the process must be fixed for CURRENT BALANCE. In some cases, this level of analysis is sufficient. In others, a complication arises because the turnover parameters are somewhere in the middle or one is high and the other low. CUSTOMER-ADDRESS typifies the situation. Most customers move infrequently, so the rate of replacement is low. On the other hand, new customers are being added all the time so the rate of creation is high. Thus, it is evident that both data clean-up and process improvement will be required. As a rule of thumb, it is usually better to fix the process first and then clean up remaining data. This makes the clean-up job smaller. Many enterprises are tempted to clean up the data first and fix the process later. This is dangerous for two reasons.

- First, they've created a tremendous amount of new and unclean data, while cleaning up the old data. These, too, will have to be cleaned up.

- Second, sometimes priorities and budgets change and the process improvements may be deferred. Then, slowly, the gains made by cleaning up data will be lost.

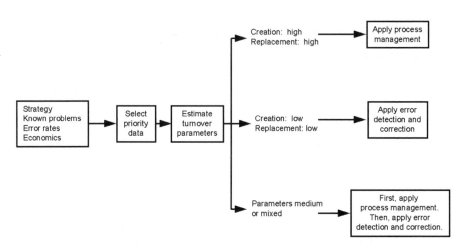

Figure 2.2   This is the sequence of steps for creating an operational plan to select and improve data: "one database" case.

In contrast, if the process is first improved, the overall quality level will continue to increase. And the size of the clean-up will be minimized.

To conclude this section we summarize the key steps in developing an operational plan for the "one database" case. First, business needs, including strategy, known problems, error rates, and economics, are considered to specify a set of data for improvement. Then the rates of data creation and replacement are estimated at a very granular (field) level. Finally, the appropriate improvement method is selected and applied. In some cases, process improvement is followed by clean-up. This sequence of steps is summarized in Figure 2.2.

2.5   Improving Data Accuracy for Two Databases

We now consider the situation in which data selected for improvement are stored in two databases. Naturally, the following points may be extended to any number of databases. We consider three situations of increasing complexity.

In the first situation, selected data are stored in two databases, but there is no overlap. Essentially, then, one has two "one database" cases and the method for developing the operational plan should be applied to each database.

In the second situation, the selected data are stored in both Databases A and B, and Database B uses Database A as a source. An alternative description is that

Databases A and B exhibit a master-slave relationship, with B the slave of A. It is clear that the secret is to treat Database A as in the single database case, and let Database B derive its corrections and improvements from A.

In the third situation, Databases A and B overlap and are fed by separate processes. This situation is of greatest concern and the most difficult to address. Unfortunately, it is also a common situation and one that is often disguised by the goals of disparate organizations.

We've already cited two such examples: the manufacturing enterprise in which Purchasing and Engineering each created the same "parts" data and, even more subtly, the Accounts Payable organization, which developed separate data for bill verification. Note that each organization was doing the right thing, at least from its own perspective. Thus, the most obvious approach is to treat Databases A and B separately and then use some form of database bashing to resolve discrepancies. Such an approach will work, but it will require database bashing on an ongoing basis and is, therefore, not recommended.

Mark Twain once observed that, "A man with a watch knows what time it is. A man with two is never sure." This thinking applies to processes that create data as well.[3] And there are relatively few situations in an enterprise that can justify maintaining two processes to create essentially the same data, especially over the long haul.[4] One or the other process must be eliminated. The Accounts Payable organization has two choices.

- It can work with suppliers to ensure that bills are accurate. It may even demand evidence of accuracy on an ongoing basis, audit the results, and take other steps to protect itself. And once bills become accurate, it must eliminate its own database and process for creating bill-verification data.

- If Accounts Payable feels it can do a better job billing than the suppliers, it can decide to pay suppliers based on its own data. In this scenario, Accounts Payable does not accept invoices from suppliers, effectively eliminating their database and data-creating process.

---

3.   Bob Kotch, at the time CIO of the Global Real Estate organization at AT&T, advocated the "one lie" approach. He reasoned that the organization was far better off with a single database, even if some data were wrong. Not only did it reduce the expense and confusion of multiple databases, it forced the organization to concentrate its efforts on the remaining single copy of the data.

4.   There are a few notable exceptions. News agencies, for example, have procedures that specify when a second source is required, even when the first source is "usually reliable." These situations are the exception rather than the rule.

Each scenario has advantages. Many factors may dictate which alternative is selected. For example, many enterprises are working on quality initiatives with key suppliers, and adding bill quality to the initiative may be a good choice.

Note that the focus of this discussion has been on processes that create data, not the databases. One of the promised benefits of database technology is to make data available for use by many people. In principle, this should make it possible to eliminate one or the other database as well. In practice, this is not always the case. Backup, security, or access requirements may make it necessary to maintain the second database. Or, the second database may serve functions downstream in the larger information chain. In either case, a master-slave arrangement should be pursued.

Be advised that the passions and politics surrounding the elimination of a process and/or database are as brutal as any within an organization. It is only rarely possible to determine how two data-creating processes came to be in the first place. The organization that put each process in place can, no doubt, cite good reasons. For example, Accounts Payable was simply protecting the enterprise's best interests in an environment of caveat emptor.

2.6   Improving Data Accuracy in the Data Warehouse

We now consider the issues associated with migrating data, both at start-up and in daily operations, into a data warehouse. Celko [21] has estimated that half the total cost of implementing a data warehouse can be due to poor data quality. In addition, data warehousing intentionally increases redundancy; and in Section 2.5 we argued that redundancy should be kept under check. Similarly, the data that are migrated into the warehouse are often resident in many databases. Migration seems to require database bashing. Finally, data warehousing projects are difficult enough, even without the complications of poor data.

However, the principles discussed above can be applied to the data in a data warehouse. If an enterprise starts early, starts with small amounts of data, and proceeds in an iterative fashion, which developers will agree is a good practice anyway, it can systematically identify critical warehouse data, apply data quality principles properly, and successfully populate the data warehouse with high-quality data. We recommend the following steps.

First, identify the data that will populate the warehouse. This is similar to selecting data for improvement, but more sharply focused. It is best to select a

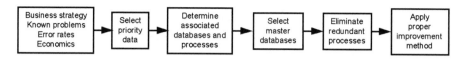

Figure 2.3 This represents a generic process for developing the operational plan for improvement.

couple of small, but critical business problems. Identify the data needed to solve those problems and define quality requirements for those data.

Next, select master data sources. For data that are stored in only one database, there is only one source, so make it the master. For data that are redundant, designate one database to be the master source, as in Section 2.5.

Third, if at all possible, estimate current quality levels of master sources. A small sample compared to real-world sources will be sufficient. Also estimate the turnover parameters for all master sources. As before, different data elements may have different rates and there may be subsets of data with different rates.

Based on these estimates, it is now possible to reduce data accuracy problems in migration to the relatively simple problems of Section 2.4 (the "one database" case). In particular, each master is treated as a single database. Error detection and correction are applied to data that are replaced slowly, and processes that create or replace data rapidly are improved.

2.7 Summary

In many respects, a database is like a lake. In the analogy, the lake is the database, water is the data, and streams feeding the lake are processes that create data. And just as those who drink from the lake benefit from clean lake water, so, too, do those who use data. If the lake is polluted, it is possible to "clean the lake." It is almost always better to eliminate sources of pollution upstream.

In this chapter we have provided necessary background and shown how to develop an operational plan for data quality improvement. There are three main methods of quality improvement and they yield predictable results.

- Error detection and correction focuses on identifying and correcting errors (cleaning the lake). It is appropriate for data that are replaced at low rates.

- Process management and improvement focuses on identifying and eliminating root causes of errors (eliminating sources of pollution). It is appropriate for data that are created and replaced at high rates.

- Process design focuses on making processes less error prone and should be used whenever new processes are designed.

One key to a good operational plan is properly applying these three methods. Two other keys are to focus on the data that are most critical to the enterprise and to eliminate redundant data-creating processes. Even complicated situations, such as multiple databases and data warehouses, can now be reduced to a series of simpler situations, each addressed by applying the proper method of quality improvement. Figure 2.3 summarizes this process.

REFERENCES

[1]   Porter, M. E., *Competitive Advantage: Creating and Sustaining Superior Performance*, New York: The Free Press, 1985.

[2]   Buchanan, L., "Cultivating an Information Culture," *CIO*, Vol. 7, No. 6, December 15, 1994/January 1, 1995, pp. 47–51.

[3]   Ishikawa, K., *Introduction to Quality Control*, Tokyo: 3A Corporation, 1990.

[4]   Juran, J. M., *Managerial Breakthrough*, New York: McGraw-Hill, 1964.

[5]   Deming, W. E., *Out of the Crisis*, Cambridge, MA: Massachusetts Institute of Technology, 1986.

[6]   Wadsworth, H. M., K. S. Stephens, and A. B. Godfrey, *Modern Methods for Quality Control and Improvement*, New York: John Wiley & Sons, 1986.

[7]   Fellegi, I. P., and D. Holt, "A Systematic Approach to Automatic Edit and Imputation," *Journal of the American Statistical Association*, Vol. 71, 1976, pp. 17–35.

[8]   Little, R. J., "Editing and Imputation of Multivariate Data: Issues and New Approaches," in G. E. Liepens and V. R. R. Uppuluri (eds.), *Data Quality Control: Theory and Pragmatics*, New York: Marcel Dekker, 1990.

[9]   Little, R. J., and P. J. Smith, "Editing and Imputation for Quantitative Survey Data," *Journal of the American Statistical Association*, Vol. 82, 1987, pp. 58–68.

[10]   Rubin, D. B., *Multiple Imputation for Nonresponse in Surveys*, New York: John Wiley & Sons, 1987.

[11]   Liepens, G. E., and D. J. Pack, "A Simulation Study of Selected Methods for Dealing with Survey Errors," in G. E. Liepens and V. R. R. Uppuluri (eds.), *Data Quality Control: Theory and Pragmatics*, New York: Marcel-Dekker, 1990.

[12] Ross, R., *The Business Rule Book: Classifying, Defining and Modeling Rules*, Boston: Database Research Group, 1994.

[13] Brodie, M. L., "Specification and Verification of Database Semantic Integrity," Ph.D. diss., University of Toronto, 1978.

[14] Date, C. J., *An Introduction to Database Systems, Vol. 2*, 3rd ed., Reading, MA: Addison-Wesley, 1983.

[15] Naus, J. I., *Data Quality Control and Editing*, New York: Marcel Dekker, 1975.

[16] Tsichritzis, D. C., and F. H. Lochovsky, *Data Models*, Englewood Cliffs, NJ: Prentice Hall, 1982.

[17] Parsaye, K., M. Chignell, S. Khoshafian, and H. Wong, "Intelligent Databases," *AI Expert*, Vol. 5, No. 3, March 1990, pp. 38–47.

[18] Deming, W. E., *Quality, Productivity, and Competitive Position*, Cambridge, MA: Massachusetts Institute of Technology, 1982.

[19] Caby, E. C., R. W. Pautke, and T. C. Redman, "Strategies for Improving Data Quality," *Data Quality*, Vol. 1, March 1995, pp. 4–12.

[20] Scholtes, P., *The Team Handbook*, Madison, WI: Joiner Associates, 1988.

[21] Celko, J., "Don't Warehouse Dirty Data," *Datamation*, October 15, 1995, pp. 42–52.

Chapter 3

Data Quality Policy

"Eyesight should learn from reason."
—Johannes Kepler

3.1 Introduction

Chapter 1 reviewed business reasons to care about data quality and Chapter 2 discussed how leaders develop operational plans for making sustainable improvements to data accuracy. We now turn our attention to the third element of successful enterprise-wide data quality programs, namely management accountability. Enterprises quite naturally hold managers accountable for those things they recognize as business assets. Most recognize capital, raw materials, plants and equipment, and employees as assets. Others may recognize such knowledge-based resources as expertise in manufacturing, marketing, or product innovation as assets. Enterprises hold managers accountable for protecting all such assets and using them to produce value for customers, returns to owners, and so forth. Enterprises that wish to possess good data, to create data of high value on an ongoing basis, and to put those data to effective use must also recognize data (and information) as assets and define explicit management accountabilities for them.

Some of the principles that are helpful in managing other assets apply to data as well. But data are different from other assets in some crucial ways, and so many principles don't readily extend to data. In fact, because data are less tangible than other assets (except perhaps knowledge-based assets), many enterprises don't recognize the need to manage data and information as assets. And some organizations, correctly recognizing that data are "stored in the computers," implicitly assign ownership for data to the Information Technology organization or the Chief Information Office. Unfortunately, failing to assign management accountability or making data solely the province of IT or the CIO yields unacceptable results.

The principal purpose of this chapter is to describe a "model data policy" for the entire enterprise that assigns specific responsibilities to people and organizations as they create, store, process, and use data. While our interest here is in data quality, data policies should extend beyond quality per se, to issues such as security, privacy, and redundancy.

In the next section we discuss issues that a data policy can cover. We take as a given that enterprises should define policies that address their most important ongoing business issues. Equally important, enterprises should *not* define policies that they cannot deploy. Each enterprise must decide for itself exactly what it can deploy at any point in time. We then give a brief summary of several features of data pertinent to their management. These features, together with good management practice for other assets, lead to the model policy.

We conclude with a discussion of deployment issues. While the model policy is a useful starting point, enterprises are well-advised to craft policy with deployment in mind. A well-deployed policy, even if it doesn't cover everything, is far superior to a technically excellent policy that everyone ignores.

3.2 What Should a Data Policy Cover?

3.2.1 The Data Asset in a Typical Enterprise

Chapter 1 discussed the consequences of poor data quality in great detail. Increased operational expense, lowered customer satisfaction, and the inability to implement strategy are the results. Addressing these problems ought to be reason enough to cause most enterprises to define explicit management responsibilities for data. Most enterprises face other issues as well. Indeed, while most enterprises readily agree that "data (and information) are among our most important assets," most are faced with at least some of the following.

- Many enterprises don't have a current inventory of their data and information assets. Can you imagine an enterprise that didn't know how many employees it had or where its plant and equipment were located? An enterprise simply can't manage those things that it doesn't know it has.

- In many enterprises data are not shared across organizational lines. The most serious situation arises when data are implicitly considered organizational (or even personal) property and others cannot get them.

- People cannot easily find out what data the enterprise has. Many development organizations do a fairly good job at defining their "data dictionaries." But even the good data dictionaries are accessible only by the development community. The rest of the enterprise is left pretty much in the dark. As Negroponte [1] points out, the data about data (often called the "metadata") are often even more valuable than the data themselves.

- Data are hard to access. In some cases, the data are bound up with application programs; in others, special hardware or software is needed.

- There are no data standards and common terms, such as "vendor," for example, which has different meanings across the enterprise. Thus, a set of data can meet only narrow needs. And this defeats the whole purpose of database technology.

- Many enterprises have too much data. There are two principal contributors: First, in many enterprises data redundancy is out of control. Each organization seems to have its own copy of data. Of course, this is the expected result if data are not shared. Second, many organizations continue to develop and store much data that have outlived their usefulness.

- As the enterprise evolves, it may require new data and data sources. Obtaining needed data may require long lead times. Many enterprises do not have adequate processes in place to ensure that they will have the data they need next year, the year after, and five years hence.

- In many enterprises data are at risk of being stolen or destroyed.

- In many enterprises rules governing confidentiality and privacy are not clearly spelled out. People and organizations make their own decisions regarding what can be shared outside the enterprise, even what data may be sold. As yet, legal and social frameworks governing privacy and confidentiality are not in place, so the impact is unpredictable (see [2] for a discussion of these and related issues).

- In many enterprises, data are neither explicitly nor implicitly assigned monetary value, so they are treated as low priority.

3.2.2   What a Data Policy Can Cover

We group issues that a data policy can cover into six broad and interrelated categories.

- *Quality* in its broadest sense. This implies data that are relevant to their intended uses and are of sufficient detail and quantity, with a high degree of accuracy and completeness, consistent with other sources, and presented in appropriate ways.

- The *inventory of data assets*. The enterprise should know what data it has; where they are located; what they mean; who, both inside and outside the enterprise, is allowed access; and how those allowed access can obtain them. I call this information the *data library*. The library is a bit more involved, though, due to the nature of the data asset. As we will discuss, data are created at enormous rates, used in novel ways, and aggregated or disaggregated to serve any number of needs. And the value of many data deteriorates rapidly. So in many cases, it is not the data per se that are of value, but the ability to create new data and rapidly use them that is the true asset. This implies that end-to-end information chains are often the real data assets, and they should be included in the library.

- *Data sharing and availability*. Data can, in principle at least, be shared by any number of organizations and individuals. But as noted above, data sharing, in practice, is often the exception rather than the rule. While all data sharing is not necessarily good (we'll discuss privacy momentarily), enterprises should promote and otherwise manage data sharing. Of course, if data are to be shared, people need to know of their existence, be able to find them easily, and obtain what they need without undue hardship. Thus, the data library, or at least parts of it, must be readily accessible.

- *Data architecture*. Many data issues can best be addressed through simple, practical architectures. Data architectures should (in time, anyway) create and enforce data standards, minimize unneeded redundancy, provide backup and disaster recovery, and ensure that data and applications programs are separated (separating data from applications helps reduce redundancy and promotes sharing).

- *Security, privacy, and appropriate use.* Naturally, enterprises must protect data from harm, including unwanted destruction or changes and unauthorized access. They must also protect privacy and confidentiality rights, even though guidelines for doing so, both legal and social, have not yet emerged.

- *Planning.* The enterprise must plan for its future data and information needs on an ongoing basis. A planning process should be driven by business strategy and look ahead at least 2 to 5 years for the new kinds of data, sources of supply, and technologies that help turn data into information that will be needed.[1]

3.3 Needed Background on Data

3.3.1 Differences Between Data and Other Assets

Most enterprises know how to manage traditional assets such as capital and human resources.[2] And a vast body of theory and practical experience has been developed to help managers increase the value of such assets. As yet, there is no such management theory for data and information. Of course, if data were similar to traditional assets, one could simply apply other management sciences to data. But there are critical differences.[3] We'll discuss critical differences and several models of data in detail in Chapter 12. Here we highlight the most important points for managers and leaders.

---

1. For an interesting perspective on the importance of turning data into information, see *Understanding Information* [3].

2. See Levitin and Redman [4, 5] and Fox, Levitin, and Redman [6] and references therein for original sources. Anany Levitin of Villanova University, Christopher Fox of James Madison University, and Robert Pautke of AT&T Bell Laboratories have done a great deal of work to understand critical differences between data and other assets and the management consequences thereof.

3. The most important principle, that management accountability must be assigned for those things that the enterprise values, does apply.

First, we have already noted that data are not tangible. You never really see data, just its representation. All other assets can be seen and touched. And in many enterprises "out of sight, out of mind!"

Second, data are copyable and transportable to an almost unlimited degree. These features can be a double-edged sword. They mean that people need never be denied access, but they can lead to redundancy, which, we noted, is out of control. And copying data doesn't necessarily increase their value.

Third, data are not consumed with use. This, too, is a double-edged sword. On the one hand, once obtained, they are always available. On the other, they may be kept long after they have outlived their usefulness.

Fourth, most useful data are novel or unique in some way. It is how people differ, for example, not how they are the same, that is usually of interest to marketers. This point has two important consequences. First, one unit of data cannot be substituted for another unit of data (that is, data are not fungible). Second, for most mass-produced assets, managers strive for uniformity of output. Uniform data are of no interest whatsoever.

The fifth important difference is in the way data assets are valued. While there are a few exceptions, for most data there is nothing equivalent to a marketplace, where they can be bought and sold. Perhaps as a consequence, data aren't usually assigned any monetary value (intangibility may play a role as well). There is no place in the accounting structure for "value of data," as there is for value of fixed assets and inventory.

Finally, and perhaps most importantly, data and information are far more dynamic than other assets. They cross organizational and enterprise boundaries in the blink of an eye. Other assets are far less dynamic. Organizations are usually assigned responsibility for plant and equipment, and most employees report to a single organization within the enterprise.

There are four principal activities that touch data.

- Data modeling. Data, especially data stored in databases, are the result of modeling the real world. For example, an enterprise's model of "customer" may capture facts[4] such as name, address, marital status, and so forth. Per se, the data model does not contain any actual data; it is more like the structure into which data will fit. A blank meeting calendar is a good example of a data model. The model (blank calendar) divides time into days and hours, but is distinct from the data values (meeting times and places). Data modeling is usually the province of

---

4.   Of course, these "facts" may be incorrect, but then they wouldn't be facts.

the IT organization, though, of course, many packaged software applications come complete with data models.

- Create (or obtain) data values. Data values are created by day-to-day operations, obtained from outside organizations and other sources. They (the data values) are the actual customer addresses, the details of what they purchase, logistical details, and the meeting details of the calendar example noted above.

- Store data. As or soon after data values are created, they are stored in databases, usually electronic databases. They may be restructured and reformatted to make them more easily accessible for users. Storage should protect the data from any harm, make data available to legitimate users, and prevent unwarranted access. Historically most large databases are managed by the IT organization, but recently other organizations have become capable of storing their own data.

- Use data. Sooner or later, data are put to use.[5] Most uses are routine—they support product manufacturing, customer billing, paying employees, and so forth. Data are also used for making decisions where large amounts of data are combined and put into new contexts. In a typical enterprise, most users of data for routine purposes are in the operating units, and users for decision-making purposes are managers. Importantly, some data are never used for any purpose. Other data are used in literally dozens of contexts, many far removed from the context(s) in which they were originally collected.

Because data are so dynamic and so many organizations may touch even the most mundane data, centralized organizations cannot be expected to assume much accountability for data. For example, it is simply unrealistic to assign responsibility for the accuracy of data created in Order Entry to the Chief Information Office.

---

5. There are many possible definitions of data and information, each leading to different distinctions between the two. In daily conversation, most people apply the term "information" to data that are being put to some use. Note that this distinction between data and information is subjective. For example, one person may take data and summarize them in some fashion. From this person's perspective, he or she has created information. Someone else may use this "information" in a different context. From the second person's perspective, the information is simply raw data.

3.3.2   Who Uses the Data

The typical enterprise possesses enormous quantities of data.[6] Some data cross organization and enterprise boundaries; other data spend their entire lifetime in a single department. Some data are used solely in operations; other data become part of larger information bases used strategically. Here we review two classifications of data, based on their use and the boundaries they cross.

First, we recognize operational, tactical, and strategic uses of data.

- *Operational data* are those data used in the day-to-day operation of the enterprise. In terms of quantity, the vast bulk of an enterprise's data (if they are used at all) are used in billing, financial, customer service, manufacturing, logistical, and other basic operations. Similarly, most data that an enterprise creates or obtains are for operational purposes.

- *Tactical data* are used in routine, though perhaps not day-to-day, management functions. Most, but not all, tactical data are derived from operational data. Thus, individual sales are summarized and used by the sales manager to reassign sales associates, and summaries of logistics data are used to help identify preferred sources of supply.

- *Strategic data* are used to make long-term decisions that affect the health of the enterprise or its important organization over the long term. Strategic data are usually rooted in summaries of operational or tactical data. Thus, revenue history, by industry segment, may be used to project growth rates, which in turn are used to evaluate markets to enter, investment strategy, and long-term organizational needs (e.g., acquisitions). Importantly, a greater fraction of strategic data originates outside the enterprise. Such data may not be as trustworthy as data developed from within.

An enterprise might be tempted to treat strategic data with greater importance than tactical data and tactical data with greater importance than operational data. Unfortunately, the enterprise can never be sure that operational data will not be used to make higher level decisions. We noted in Chapter 1, for example, how poor operational data can compromise a re-engineering project. Enterprises can and should distinguish the important data from the unimportant, but strategic use is not a reliable way to do so.

---

6.   Unfortunately, most organizations have considerably less information, however information is defined.

With few exceptions (a person's salary, for example), most individual operational data can and should be shared broadly. Data sharing mitigates the "white space" on the organization chart and more effectively connects the enterprise with customers and suppliers. Tactical data are generally held more tightly and strategic data, more tightly still.

The second classification is based on the ideas presented by Paul Strassman in *The Politics of Information Management* [7]. Strassman considers the most important issues of managing information technology that have arisen in the last several decades and continue to arise, such as centralized versus decentralized computing power, standards versus local initiative, and outsourcing. He argues for an "Information Constitution," which specifies a system of checks and balances much like the American Constitution, including how governance issues will be addressed, and how the roles of the Chief Information Officer and the Policy Board will be defined. Strassman does not make much of the distinction between technological assets, such as computers and networks, and data and information, but many of his points are directly applicable to data.

Of special interest here is Strassman's "Information Configuration Policies." He defines a seven-level hierarchy, which determines who has decision-making rights, based on the scope and impact such decisions may have. As adopted for data, "extent of data sharing" replaces scope, and four levels are of particular interest.

- Global: Data that are acquired or shared outside the enterprise are *global data*. All organizations bill their customers, so "billing data" are global. Indeed, any data needed to conduct day-to-day operations with customers and suppliers are global data. Public corporations share summaries of billing data, called "revenue," in their annual reports. Such data are also of a strategic nature, but most strategic data are not shared so widely.

  Once data leave, an enterprise has relatively little control over how they are used. Therefore, it should take care in designating data as global data. Similarly, special care must be taken before using data obtained from outside to ensure they are of sufficient quality.

- Enterprise: Data that are needed by a number of organizations and/or unrelated processes or are critical to the entire enterprise are considered *enterprise data*. Data about employees and certain financial data are good examples. However, just because data are designated as enterprise data, does not imply that any person or organization should be granted access. For example, data about employees may well be enterprise data, but people should be able to expect that their salary histories remain private.

- Process: Data needed to support information chains that cross organizational lines are considered *process data*. The distinction between enterprise data and process data may be subtle in some cases, as data designated as process data are used across the enterprise. The most important distinction is that one may expect an information chain manager to be accountable for process data. There is no such obvious manager of enterprise data.

- Organizational, Application, Local, and Personal: Data developed and used wholly within a single organization are considered *organizational data*. Within the organization, data may be used by a single department or person. Our principal concern will be with data flowing into/from the enterprise and among organizations within the enterprise. Naturally, the same issues may arise within an organization as, for example, the penetration of personal computers and wide availability of cheap storage devices have led many people to view some data as their personal property.

3.4   A Model Data Policy

In this section, we discuss a "model" data policy, and in the next section, we discuss implementation. Our main concern is data quality. The dynamic nature of data, especially the number of organizations that touch data and, thus, may compromise their quality, leads to a policy where responsibility is highly decentralized. As noted, Order Entry (and clerks therein) must be held accountable for data accuracy. We reserve, for centralized organizations such as the Chief Information Office, only those responsibilities that meet two criteria.

- Functions that individual organizations cannot be expected to perform on their own (a privacy policy, for example).

- Functions that the centralized organization can reasonably be expected to perform.

The Model Data Policy is as follows. We expect that enterprises will tailor the policy based on their individual needs and styles.

3.4.1 Model Data Policy

Overall

1. Data and information, and the business processes that create, store, process, and use them, are the property of the enterprise.

2. An organization must share any data and information that it creates, stores, or uses within the enterprise, unless privacy or legal considerations dictate otherwise. Since an organization cannot own data, it may not charge another for the data it supplies. It may, however, charge an "access price" based on its legitimate costs to make the data available.

3. Efficient business operation requires that data be shared with customers, vendors, and others. Those who need or otherwise desire to share data beyond the enterprise must obtain permission from the Data Council. Unless specifically noted, those outside the enterprise who either supply us data or receive our data will be made aware of this policy and asked to follow it. Adherence to the policy (at least for data that involves us) is a requirement of all major, long-term suppliers unless explicit provisions otherwise are made.

Centralized Functions

1. The Chief Information Office (or other named organization) is responsible for maintaining a current inventory of our data and inventory assets, including our major databases, data and information chains, and reusable data models. The inventory will include data definitions, sources, and access information and will be made available to any person or organization with a legitimate business purpose.

2. The Chief Information Office is responsible for ensuring that the enterprise will have, on an ongoing basis, the data and information, data sources, and technologies for managing data needed to support the enterprise's strategies.

3. The Chief Information Office is also responsible for minimizing unneeded data redundancy across the enterprise.

4. The Data Council will be responsible for a "data standards process," which:

- specifies which data are designated as global and organizational data. Data are assumed to be either enterprise or process data unless otherwise designated.
- develops and supports standards for data elements, tools for measuring and improving data quality, privacy, security, and so forth.

5. The Chief Quality Office will establish and report overall measures of data quality, obtain and make available methods organizations need for measuring and improving data quality, and coordinate major improvement efforts as needed.

6. A Conflict Resolution Board, comprised of senior executives across the enterprise, will resolve conflicts in a timely manner.

Throughout the Enterprise

Individuals and organizations that conduct the following activities involving data have specific responsibilities to manage data as an asset to the entire enterprise [8].

Suppliers and Creators of Data

1. Understand, on an ongoing basis, who uses the data they create and for what business purposes. Actively solicit their needs for data and their data quality requirements. Creators of operational data are especially encouraged to seek out tactical and strategic users.

2. Implement measures of data quality and/or other measures to ensure that users' requirements are met.

3. Implement process management for the data they create. Establish statistical control, assess conformance to users' requirements, and make needed improvements.

4. For the purposes of this policy, those who obtain data from outside the enterprise are directly responsible for point 1 on behalf of the entire enterprise. They are also responsible for ensuring that suppliers satisfy points 2 and 3.

Those Who Store and Process Data

1. Provide databases and data architectures that minimize unneeded redundancy.
2. Safeguard data from harm and unwanted and/or unauthorized access.
3. Make data readily accessible for legitimate business users.
4. Ensure that new Information Technology is designed to promote data quality.

Users

1. Proactively seek out and work with data suppliers. Develop clear and operable data requirements. Tactical and strategic users of data are especially encouraged to seek out original sources.
2. Provide feedback as part of supplier partnerships.
3. Ensure that data are correctly interpreted.
4. Ensure that data are used for legitimate business purposes only.
5. Seek out and understand customers', employees', and others' rights to privacy. Protect those rights.

3.5   Deploying the Policy

In this section we provide some practical advice for making the data policy effective. In many respects, deploying a data policy is similar to deploying any other policy within the enterprise. It requires energy, time, patience, and political acumen. All enterprises are different. Some actively resist top-down policies; others require strong leadership. In many enterprises, once people are pointed in the right direction, they determine how to implement policy on their own. In other enterprises, people require more support. In many enterprises, role models play a critical role. The most important advice is to define a deployment plan that takes advantage of the enterprise's culture. Work with, not across or against, the culture. Davenport, Eccles, and Prusak [9] recognize five models of information politics: feudalism, anarchy, technocratic utopianism, monarchy, and federalism. Each has its own "information politicians," whose leadership and support will be vital to successful deployment. Davenport et al. note that the federal model is likely to produce both the best overall results and the highest levels of data quality. It also requires the most energy, patience, and skill.

Second, we have already noted that enterprises should not promulgate policies that they cannot deploy and support. It is particularly easy to craft data policies that are technically excellent, but not deployable. With data, the hardest points to implement usually involve the centralized functions. People place low priority on supplying information to organizations they view as "bureaucrats," resisting data standards (more will be said about this point below), and hiding serious conflicts. Enterprises should tailor their data policies with deployment in mind. Policies can be deployed in stages and difficult points can be reserved for later stages. It is far better to deploy a relatively straightforward policy first and then expand it, than to struggle with a more complete policy. Similarly, it is usually better to deploy the policy to organizations that are most receptive first, saving the more difficult ones for later.

It is usually easiest to obtain buy-in for the portions of the policy that apply to data suppliers and users (and from a data quality perspective, these portions are the most critical). As an example, few dispute that creators of data values must be responsible for the accuracy of those values. Assigning accountability for accuracy elsewhere does not work, as those who perform data clean-ups attest. Many wonder what would compel one organization, under tight budget constraints and other pressures, to care much about the data quality requirements of downstream organizations. In my experience, this issue usually resolves itself when the first organization understands the impact that poor data has downstream. The first organization is usually the recipient of poor data itself and so has an innate understanding of the problem. Of course, downstream organizations must work with the first organization to ensure that their requirements are understood. Almost all organizations will then make a real attempt to meet such requirements. Thus, the key is getting data creators and users to work together.

The point also underscores the advantage of information chains. Managers of such chains clearly have horizontal management responsibilities and, thus, accountability for those portions of the policy. And, since most global data are at one end of an information chain or the other, chain managers can be expected to assume data responsibilities on behalf of the enterprise.

Enterprises should focus their efforts on their most important data. This subject was discussed in Section 2.3. The most important data, quite simply, are those data that are most important to implementing the enterprises' business strategies. Enterprises pursuing a strategy of customer relations will, of necessity, designate "customer data" as most important. Data about other critical assets may also fall into the "most important" category as well. Enterprises that must make efficient use of plant and equipment (as does an enterprise that derives competitive advantage through capacity planning) or employees (as does an enterprise that depends on product innovation) to succeed would designate data about these assets as "most important." Such data will not be readily shared outside the enterprise. Data custodians, data stewards, or data trustees can be designated to coordinate policy accountabilities for the most important enterprise data.

One of the biggest traps in deploying data policy is standards. I know of no enterprise that has had much success with data standards.[7] There are several reasons. Most obvious is the lack of support mechanisms. People may be unaware of standards and/or unable to implement them.[8] It is usually easy to explain that one didn't follow a standard by citing ignorance of its existence. And many promulgators of many standards seem to think that responsibility for seeking out and following standards lies with the rest of the enterprise. Another reason standards don't work is that enterprises attempt to standardize things that shouldn't be standardized. For example, I know of people in one enterprise who would like to develop a standard definition of "customer." They fail to recognize that the enterprise is in at least six separate (and fairly autonomous) businesses. Each deals with its customers differently; and, as a result, each thinks about customers differently. Each truly has a different definition of customer and so, of necessity, has a different data model. Any attempt to impose a standard definition is, at best, fruitless. At worst, an imposed standard will force businesses to change the (successful) ways they interact with customers.

To be successful with standards, an enterprise must have a "standards process," adequate representation on the standards body, and support mechanisms in place. If it is not prepared to make the investment required, the enterprise should forego standards in its Data Policy.

Another difficult issue is data redundancy. For whatever reasons, many organizations seem to like to have their own copy of data, even though there may be other sources readily available. This is very costly, of course, but only enterprises under tight budget constraints can expect to be successful in reducing redundancy. As a first step, however, enterprises can minimize the creation of further redundancy on a going-forward basis. Of course, managing redundancy requires a good data library.

---

7. The evidence for this statement is anecdotal only.

8. One story that illustrates this point involves reuse of data objects. Lore has it that the typical developer will spend 10 seconds looking for an object to reuse before initiating work to define his or her own.

Privacy is perhaps the murkiest data issue. We've already noted that legal and social frameworks defining privacy rights are yet to emerge. As a consequence, Strassman [7] recommends that enterprises adopt very conservative privacy policies.

Finally, the Model Policy clearly states that all data are owned by the enterprise. Strassman agrees, noting that all data and information must unequivocally be owned by the entire enterprise. This implies that there is no such thing as *personal data*. This implication conflicts with the fact that many people view their PCs, including the data thereon, as personal property. I don't see a resolution that will make everyone happy. Strassman notes that PCs are now affordable, so people ought to buy their own and keep personal data there. On the other hand, I can't imagine an enterprise that could afford to check what people placed on their desktop PC. An informal policy that people can put their personal data on the PC, with the understanding that there are no privacy rights, might be best.

3.6 Summary

Despite the fact that management science and legal frameworks for data and information have not yet become established, enterprises desirous of improving data quality and getting full benefit from data can and should establish clear management responsibilities for data. Based on the issues it faces and its deployment capabilities, an enterprise should consider a data policy that covers the following areas.

- Quality in its broadest sense;
- Data inventory;
- Data sharing and availability;
- Data architecture;
- Security, privacy, and rules of use;
- Planning.

A knee-jerk response, such as assigning most responsibility to the Chief Information Office, is unlikely to be successful. And data differ from more traditional assets, which enterprises know how to manage, in critical ways. They are not tangible, but they are easy to copy and transport. They are easy to share, but many people are reluctant to do so. And, of course, sharing is not always appropriate. Data are incredibly dynamic and any number of people and organizations may touch them as they traverse the enterprise. Useful data are novel and short lived, but they can be stored for an almost unlimited time. It is very difficult to predict how data will be used. Many are used again and again in any number of low- and high-level applications. Others are never used for anything.

The policy recommended here takes these features of data into account. Most responsibilities lie with line organizations. In particular, organizations that create data values assume responsibility for their accuracy. Deploying any policy is difficult, although certain areas are easier to deploy than others. The enterprise is advised to start with those items that are easier to deploy.

REFERENCES

[1]   Negroponte, N., *Being Digital*, New York: Vintage Books, 1996.

[2]   Branscomb, A. W., *Who Owns Information?: From Privacy to Public Access,* New York: Basic Books, 1994.

[3]   *Understanding Information,* Surrey, England: P-E Centre for Management Research, 1994.

[4]   Levitin, A. V., and T. C. Redman, "A Model of Data (Life) Cycles with Application to Quality," *Information and Software Technology,* Vol. 35, No. 4, April 1993, pp. 217–223.

[5]   Levitin, A. V., and T. C. Redman, "Data vs. Traditional Resources: Properties and Management," submitted to *Communications of the ACM.*

[6]   Fox, C., A. Levitin, and T. Redman, "The Notion of Data and Its Quality Dimensions," *Information Processing and Management,* Vol. 30, No. 1, 1994, pp. 9–19.

[7]   Strassman, P., *The Politics of Information Management,* New Canaan, CT: The Information Economics Press, 1995.

[8]   Redman, T. C., "Opinion: Improve Data Quality for Competitive Advantage," *Sloan Management Review,* Vol. 36, No. 2, Winter 1995, pp. 99–107.

[9]   Davenport, T. H., R. G. Eccles, and L. Prusak, "Information Politics," *Sloan Management Review,* Vol. 33, Fall 1992.

Chapter 4

Starting and Nurturing a Data Quality Program

"A little rebellion every now and then is a good thing."
—Thomas Jefferson

4.1 Introduction

The fourth leg of a successful data quality program is program administration, including, and maybe especially, change management. Program administration and change management provide the vision and courage to nurture the data program as it gets started, the planning to help it grow, the discipline to keep it on track and focused on the most important problems and/or opportunities, and the management to help the data program become part of the enterprise's mainstream.

It provides the leadership to garner support, to help people understand their roles and responsibilities, and focus the effort. It performs the day-in and day-out planning, resolves conflicts that are sure to arise, and ensures that the myriad of details are covered. Program administration helps place key people in the right positions. When standard reference materials, training programs, or benchmarks are needed, program administration arranges to acquire them. If a few malcontents are holding up progress, program administrators find a middle ground. When technical or management problems arise that people can't resolve on their own, program administration finds solutions. And it celebrates success!

Few people openly admit that they are opposed to data quality. Still, neither starting a data quality program nor advancing a solid program is easy. If this sort of progress was easily made, then every enterprise would already have good data. Actually, most enterprises already have data quality systems, even if they are only implicitly defined. Here the phrase "data quality system" is the totality of the enterprise's efforts to impact data quality. Included are efforts to respond to errors, find errors before others do, manage and improve processes that create data, and prevent errors. In this chapter we consider an enterprise with a so-called "first-generation" data quality system.

First-generation methods for information chains were described in Chapter 2, and characteristics of enterprise-wide, first-generation data systems are given in Figure 4.1. An enterprise with a first-generation data system may be responding to customer billing or delivery complaints, conducting a clean-up exercise, or editing "dirty data" before they enter a data warehouse. These efforts are likely to be uncoordinated, expensive, and of uncertain value. The enterprise is likely experiencing other data issues, such as redundancy and privacy concerns.

Second-generation methods for information chains were also discussed in Chapter 2 and characteristics of enterprise-wide, second-generation data systems are also given in Figure 4.1. In this chapter, we'll discuss how to move from a first-generation system to a second-generation system.

An enterprise will not be able to move from a first-generation system to a second-generation system overnight. Early on, it will do well to implement one or two projects on a single information chain. It can then expand the program, enlarging its scope and impact. Finally, the data quality program can become part of the enterprise's mainstream, with data quality just a part of everyone's everyday job.

Figure 4.1 depicts these stages. There is nothing special about the specifics of the three transition periods. In some enterprises the distinctions among stages may be blurred; other enterprises may require more than three stages; still others may have to repeat the three stages in each organization. The focus of this chapter is on the transition periods—starting the data quality program, expanding it, and

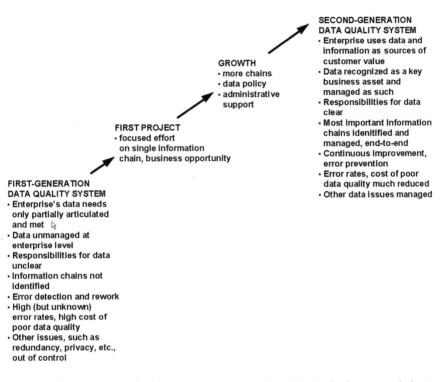

Figure 4.1 Transformation cannot happen in a single step. Here we consider the case in which an enterprise starting with a "first-generation" data quality system implements changes necessary for it to have a "second-generation" data quality system as part of the mainstream.

becoming mainstream. Obviously, working within each stage is also important. But our focus here is on the transition periods.

The need for change, rapid and continual, is no longer news to the Information Age enterprise. The pressures that demand change are enormous—shorter product life cycles, global competition, and demands of owners for higher profits and leaner organizations. In many industries these pressures have predominated for two decades and there is no letup in sight. "Re-engineering" was the norm long before the term was coined.

Yet, change is risky and uncertain. We noted earlier that three-quarters of re-engineering projects fail. There are any number of reasons that data programs are especially difficult, as discussed in Chapter 3. But experience suggests that at least some of the uncertainty can be reduced. We begin the chapter with a model useful for reducing the uncertainty in implementing any change program, not just data. We'll then discuss its application to data quality during the three critical transitions: getting started, expansion, and becoming mainstream.

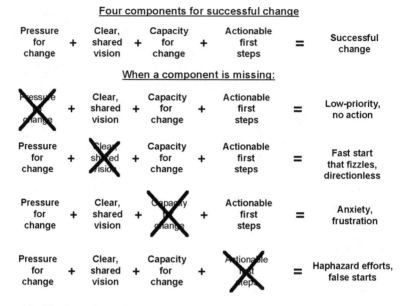

Figure 4.2   This figure depicts four components needed to successfully implement any change program. If any are missing, the change program is unlikely to succeed!

4.2   A Model for Successful Change

Figure 4.2 depicts a model with four components needed for successfully implementing change, along with the likely result when each component is missing.[1] These elements are:

- Pressure for change (a sense of urgency);
- A clear, shared vision;
- Capacity for change;
- Actionable first steps.

We'll briefly explore each element in turn.

4.2.1   Pressure for Change

Enterprises in stable environments, with assured customer and product bases and financial returns, historically have not usually shown much interest in

---

1.   Steve Michaele of AT&T's Chief Information Office provided me with this model. He claims it has been around AT&T for at least a dozen years, but he can't recall the original source.

change. Nor have those in rapid expansion periods. Such enterprises usually believe, with good reason, that they must be doing something right. Change is risky, so why bother? Indeed, it seems that few enterprises change without crisis.

But, let's face it. Few enterprises are in stable environments with assured customer and product bases and financial returns. The norm is that there is already too much to do. Customers want more for less, shareholders seek greater returns, employees are already working beyond what can reasonably be expected, and competitors are becoming more aggressive every day. People are worn out from the continuing demands to do more with less. How can "something new" command any attention under such circumstances? Clearly, without significant pressure, it will not.

The pressure for change almost always comes from the outside. Customer and/or shareholder dissatisfaction, loss of market share, or competitors' actions may cause a crisis situation. For an organization within the enterprise, the crisis may be as simple as a budget cut or an overbearing boss. The pressure for change can also come in the form of an opportunity—to increase market share, to crush a competitor, or establish a marketing niche. And the opportunity may be as simple as a personal opportunity to take and show leadership.

The most important implication is that leaders of a data quality program should not appeal to "quality is good" type arguments in building support for the program. Data quality must address specific issues/opportunities and make specific contributions to the business. In building support, data quality is not the "ends," but the "means," for responding to the business need or creating an opportunity.

4.2.2 Clear, Shared Vision

The second component necessary for implementing change is a clear, shared vision of the desired end result. Let's take the phrase apart a word at a time. First, the word "vision." Here, vision connotes what is to be achieved, or the "end-in-mind" in Stephen Covey's language [1]. The vision must address the pressure for change, but it must say more than "this incredible pressure we're under will go away."

The first of the two descriptors is "clear." The end-in-mind should be stated in simple business language that people can understand. A statement such as "our data will be 99.9% accurate" is a terrible vision statement, because it doesn't address a business need and because most people simply don't understand it. There is a tendency to try to squeeze a vision into as few words as possible. Often a single picture can convey the image much more clearly than words.

The third word is "shared." All important changes demand that a community of people work together. Any number of clichés capture this thought: "Let's all row in the same direction!" "Let's get on the same page!" Obvious as this point is, few groups can achieve a shared vision. Even at the highest levels of team sports, it is extremely difficult to get everyone to subscribe to a larger "end-in-mind." Without a clear, shared vision, a change program tends to go in all directions at once. A fast start is sometimes made, and a few initial results achieved. Some efforts cancel each other out, the effort fizzles, and no sustainable changes are made.

Again, the implications for leaders of data programs are clear. They must be able to convey their visions in simple terms that people throughout the enterprise, or at least those involved, understand and find compelling.

4.2.3   Capacity for Change

Obviously, the enterprise must be capable of doing things in new ways if it is to succeed. It must have any needed equipment, time, and knowledge. There are plenty of trite examples. You can't expect people to use new desktop software if it requires more memory than people have on their PCs, nor can you expect them to use it unless they have proper training or the time to figure it out for themselves. Nor can you expect someone to computerize an operation without needed capital resources. Similarly, you would not expect someone to implement process management on an information chain unless he or she understood process management.

Knowledge, capital, and time are all important elements of the "capacity to change" component. But the most important element is the *emotional* ability to change. People get used to doing their jobs and thinking about things in particular ways, and they don't like to change. Much resistance to change is purely emotional, although, of course, it is seldom articulated as such. In many cases, people (and organizations) feel that a proposed change invalidates cherished beliefs or their lives' work. Even scientists, whose tradition highlights the importance of new theories replacing old, hold onto paradigms long after evidence has discredited the old thinking (see Kuhn [2] for a discussion of paradigm shift in science). Kuhn's points seem to me to be equally valid for all individuals. Finally, the required ability to change applies to entire organizations in the same way it does to individuals.

As applied to "quality," specifically, there is strong evidence that emotional reactions to quality have deep psychological and cultural bases [3]. In America, people react strongly to the notion that they "aren't doing their jobs well enough." But when they get "turned on," they do amazing things.

Individuals can be motivated to overcome their emotional resistance to change through one or more of the four Fs: Fear, Fame, Fun, and Fortune. Some people are motivated by the fear that failure to change will be more painful than changing; others, by the possibility of personal recognition; others, by the adventure of a project that may "succeed against all odds" ; and still others, by personal financial gain.

Leaders of data quality programs should be prepared for emotional resistance. They may be able to partially address emotional reactions if their vision is compelling enough. They can develop compelling arguments for their programs that appeal to each individual's motivations to change. Finally, in the early stages of their program, they should avoid people whose resistance is purely emotional.

4.2.4 Actionable First Steps

All this philosophy is fine, but people have to actually *do* things differently, not just feel inspired or part of a team. Progress has to actually be made, one small step at a time. The first steps are particularly important for several reasons. First, visions are not always practical and have to be tested. Second, many people "on the team" need to see progress or they become disillusioned. Third, those who opposed the change program are all too eager to cite failure to show results as evidence of the program's wrong direction.

4.3 Getting Started

This section focuses on getting a data quality program started. The essence of our advice is focus carefully, start small, and move quickly to achieve the first couple of successes.[2] Doing so makes it much easier to achieve and sustain the four required elements of success. Thus, it is best to select a specific business problem and a single information chain, implement process management on a portion, make some improvements, and reap the first few benefits. As always, the intended benefits should make a tangible contribution to the enterprise's business.

The selected project should balance a number of tradeoffs. First, the selected information chain and business problem should be big enough that people agree that making progress adds business value, but small enough that it

---

2. In the context of Figure 4.1, successfully completing the first project is the "actionable first step."

can be completed fairly quickly and doesn't attract too much controversy. The project should be fairly broad, as most interesting data quality issues cross organizational boundaries. But, breadth breeds complexity. A small cross-organizational team, of say three to five volunteers, called the process management team (see Chapter 7), should be responsible for the project. Collectively, team members should be able to effect needed changes where required and have technical knowledge of the selected information chain. Each individual should be respected within his or her own organization. It is usually fairly easy to find a small number of people who intuitively understand the impact of poor data quality and are willing to invest time into the first project. Too few team members reflect a project of insufficient breadth; too many, and it will be impossible to "share the vision."

It is best when the first project is sponsored or led by a senior executive, ideally an executive whose business results are affected. Other good project sponsors include the Chief Information Officer, the Chief Quality Officer, and the Chief Financial Officer.

This project will later be called a "prototype" or "skunkworks." If successful, it will serve as a role model to the rest of the enterprise. Therefore, it is important that the process management team work through the entire process management cycle, as described in Part II. At the same time, the team needs to move quickly. It is almost always best to quickly obtain definitive successes on some of the easier opportunities than to address the harder ones, even if the harder ones yield bigger returns. Small successes make it easier to address the larger issues later.

The usual temptation is to select first projects that are too big. Most important business issues are multidimensional and addressing them requires both breadth and depth. It is best to resist temptation and focus carefully. For example, if various types of data from several sources compromise the enterprise's Decision Support System, there is a temptation to develop and implement a comprehensive solution. Unless the enterprise has a great deal of experience with data quality, this is unlikely to work. Instead, select a single source or type of data. Better still, focus on a single source *and* type of data. To be sure, select important data and a big source, but make the problem manageable. And, given the choice, pick a *willing* source. Similarly, if poor billing is the business issue, focus first on a single product line, category of customers, and billing option.

This advice goes a long way to providing each of the four elements of successful change.

- The "pressure for change" stems from the need to achieve results quickly.
- The vision is focused, short-term, and defined in business terms. Only volunteers who subscribe to the vision are included. This also helps lessen the initial resistance to change.
- Capacity for change is achieved through the formation of the team.
- Actionable first steps are the steps of the process management cycle, discussed in Part II.

One final piece of advice to team members. Don't fight the naysayers. They come out of the woodwork with all kinds of reasons that this first project is silly, of no importance, and that process management won't work. In fact, of course, these reasons simply camouflage emotional resistance to change. These emotional reactions are completely valid, but there is simply no way for team members to address them and attempting to do so is a waste of time. Most naysayers are completely harmless. If and when they do slow progress, the executive sponsor should provide relief.

4.4 Growth Stages

Joe Juran[3] has noted that enterprises do not move forward in lockstep. There are usually a few intrepid souls willing to try something new. They are the volunteers for the first projects. Then there is a second layer of people who like to be early adopters of new ideas, even if they aren't the first. These people often like to let others work out some of the details and take the initial risks. They keep an active eye out for new ideas and select some promising ones. The third layer is the majority of the enterprise. There is a fourth layer of people who will never change.

The second layer is the key to the second transition phase, growth. The first successful project may serve as a role model for the next several, but expanding it and identifying and conducting the next several projects is probably the most difficult transition for most enterprises. Some of our advice for getting started had the impact of hiding the first project from the scrutiny of the rest of the

---

3. I heard Juran explain this model for organizational change in a lecture in the mid-1980s, but I have not seen it in his writings.

enterprise. We advised moving fast, selecting only a piece of a business problem, and ignoring naysayers. Obviously this advice is not practical during the growth stages—nor is it wise. If you want a program to grow, it hardly seems wise to keep people from knowing about it. But growth places new strains on all four elements needed for successful change, and leaders must work continually to ensure that all four elements are in place. People in the second layer are not too patient. They will try something that looks promising, but they want good results fast.

Thus, selection of business problems, information chains, and projects is even more critical during the growth stage. If the first-stage project was a carefully selected prototype, then expanding it is one good growth project. Other candidate projects stem from the enterprise's most critical business strategies and/or most important data, as discussed in Section 2.3. Each project should be just as carefully focused as the first. The growth stage is the proper time to develop and begin implementing the data policy. As discussed in Chapter 3, it is often best to deploy the policy in layers as well.

Numerous support elements are needed if the new projects are to succeed and the policy is to be successfully deployed. These include:

- Frequent and clear communication of the program's urgency, the end-in-mind, the data policy, and success stories.

- Training and education programs. People and teams need to know what to do when. They need to know what tools to use and they need a common language.

- A means of tracking overall progress. Data quality can become a part of the Chief Quality Office or the Chief Information Office's overall program, and data quality metrics may be added to their existing reporting "scorecards."

The enterprise's total resistance is greatest during the growth phase, so, visible, committed senior leadership is essential. Senior leadership helps select the right projects, build the right teams, and ensure that needed support elements are in place. It also settles disputes.

4.5   Becoming Part of the Mainstream

The best quality programs are those that are simply part of the fabric of the enterprise. No one will be surprised to learn that this takes years and cannot be rushed. Attention to data and understanding what is needed to develop and sustain high-quality data is simply built into the culture. Enterprises that are proponents of the Deming philosophy or have embraced Total Quality Management can usually embrace data and information quite easily.

There is no better advice for creating a culture, enterprise-wide, that supports data quality than W. E. Deming's Fourteen Points [4, 5]. They are repeated here, focused to apply specifically to data and information.

1. Recognize the importance of data and information to the enterprise's objectives and create constancy of purpose in improving them and their use.

2. Adopt the new philosophy. The enterprise can no longer live with currently accepted levels of data quality and the lowered customer satisfaction, expense, and delays they cause.

3. Cease dependence on error detection. Eliminate the need for error detection by building accuracy and other quality attributes into processes that create data and information.

4. End the practice of awarding business on the basis of price tag. In particular, require that associated data and information be of high quality. Encourage suppliers to provide statistical evidence and eliminate those who will not.

5. Constantly improve the systems by which data and information are produced and used to create value for customers, the enterprise, and its stakeholders.

6. Institute job training. Help individuals and organizations understand how their actions impact data and others downstream. Teach them how to solve problems they can solve on their own and bring those they cannot to the attention of others.

7. Teach and institute leadership for supervisors of workers who produce data. Managers of organizations that produce data must become responsible for quality, not simply numeric production. The entire enterprise's productivity will improve with improved data.

8. Drive out fear so people may focus their efforts for the good of the enterprise.

9. Break down barriers between organizations. In particular, ensure the free flow of high-quality data and information across organizational boundaries.

10. Eliminate slogans and numerical goals that seek improved productivity or quality without providing the means. Don't simply expect improved data; show how this may be achieved.

11. Eliminate production quotas and management by objective. They lower data quality and harm the enterprise as a result. Instead, learn how to manage and improve processes that create and use data and information.

12. Remove barriers standing between data producers and their rights to pride in their work.

13. Institute training on data and information, their roles in the enterprise, and how they may be continuously improved.

14. Create a structure in top management that recognizes the importance of data and information and their relationships to the rest of the business. Develop and implement a plan to put everyone's talents toward the transformation.

4.6 The Role of Senior Management

Early in my career, I was critical of many people in the Total Quality Management movement because I thought they placed undue emphasis on the role of an enterprise's senior management, especially its CEO. Frankly, I thought that their criticisms were merely an excuse for ineffectiveness. I've changed my mind. I still think an enterprise can make important strides to improve quality, including data quality, without the leadership of the CEO—I've seen it happen. Leaders are needed at all levels. In almost all enterprises, middle managers can identify and lead the projects needed to get a data quality program started. They can do so without visible support from their bosses, but the failure rate of such unsupported projects is too high. The active, committed leadership of senior management can reduce the failure rate—the sooner the better, the higher the better.

After the prototype stage, programs move further and faster with senior leadership. No enterprise can hope to build data quality into its mainstream without it.

4.7 Summary

Starting and nurturing any quality program is fraught with difficulty and danger. Data quality is especially difficult. Programs yield disappointing results for any number of reasons. But the risks can be managed. By recognizing what is needed to successfully implement change, leaders of a data quality program can minimize risk. They should start small and tackle data quality issues that produce definitive results recognized by the business. They should recognize emotional resistance to change. And they should build a culture that puts data quality squarely in its mainstream by advancing Deming's Fourteen Points.

The difficulties are counterbalanced by the rewards. For individuals and small teams, starting and nurturing a data quality program can be exhilarating! The benefits that accrue to their organizations and enterprises are enormous. Most quality programs cannot be delegated far down in the organization chart. This is particularly true of data and information, since data ownership is elusive. Senior managers simply must lead if long-term, sustained, enterprise-wide success is to result.

REFERENCES

[1]   Covey, S., *The Seven Habits of Effective People*, New York: Simon & Schuster, 1989.

[2]   Kuhn, T., *The Structure of Scientific Revolutions*, 2d ed., Chicago: The University of Chicago Press, 1970.

[3]   Zuckerman, M., and L. Hatala, *Incredibly American: Releasing the Heart of Quality*, Milwaukee, WI: ASQC Quality Press, 1992.

[4]   Deming, W. E., *Quality, Productivity, and Competitive Position*, Cambridge, MA: Massachusetts Institute of Technology, 1982.

[5]   Deming, W. E., *Out of the Crisis*, Cambridge, MA: Massachusetts Institute of Technology, 1986.

Chapter 5

Data Quality and Re-engineering at AT&T

"A man with a watch knows what time it is.
A man with two is never sure."
                              —Mark Twain

5.1 Introduction

We mentioned earlier that data quality and re-engineering are intimately related and that poor data quality can derail many re-engineering projects [1]. Many re-engineered process designs call for IT to get data in the right place at the right time to complete some sequence of value-added activities for a customer. But if the data are wrong, either one or more activities can't be completed, or they will be completed incorrectly. Either way, the re-engineered process is ineffective. You simply can't get the benefit from a re-engineered process when the data are wrong.

On the other hand, improving data quality offers a proven method to re-engineer processes, especially financial processes. Many financial processes involve a long series of simple operations: The customer orders something, gives some account data, a credit check is run, an account is set up, the merchandise is shipped, a charge is applied to the account, a bill is prepared and sent to the customer, payment is received, the account credited, and so forth. Such financial chains also process large numbers of items. They were among the first uses of computers in industry. Most financial chains also feature a large number of integrity checks, database bashes, and edits. I suppose this is natural. When money is involved, most people and organizations are more careful, and the natural way to be more careful is to check that what you received is what you expected to receive. Maybe this checking is justified, as so many financial processes don't seem to work very well. But checking is not value-added work. It is just the kind of work that Hammer and Champy envision should be eliminated [2]. And when there are lots of non-value-added steps, eliminating them all dramatically simplifies the process, effectively re-engineering it. In this chapter we give a brief description of efforts initiated by the AT&T access management organization in this regard.

5.2 Background

In 1984, AT&T divested itself of its companies that provided local telephone service. AT&T itself continued to provide long-distance service, manufacture and install telecommunications equipment, and manufacture computer equipment. These local telephone companies (Telcos) provided local service, directory services, and "access services," which connected the long-distance providers to end users. It is long-distance and access services that are pertinent to this case study. Figure 5.1 depicts an example call. The caller on the left, in Somerset, New Jersey, dials her friend in Nashville, Tennessee. New Jersey Bell (a Bell Atlantic company) receives the digits, recognizes the long-distance carrier preferred by this customer, and switches the call to that carrier (in this case, AT&T). AT&T carries the call through its network to the Nashville area, where it is handed off to South Central Bell. South Central Bell completes the call. The hookups from the customer to AT&T, on both ends of the call (Bell Atlantic on the originating end, South Central Bell on the terminating end), are examples of access services. Access is thus critical to all parties: It is needed by long-distance providers to connect to customers. Without it, customers simply can't complete calls. It is a significant source of revenue to the Telcos, and long-distance

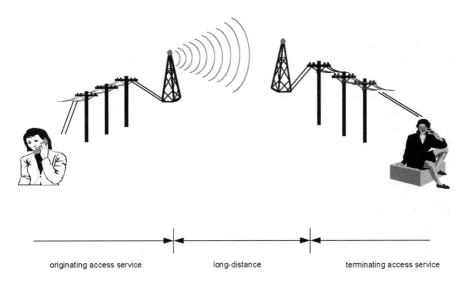

originating access service	long-distance	terminating access service

Figure 5.1 A long-distance phone call. On the originating and terminating ends, access between the customer and the long-distance carrier is provided by the local telephone company (e.g., Southwestern Bell). Long-distance providers (such as AT&T, MCI, and Sprint) carry the call between distant cities. They view the calling and called parties as customers and the access providers as suppliers.

providers are some of their biggest customers. Finally, much of the impetus behind divestiture was to ensure fair access to customers to all long-distance providers. Thus, judicial and regulatory bodies had great interest in access.

Our concern here is with the billing for access services. Roughly, AT&T spends $15 billion per year on access. There are many complexities in the billing access services, so here we'll concentrate on so-called "private-line" services. Here, end users, usually business customers, are connected to their long-distance provider by means of a dedicated line, not shared with anyone else (consumers, in contrast, share most portions of the network). Billing is relatively simple. Price is based on the capacity of the dedicated line, its length, and several other factors. And the price is the same no matter how long the circuit is used.

Divestiture was accomplished very quickly considering the magnitude of the job in splitting up over $100 billion worth of plant and equipment. All telecommunications providers had a hard enough time providing service. In many cases it wasn't clear which lines were connected where or even who owned them. So perhaps it is not surprising that access billing was a low priority and was not done well. So AT&T, to protect its financial interests, developed a "bill verification process." When AT&T received a bill, it paid the bill, then checked the bill against a "predicted bill" developed using its own sources. If the real bill and the predicted bill differed by too much, a claim was issued to the Telco (this policy of paying the bill and then claiming a rebate for overbilling is the so-called "pay and claim" policy). If the Telco thought the claim was strong, they could rebate the overcharge; if not, they could reject the claim and submit additional proof of the validity of their bill. Further, the Telco could issue bills for some time past the normal bill date and issue counterclaims to AT&T claims. In many cases, neither side could satisfactorily demonstrate its claims or counterclaims. So they were lumped together and an overall settlement reached. The key features of access billing and bill verification are depicted in Figure 5.2. It is especially pertinent to note that neither side was doing anything wrong. The Telco was doing the best billing job that it could. Much of the data needed by the Telco were a casualty of divestiture. They were wrong, out-of-date, or missing. Similarly, AT&T was trying to protect its financial interests.

Before proceeding, it is important to note just how typical the situation depicted by Figure 5.2 is, especially when money is involved. Even within enterprises, departments don't always trust one another, and they often develop elaborate error-detection and error-correction procedures of one sort or another. Except in unusual situations, this error detection and correction is non-value-added work, and almost all of it should be eliminated.

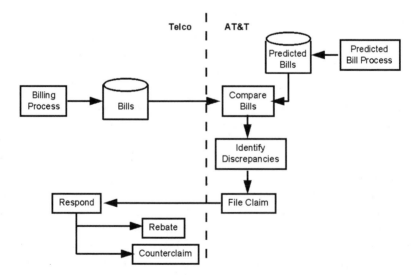

Figure 5.2 This diagram captures key features of the bill verification process. Note that bill verification is really a form of database bashing.

5.3   First Steps

5.3.1   Improve Bill Verification

The reader will immediately recognize that bill verification is really "database bashing," as described in Chapter 2. We noted there that database bashing was especially dangerous because it is easy to be seduced into bashing on an ongoing basis. That was certainly the case here.

But in many ways, bill verification worked. Over time, ownership and correct bills for a majority of private lines were determined. And the number and dollar value of claims decreased. AT&T could even view bill verification as a revenue producer. Even at their lowest, rebates and claims far exceeded the costs of obtaining them, and money coming in is revenue—no matter what the source.

Naturally, there was some dissatisfaction with bill verification. We already noted that a second problem with database bashing is that it is very hard to do well. This was also true of bill verification. As noted, a large number of claims were simply lumped together and settled because neither side could develop enough evidence to convince the other. Incremental improvements to bill verification were continually being developed to reduce the number of claims being settled.

The most critical problem, of course, was that the private-line business is very dynamic. Customers need more or fewer circuits, they need different features, they move, new customers need new services, and some businesses fail. The data associated with all these changes (and, as noted, the number of changes was considerable) added to the base of data issues each month. A sort of dynamic equilibrium evolved. New issues were created each month: Some issues were resolved, and many unresolved issues were lumped together and settled.

For its part, AT&T management decided that it had to do a better job of bill verification. That required better data. So it embarked on a small trial of data tracking (see Chapter 11). It focused first on the process by which new customers are "provisioned" private lines. That process is depicted in Figure 5.3. In the first step, a universal service order (USO) is created based on customer input. The next step creates an access service request from the USO. This request is translated into an industry-standard language and sent to the telephone company via a "firm order." The telephone company confirms that it will provide the requested service via a "firm order confirmation." When service is provided, data are stored in an access inventory database. The data created in this provisioning process were fed directly to the bill verification process. In the trial, about 50 records were tracked by hand. People did not believe the initial results.

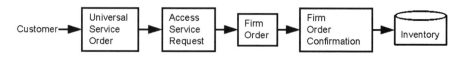

Figure 5.3   This diagram illustrates those portions of the access provisioning process that involve AT&T.

Virtually every record had at least one error. Not all the errors would affect bills, but a high enough proportion did. So the trial continued for several more months. Gradually, acceptance grew. Acceptance was greatly increased when a couple of nagging problems were solved. Figure 5.4 presents one tracked order [3]. A number of changes, as described in Chapter 11, are shown. Of interest here are the changes of a serious nature in the LSO-SECLOC (the Telco serving office) and BAN (billing account number) fields. Note in Figure 5.4 that both these fields change between AT&T and the telephone company. Figures 5.5 through 5.8 illustrate how the root cause was localized, improvements made, and the gains sustained. First, Figure 5.5 confirms that the most serious errors occur in the BAN and LSO-SECLOC fields. While BAN has fewer errors, these are more costly, so it is the appropriate field to concentrate on first. Figure 5.6, a "process-overview-of-differences chart" (see Chapter 10) for BAN, shows that almost all BAN errors occur on the AT&T/Telco interface. Figures 5.5 and 5.6 have thus pinpointed a specific problem and where it occurs. Figure 5.7 depicts the process used to determine the root cause. It is evident that one administrative region (Region 6) experienced far fewer BAN problems. Upon investigation, it was learned that Region 6 managed the interface with the Telco differently, and when those methods were implemented in other regions, improvements were quickly made. Figure 5.8 is a control chart (see Chapter 10), which illustrates the magnitude of improvements made. The control chart is also the primary vehicle for sustaining gains.

field ＼ step	USO	ASR	FO	FOC	Inventory
CKR	.DHBC.728534.ATI	**DHBC 728534 ATI**	DHBC 728534 ATI	DHBC 72853 ATI	DHBC 728534 ATI
BAN			272-791-9089	**272-791-9100**	272-791-9100
S25	SRBEX	**A**	A	A	A
LSO SECLOC	408727	408727	408727	**408970**	408970

Figure 5.4   Several fields tracked through the access provisioning process are shown.

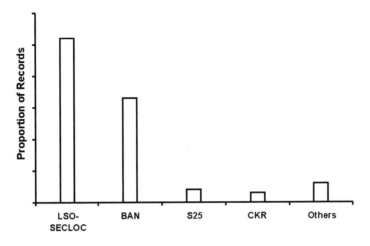

Figure 5.5 A pareto plot shows the proportion of fields experiencing serious changes in the access provisioning process.

As acceptance of data tracking grew, a number of people became increasingly dissatisfied with bill verification. A simple analogy to a gold mine evolved. In the analogy, one party seeded a mine with the other's gold. The second party used its best means to find and mine the gold. Since it was the second party's gold to begin with, there was no way to come out ahead. These people also recognized data tracking as "the right technology," but applied in the wrong place.

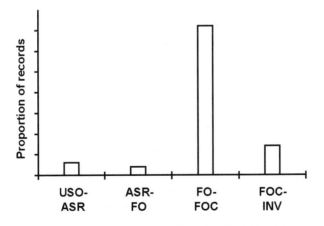

Figure 5.6 A "process-overview-of-differences chart" for the BAN field and the access provisioning process is shown.

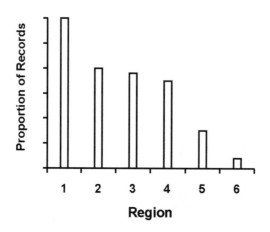

Figure 5.7   A plot of the proportion of BAN changes in six administrative regions. The fact that Region 6 is performing so much better suggests that the process is operated differently in Region 6.

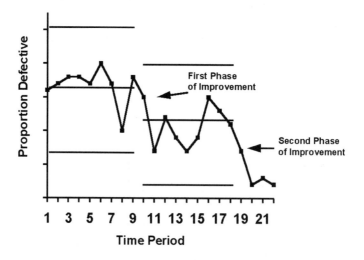

Figure 5.8   A control chart (p-chart) of the BAN changes between the FO and FOC steps. The first part of the chart indicates performance before improvements were made, the second part indicates when Region 6 procedures were tried in a second region, and the third part indicates when Region 6 procedures were implemented company-wide.

5.3.2 Prototype with Cincinnati Bell

But no consensus developed, so AT&T continued to try to improve bill verification.

As luck would have it, the AT&T unit leading implementation of data tracking was based in Cincinnati, Ohio, and shared a building with Cincinnati Bell. Many people were colleagues and personal friends. One day a few AT&T and Cincinnati Bell employees shared lunch and the discussion turned to billing issues. The AT&T employees noted their excitement about data tracking and their frustration with bill verification. Cincinnati Bell employees also shared their frustration with bill verification. They also noted that the data they needed from AT&T were suspect, although they thought it unlikely that any of their own data were corrupt. But they agreed to give data tracking a try.

To its credit, Cincinnati Bell only needed to track a couple of records to convince itself that there were problems with its data. Cincinnati Bell has a strong service ethic and any billing errors that resulted were simply unacceptable. So AT&T and Cincinnati Bell employees worked together to improve the quality of bills. They began by tracking new customer orders across company boundaries—from receipt of a customer order, through Cincinnati Bell provisioning, and into billing. The most important results are as follows.

- The information chain, including the ordering and provisioning processes that created data needed for billing (or predicted billing), produced large numbers of errors. A few errors were the fault of one company or the other. But it was not possible to assign blame for most errors. Almost all errors occurred on interfaces, either between the two companies or between departments of either company.

- Almost all of these errors could be eliminated.

- Neither AT&T nor Cincinnati Bell had done a very good job explaining exactly what it needed from the other.

The trial was continued for about 6 months and a number of root causes were eliminated.

5.4 Re-engineering

One of the most interesting dynamics associated with re-engineering is paradigm shift.[1] Even with the success of data tracking and the Cincinnati Bell prototype, only a relatively small fraction of AT&T people thought that bill verification could be successfully eliminated. After all, Cincinnati Bell was a small company and other Telcos would not be impressed. But AT&T leadership had became convinced, and they wanted immediate action. The following sections describe briefly the four components of the successful data quality programs, as implemented here. The re-engineering project was given the name "Future Optimum State," or FOS.[2]

5.4.1 Business Direction

As senior management and a few others at AT&T developed a better understanding of the Cincinnati Bell trial, they decided that AT&T should at least try to eliminate bill verification. This would save lots of money—tens of millions of dollars per year. But would all Telcos be willing partners? They certainly would have to make some investment and why should they?

The answer to that question became readily apparent. Telcos didn't like bill verification any better than AT&T did. For them it was an expense—and an unpredictable one at that. Telcos incurred two types of expense: the monies they returned to AT&T and the cost of responding to the claims. This second type of expense was incurred even if a claim turned out to be unjustified. Minimizing these expenses, or at least making them predictable, was in the Telcos' best interest. So the long-term goal of a claimless environment developed rather quickly—where "long-term" meant "as soon as possible."

There are, of course, many ways to eliminate bill verification. Neither side doubted the other's integrity, and many people felt that the total of all billing errors, if they could be properly calculated, would net to zero or close to it. In other words, some billing errors were "undercharges," meaning the Telco charged less than the correct amount for the circuit; others were "overcharges," meaning the Telco charged more than the correct amount for the circuit. Some felt that overcharges and undercharges were about the same. Why not simply eliminate bill verification and let the chips fall where they may?

---

1. Personally, I feel the term "re-engineering" has become overused and corrupted in recent years. Any minor process improvement seems to qualify as re-engineering. Real re-engineering involves fundamental change, or paradigm shift, and paradigm shift is the most difficult component of successful re-engineering. Most re-engineering projects take time—2 to 3 years seems typical. Much of this time is spent in paradigm shift.

2. Pat Baker, Becky Bennett, Errol Caby, Sandra Fuller, Arnold Lent, Monica Mehan, Kerin Montogomery, Carol Spears, and John Tomkas led AT&T's efforts.

Independently, both sides decided that eliminating claims immediately might not serve their financial interests. Further, each company had short-term financial commitments that it had to meet while pursuing the claimless environment. This led to the FOS goal: Move to a claimless environment as quickly as possible while protecting the financial integrity of all parties. As a practical matter, this meant building the FOS system while continuing to operate bill verification. Bill verification would be eliminated when FOS proved itself.

Two specific measures were developed to verify progress toward the goal.

- *"Risk"* is the sum of estimated overcharges and undercharges. It represents the total magnitude of billing errors, without respect to which party they (the errors) might favor.

- *"Consequence"* is the difference of the estimated overcharges and undercharges. It represents the amount of money that should change hands.

In terms of these parameters, the FOS goal was to keep the *consequence* as small as possible each month and drive *risk* to zero as quickly as possible.

5.4.2 Program Administration

There are literally hundreds of telephone companies in the United States, all providing access services. Most are small, with only a dozen or so providing the bulk of private-line service. AT&T decided that it would first achieve FOS with these larger Telcos and worry about the smaller ones later. Even for the larger Telcos, AT&T did not want a separate FOS program for each, so it decided to manage FOS implementation as it would manage any other project. Local differences would, of course, be permitted, but certain core components of FOS would be the same for all providers.

A number of design and implementation teams were set up.

- An FOS core team. This team was made up solely of AT&T people and had responsibility for overall definition of the FOS implementation process (discussed in Section 5.4.4), definition of AT&T requirements, certification that a Telco had properly implemented FOS, and overall program management.

- Implementation teams (one per Telco). Implementation teams had the responsibility of taking AT&T requirements, translating them into a specific plan, and implementing the plan. Most members, including team leaders, were from the Telco. One member of the AT&T core team also served on each implementation team. Each Telco was allowed a certain amount of latitude in determining how to meet AT&T requirements, and the core team member was available to help make day-to-day decisions about what would be acceptable to AT&T.

- Steering committees (one per Telco). The leader of the AT&T core team, the leader of the implementation team, and senior leaders from both companies formed a steering committee, which met quarterly. The steering committee helped the implementation team with any problems they were having, resolved differences, and ensured that implementation was proceeding on schedule. The steering committee bore ultimate responsibility for successful implementation.

The cooperation of the teams helped ensure successful communication among parties.

5.4.3   Management Responsibilities

Perhaps AT&T's most important realization was that it bore full responsibility for the persistence of bill verification. It was easy to blame the Telcos for bad billing and to justify its actions on the basis of protecting its financial interests. But, subtly perhaps, when one organization checks the work of a second, the first assumes responsibility for the quality of the second.[3] FOS had to shift responsibility back to the Telco. AT&T's second important realization was that it had not been a good customer. In conversations with many Telcos, it was clear that they really did not understand what AT&T meant by a "timely and accurate bill." A clear definition had to be developed. These two realizations inspired definition of responsibilities along the lines of the data policy (Chapter 3) and the customer-supplier model (Chapter 7). In particular, AT&T would:

- Define exactly what it wanted and make sure the Telco had a fair chance to understand these requirements.

- Provide the Telco with correct data so the Telco could provision and bill correctly.

- Replace bill verification with supplier management. Results would be reviewed each month and AT&T would work with the Telco to address any shortcomings, plan responses, and manage their long-term relationship.

---

3.   Parents who check their children's homework know how quickly the children become dependent on their parents to find their mistakes.

The Telco would:

- Assume full responsibility for bill accuracy.
- Provide evidence of bill quality.
- Work to identify and eliminate root causes of error quickly.

5.4.4   Operational Plan for Improvement

The AT&T core team first defined what exactly AT&T meant by a "timely and accurate bill" and worked with each implementation team to ensure the definition was understood. Innocuous as the phrase "timely and accurate" may seem, a seemingly endless series of special cases had to be worked through.

The core team also defined the "implementation process" as a series of 12 milestones, which each implementation team would have to meet. Highlights include:

- Specification of an implementation schedule for other steps.

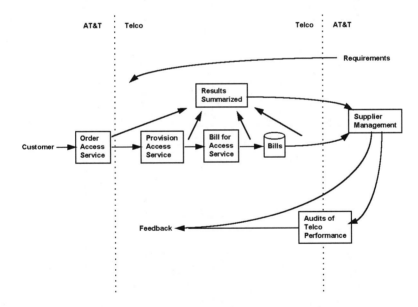

Figure 5.9 Key features of FOS implementation. Note three things: First, that AT&T ordering, telephone company provisioning, and telephone company billing were tracked as a single information chain. Second, note that results were summarized and sent along with the bill each billing cycle. Third, AT&T replaced bill verification with supplier management. Results were carefully reviewed, opportunities for improvement identified, and progress carefully tracked. An audit is conducted annually.

MILESTONE

TELCO	1	2	3	4	5	6	7	8	9	10	11	12
A	complete	complete	complete	complete	due 1/15	due 1/15	due 3/1	due 4/1	due 6/1	due 6/15	due 7/1	due 9/1
B	complete	complete	complete	complete	due 1/15	due 1/15	due 3/1	due 4/1	due 6/1	due 6/15	due 7/1	due 9/1
C	complete	complete	RED	YELLOW	due 1/15	due 1/15	due 3/1	due 4/1	due 6/1	due 6/15	due 7/1	due 9/1
D	complete	complete	complete	complete	complete	complete	complete	complete	complete	complete	complete	complete
E	complete	complete	due 2/1	due 2/1	due 2/15	due 3/1	due 4/1	due 5/1	due 6/15	due 6/15	due 8/1	due 9/15
F	complete	complete	YELLOW	YELLOW	due 1/15	due 1/15	due 3/1	due 4/1	due 6/1	due 6/15	due 7/1	due 9/1
G	complete	due 2/1	due 3/1	due 4/1	due 4/15	due 4/15	due 6/1	due 7/1	due 9/1	due 9/15	due 10/1	due 12/15
H	complete	due 1/15	due 3/1	due 4/1	due 4/15	due 4/15	due 6/1	due 7/1	due 9/1	due 9/15	due 10/1	due 12/15
I	RED	N/A	N/A	N/A	N/A	N/A	N/A	N/A	N/A	N/A	N/A	N/A
J	due 1/15	N/A	N/A	N/A	N/A	N/A	N/A	N/A	N/A	N/A	N/A	N/A

Figure 5.10 An FOS implementation scorecard. The first milestone is to schedule completion of the other 11 steps. The due date is replaced with "complete" as milestones are completed. Missed milestones are signaled first by a "YELLOW" and then by a "RED" flag. Note that as of the time of this scorecard, one Telco had completed all milestones, two showed RED flags, and two showed YELLOW flags.

- Implementation of an in-process measurement system, using data tracking.

- Demonstration that the in-process measurement system led to acceptable estimates of *risk* and *consequence* (defined above).

- Making the *risk* acceptably small and showing it to be in a state of control.

Then bill verification was turned off.

Third, the core team provided a detailed description of one acceptable implementation of the requirements. Figure 5.9 depicts a number of key features [4]. Note that an information chain, consisting of AT&T's ordering process, the telephone company's provisioning process, and the billing process, was tracked. Orders were randomly sampled and tracked and the billing impacts were calculated. Root causes of errors were systematically uncovered and eliminated. As was noted in the discussion of the Cincinnati Bell trial, most errors occurred on the interfaces of organizations within one company or the other or between companies. Almost all were relatively easy to fix once they had been identified and all implementation teams were able to reduce the *risk* by at least 90% in a relatively few months of serious work.

Finally, the core team tracked progress. A simple scorecard, such as that illustrated in Figure 5.10, gave an overall summary and provided needed detail at any point in time.

5.5 Summary

Once begun, AT&T completed its FOS re-engineering project in a little over 2 years, not counting time spent with Cincinnati Bell on the prototype. Billing errors were reduced by two orders of magnitude. Both AT&T and telephone companies benefited. Each saves millions of dollars per year by eliminating bill verification and associated claims processes. They improved their overall level of financial assurance and the predictability of expense and cost, respectively.

But the most striking feature of the FOS project is not its success. Rather, it is how typical the original situation, as depicted in Figure 5.2, actually is. The boundaries need not always be between enterprises—organizations within a single enterprise may exhibit the same behavior. The FOS formula of identifying the critical information chain, understanding the data requirements, making proper measurements, identifying root causes of data errors, eliminating those root causes, and then taking full advantage of this formula by eliminating non-value-added work is applicable anywhere.

References

[1]   Light, M., "Data Pollution Can Choke Business Process Reengineering," *Inside Gartner Group This Week*, Vol. 23, April 1993, pp. 5–6.

[2]   Hammer, M., and J. Champy, *Reengineering the Corporation: A Manifesto for Business Revolution*, New York: HarperCollins, 1993.

[3]   Redman, T. C., "Data Quality for Telecommunications," *IEEE Journal on Selected Areas in Communications*, Vol. 12, No. 2, February 1994, pp. 306–312.

[4]   Redman, T. C., "Opinion: Improve Data Quality for Competitive Advantage," *Sloan Management Review*, Vol. 36, No. 2, Winter 1995, pp. 99–107.

Chapter 6

Data Quality Across the Corporation: Telstra's Experiences

"The reasonable man adapts himself to the world;
the unreasonable one persists in trying to adapt the
world to himself. Therefore all progress depends on
the unreasonable man."
                                        —George Bernard Shaw

6.1 Introduction

Telstra Corporation Limited (formerly Telecom Australia) is a very large provider of telecommunications services in Australia. It provides local, long-distance, international, cellular, directory, and other services to roughly 10 million customers, including consumers, businesses, and government agencies. Its 1994–1995 revenues and pretax earnings were $11 billion and $2 billion (approximately A$14 billion and $2.4 billion), respectively. Like most telecommunications providers, Telstra has a strong service ethic and most Australians think Telstra has done a good job providing service at reasonable rates. Telstra has a strong quality management system. Most Telstra organizations have participated in an annual "George Hams" internal assessment, Australia's equivalent of the Baldrige Award criteria. Telstra began to introduce process management in service delivery areas in the late 1980s and early 1990s. This case study begins in late 1992.[1]

While Telstra has many advantages—a large and reasonably loyal customer base, a growing industry, and a modern network infrastructure—it continues to face many challenges as well. First, Australia is a huge continent. Most of the population lives within a few miles of the coast, but even the major population centers on the east coast are hundreds of miles apart. Australians are mobile. Australia has more cellular phones per person than any other country. Second, like many national providers of telecommunications services, the competitive landscape is changing dramatically. Telephone service is being deregulated. And, naturally, competitors will attempt to target growth areas such as cellular, long-distance, and international services. With deregulation, competitors can establish partnerships that provide them with technical skills, marketing know-how, and capital to enter these markets and become strong competitors.[2] Throughout 1992, as the shape the telecommunications industry could take in Australia began to appear (however dimly), Telstra became convinced that the battle for customers would be waged on the basis of service. As noted, Australians expect excellent service, and while proud of its customer service, Telstra determined that continued improvement was to its advantage.

Telstra's decision to target data for improvement stemmed directly from relationships between poor data and lower than acceptable levels of service.

- Incorrect addresses, which often prevented technicians from installing lines and other equipment when requested.

- Customer service representatives complained that they could not provide proper service because data about customers' service were incomplete and out-of-date.

- There were many billing issues, including late and incorrect bills. In addition, billing processes were time-consuming and expensive.

1. Dennis Flentje, Brian Fuller, Gerry Gorry, Grant Salmon, and Lynne Wickens led this work at Telstra. This chapter is based on [1, 2] and follow-up conversations with Grant Salmon.

2. Just as competitors to former Bell System companies have become strong competitors.

- Service could not always be provided on time because data about network capabilities were incorrect.

And since Telstra employees have such a strong service ethic, their inability to provide service to customers was a source of job dissatisfaction. Telstra management recognized this situation, and improving employee satisfaction, particularly for service representatives, also motivated their interest in data quality. Finally, Telstra was well aware that poor data quality carried high costs, even if precise estimates were unavailable.

6.2   Program Definition

Telstra's first step was to commission an assessment of its situation. The assessment would be used to craft its overall approach. Results of the assessment, stated in terms of a Force-Field Analysis (FFA), are presented in Figure 6.1. The basic idea behind FFA is that whatever the current situation, many factors contribute. Some factors have positive impact and are called "driving forces." Others have negative impact and are called "restraining forces." The current performance level is the result of these forces pushing on one another. If performance were stable, one could say that a sort of "dynamic equilibrium" had been reached.

In Telstra, the conclusion that the level of data quality was not high enough to meet its business strategies corresponds to a need to raise the level of the horizontal line in Figure 6.1. This can be accomplished by adding or strengthening the driving forces and/or mitigating the restraining forces. Driving forces included the following.

- Common understanding of the issues. While managers and organizations may have had different ways of accommodating poor data, there was almost universal agreement that the problem existed, was serious, and warranted solution.
- Strong service ethic. As previously noted, Telstra people are highly motivated to fix service-impacting problems.
- New systems planned. Like many organizations, Telstra had, over the years, introduced a series of major operations systems, each with its own database. These systems employed their own data models, implementations, and data entry criteria. So there was little commonality in data definition, field lengths, accuracy levels, and so forth. As computer and networking technology, on the one hand, and business

May, 1993   Data Quality Needs Assessment - The Situation

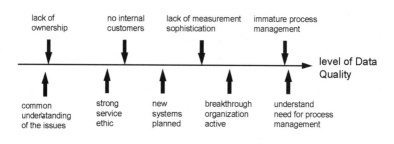

| lack of ownership | no internal customers | lack of measurement sophistication | immature process management |

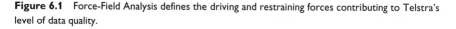

level of Data Quality

| common understanding of the issues | strong service ethic | new systems planned | breakthrough organization active | understand need for process management |

"as an organization, Telstra does not care about data quality"

Figure 6.1   Force-Field Analysis defines the driving and restraining forces contributing to Telstra's level of data quality.

needs, on the other, evolved, the various systems were interconnected. This situation contributed to data quality issues. New systems that integrated many legacy systems were on the drawing board.

- "Breakthrough" organization active. In order to accelerate the pace of implementation of process management and re-engineering, Telstra had established a special organization, known as "Breakthrough" and led by a senior manager who reported directly to the CEO. A Data Quality Center was part of this organization.

- Understanding need for process management. While process management was not yet a part of Telstra's culture, everyone—from service representatives, through middle management, to senior leadership— had a clear understanding of the need.

Restraining forces included:

- Lack of ownership. Specific management responsibilities for data were not assigned.

- No internal customers. Despite its strong service ethic, Telstra people did not recognize other Telstra people who were impacted by their work as customers.

- Lack of measurement sophistication. Most measurements of data quality were anecdotal. Telstra lacked an actionable measurement system.

- Immature process management. Telstra managers were just beginning to gain experience with process management.

With this background in mind, Telstra crafted a two-pronged strategy, as follows. The first prong was the data management infrastructure, which focused on ensuring that future system developments incorporated steps to ensure data quality. The second prong aimed at improving major processes and correcting the most important embedded data.

6.3   First Steps

For the first few months, Telstra's efforts focused on two tasks.

- Building the Data Quality Center;
- Gaining some experience with the tools of process management, understanding the nature of data, and developing high-level elements of its strategy.

The Data Quality Center was established as a part of the Breakthrough organization. Significantly, Breakthrough reported directly to and had the full support of the CEO. Its mission was set up to accelerate Telstra's implementation of process management and re-engineering, which was proceeding a bit too slowly in Business Units. Data Quality Center staff were recruited from the Business Units and the Chief Information Office. The goal was to create a focused and enthusiastic staff of people who, taken together, had good connections throughout Telstra. Staffing, of necessity, proceeded slowly and carefully.

Telstra also conducted three "alpha projects"—focused projects aimed at "learning by doing" some of the tasks their overall strategy would require. Alpha projects focused on understanding customer needs, implementing a simple data tracker to make in-process data quality measurements, and identifying Telstra's most critical data. The first two areas had been identified as weaknesses in the assessment, and the third was needed if improvement efforts were to be focused for the greatest good of the corporation. Projects were conducted in a short period of time, roughly 10 weeks, by small teams of three to four people each. Each project was led by a Data Quality Center person and assisted by an expert facilitator.

Determination of the most important data was especially interesting. Telstra has literally thousands of data elements, and to any individual the most important are those that he or she needs to accomplish a job. So there are hundreds of candidates for the designation of "most important data element." But after several discussions, a relatively simple solution was developed. Telstra used a simple model of its service chain, including customers, whom it provided with

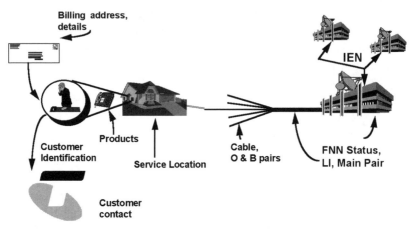

Figure 6.2 Telstra's service chain and most important data. The service chain links customers, the products and services they receive from Telstra, and Telstra's network. Critical data are those about customers (their service location, billing addresses, etc.), the products they receive (including billing details), and technical aspects of network plant and operations.

products and services, using a network to do so. Data about those major items (customers, the products and services they received, and the network) were the most critical. Figure 6.2 illustrates the service chain and the most critical data.

6.4   Full Program

As noted earlier, Telstra's overall program consisted of two components.

- The data management infrastructure, aimed at preventing problems from arising in the future;

- An operational plan, aimed at making needed improvements on specific problems.

The infrastructure component consists of several parts, as depicted in Figure 6.3. First, is a data quality policy—a high-level statement of management responsibility for data. The policy recognizes data suppliers, those who process data, and users, as well as their separate roles. The policy is supported by a set of data principles, which define specific business requirements to be met during

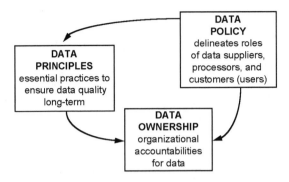

Figure 6.3   An overview of the components of Telstra's data management infrastructure program is depicted in this figure.

new systems development. These aim to ensure that data are given full consideration in new systems development, since developers are often more concerned about systems functionality than they are about data. The requirements are as basic as ensuring that data models meet quality criteria for clear definition. They also help support the concept of a single "official" store for each critical data item.

The third component is data ownership. The Chief Information Officer was made the owner of all corporate data. And a new position, called the Data Custodian, was established. Each custodian has responsibility for a related set of critical data items and works with development managers to ensure that data quality principles are followed. At the same time, Telstra's development process was modified to incorporate data quality. Development managers must obtain the custodian's sign-off that their projects adhere to the data quality principles.

Telstra had considerable success with the infrastructure component of its program and that component expanded. Figure 6.4 depicts the infrastructure component at maturity. Note the interweaving of items involving organization ("organizational structure" and "data ownership/custodianship" in the figure), management policy and practice ("data quality policy," "data principles," "corporate priority attributes," and "methodologies"), and technical capabilities ("measurement," "repository," etc.).

Telstra's operational plan for improvement is depicted in Figure 6.5. The last steps integrate process improvement and data correction and clean-up. Telstra recognized early on that the lifetimes of their data varied considerably. Some data, such as billing records, have short lifetimes and improvements must be focused "on the process." Other data, such as data about the network and about customers, are more diverse. Customers are the more familiar example.

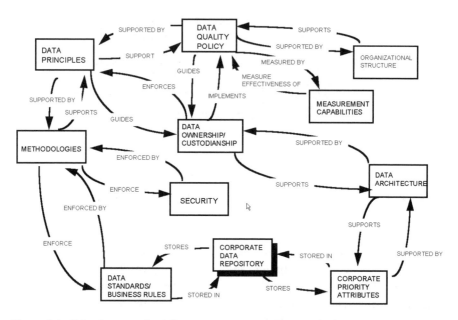

Figure 6.4   Telstra's mature data infrastructure program is shown in this figure.

There are many changes in the customer base and hence in the associated data. New customers want service, established customers want new services, and people and businesses move. But other customers establish a household or business, set up basic service, and then stay put, with the same services, for the next several decades. Data about these customers do not change over that time (unless an error is detected and corrected), although they are used frequently and are harmful when incorrect. Telstra calculations estimated that 20 years would be required for process improvements to yield the desired quality levels in customer databases. And the situation was similar for several other critical data items. Telstra's operational plan, then, aimed at properly focusing on both process improvements and data clean-ups.

With that end result in mind, Telstra's operational plan began with understanding users' data quality requirements. The focus throughout has been on the highest priority data to the entire corporation. Requirements were gathered in the usual way: first by identifying organizations and individuals using selected data, interviewing them, and then sifting through the maze of differing requirements. Extensive measurement followed. Data tracking was employed to estimate the accuracy of newly created data and the rates of new data creation. In addition, a sample of embedded data was taken and the correct values were

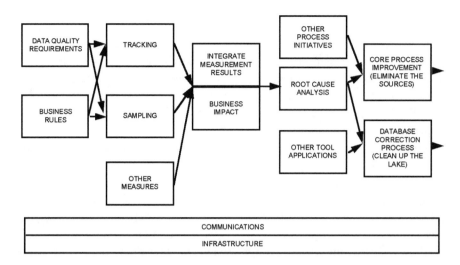

Figure 6.5 Telstra's operational plan for data quality improvement. The plan aims both to focus improvement efforts on the issues with the biggest payback and to integrate process improvement and data clean-up to improve data.

obtained by querying a customer, checking other records, and so forth. If other relevant measurements, such as customer satisfaction surveys conducted by another Telstra organization, were available, then these were also obtained.

The next stage was to estimate business impact. This step involved integrating measurements. The impact of an error was estimated, where possible in dollar terms. Then the error rates and impact were multiplied to yield an estimate of the overall impact to the business. Telstra found this step to be extremely important. First and foremost, those opportunities with the largest impact were selected for improvement. This focused improvement activities to the best advantage of the entire corporation. And over the years, of course, literally dozens of improvements were suggested. In many cases, of course, a proposed improvement activity involved some person's or organization's pet project, and business impact was not estimated. While such projects may well have been needed and valuable, Telstra had the greatest success following through when the business impact was clearly estimated.

Root causes of data quality problems were identified in parallel with day-to-day process management and other improvement activities. This required that Data Quality Center personnel work daily with process owners, members of their teams, and organizations creating data. As it expanded, the Data Quality Center could be leading a dozen or more improvement activities. In many cases process improvement and data correction were conducted at the same time. The Data Quality Center managed each improvement project just as Telstra would manage any other project. Based on business needs, resources were dedicated and a project plan, with a detailed implementation schedule, was developed. Project leaders met weekly to review status, share experiences, and resolve difficulties. Progress was regularly reported to Telstra's most senior management, including the CEO.

One other feature of Figure 6.5 deserves comment. Note that a band labeled "infrastructure," as discussed above, supports the operational plan. Sandwiched between infrastructure and the operational plan is a band labeled "communications." The Data Quality Center worked very hard to ensure that the rest of Telstra was aware of its work. It did so through a variety of means—a regular newsletter, frequent project status reports, and face-to-face communications. It also drew team members from throughout Telstra. These communications were extremely important, and any data quality project would do well to emulate Telstra's efforts. As we have noted, many data quality issues cross organizational boundaries and bringing everyone on board takes time, effort, and, above all, continual communication.

The Data Quality Center continued in the manner described above for about 2 years. Recall that it was located in the Breakthrough organization, away from customer service units and the Chief Information Office. Breakthrough had been established to provide a "greenhouse," where data quality, process management, and re-engineering could be nurtured—safe from the day-to-day pressures of line organizations. But such an organizational structure is inherently unstable. And, indeed, isn't it best if, once established, these functions are moved inside line organizations to become part of day-to-day management there? So eventually the Data Quality Center was split up. One part formed the Quality Billing Center, a second became part of the Chief Information Office's Strategy organization, and a third joined a Business Unit.

6.5 Results

Over time, the Data Quality Center participated in and led dozens of improvement projects. A large number, roughly three-quarters, were successful. The biggest gains were in billing and customer service. One of Telstra's largest internal problems was that many customer service orders did not properly enter the billing system. Ongoing clean-up had been a fact of life. Billing data and associated customer service issues surfaced as a result of this work, and measurement and impact analysis confirmed the importance of the issues. Working through the operational plan led to two major steps, conducted in parallel.

- Improving the service ordering process to ensure that orders entered the billing system successfully;

- Streamlining the error-correction process to efficiently reduce the backlog.

Note that neither activity alone provides an effective solution. But taken together, these actions produced operational, financial, and customer satisfaction returns. First, service order to billing error rates were reduced by more than half. Reduced cost of clean-ups and recovery of lost revenue produced tens of millions of dollars per year. And customer complaints were reduced. Other projects showed similar benefits—for example, errors in a customer records database were reduced by one-fourth.

It is more difficult to assign monetary benefits to the infrastructure program. In Telstra, infrastructure has lent an element of predictability—for example, in telecommunications there are literally dozens of changes to billing programs each year. Tariff changes, regulatory changes, and new services all require changes to billing programs. The infrastructure program helps make the overall process of planning for, implementing, and testing these changes more effective, efficient, and reliable.

6.6 Summary

Telstra's data quality efforts illustrate the benefits of a broadbased and broadly supported data quality program. From relatively modest beginnings and never growing beyond 20 people, the Data Quality Center defined and led a program that had broad impact and benefit across Telstra. Essential ingredients included:

- A well-developed and implemented strategy. Long-term infrastructure was built at the same time improvements were made. Telstra carefully selected and integrated the right approaches for making sustained improvements.

- Strong support of senior management. The Data Quality Center was led by a well-known and respected director. Similarly, its parent, Breakthrough, reported directly to and had the full support of the CEO.

- Focus. At each step, the Data Quality Center narrowed its efforts to embrace the most important problems. It selected the most important data based on business needs and selected improvement projects based on business benefit.

- A sense of urgency. Projects were aggressively managed and tracked.

- Teamwork and communication. The Data Quality Center worked with and through other organizations.

REFERENCES

[1]   Fuller, B. J., and T. C. Redman, "Data Quality: Lessons Learned at Telecom Australia," *Proc. QUALCON 94*, November 13–16, 1994, Melbourne, Australia, pp. 379–386.

[2]   Salmon, G., "Telstra—Data Quality Breakthrough: A Corporate Data Quality Improvement Programme," paper presented at the *GIS Partners Conference*, San Diego, CA, November 5, 1994.

Part II: For Process Owners

Chapter 7

Managing Information Chains

*"Everyone thinks of changing the world,
but no one thinks of changing himself."*
—Tolstoy

7.1 Introduction

We now describe how to improve information chains. Fundamentally, the secret is to manage these chains as *processes*.[1]

The distinction between "information chains" and "processes" is somewhat subtle. Usually, the term "information chain" is applied to a series of processes. Thus, for example, "billing" may be a process in a larger information

---

1. As a reminder to the reader, the terms "information chain" and "data-creating process" (and sometimes simply "process") are used to denote sequences of work activities involving data and information.

chain involving "order entry," "delivery," "billing," and "marketing" processes. Also, we sometimes use the term "subprocess" to denote a step of a process. Process management has proven itself on thousands of manufacturing and service processes and is just as effective on information chains. Part II of this book aims to help process owners—those assigned to manage information chains—be effective. Chapter 7 presents an overview and Chapters 8 through 11 provide more detail on the hardest steps.

As noted in earlier chapters, information chains and processes produce the data stored in large databases. More generally, processes are the means by which enterprises deliver added value to their customers—whether that added value consists of data, a service, or a tangible product. Thus, process management is fundamental to modern quality management. To motivate the discussion that follows, we contrast process management with more traditional approaches.

Our first example contrasts process management to hierarchical management. Figure 7.1 depicts a traditional high-level organization chart for a traditional enterprise. The enterprise features distinct functional organizations: Marketing, Research & Development, Manufacturing, Sales & Support, and so forth. Each organization consists of several management levels and is headed by a vice president. Each vice president is responsible for ensuring that the organization is conducted effectively and efficiently on behalf of the enterprise. Everyone below the vice president reports to someone within the functional organization and is, ideally, working for the best interests of the organization, which means understanding the organization's goals and objectives and doing their best to meet those goals. Such an organization relies on an executive committee (consisting of the president and the vice presidents) to coordinate activities. The functional areas are able to communicate with one another and work together to produce something of value.[2]

There are many benefits to this structure. Most importantly, it can create and take advantage of economies of scale. Second, with specialists in each of the functional areas, excellence in those areas can be achieved [1].

At the same time, there is one important problem with such a structure. Nowhere is there any mention of a customer, and no enterprise can survive long without a customer. It is easy to add customers to the functional organization chart—this is done in Figure 7.2. Even so, the result of hierarchically organized structures is that most management is vertical, along functional chains, not horizontal, in the direction of the customer.

---

2.   Any one-paragraph description of an organizational structure misses many points—but the purpose is to contrast hierarchical management with process management.

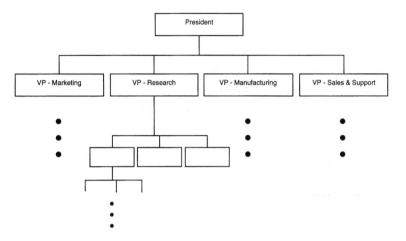

Figure 7.1 This is an example of a traditional organization chart for a traditional enterprise.

The key contribution of process management is to link various organizations, at all levels in the hierarchy, with the customer. The structure of the enterprise is then described by horizontal links, via processes, rather than by vertical links, via functions. Figure 7.3 depicts these horizontal links.

Many of the skills required to manage functions are also required to manage processes. For example, succeeding in a hierarchical organization requires understanding what the boss wants and delivering it. Succeeding in a process-

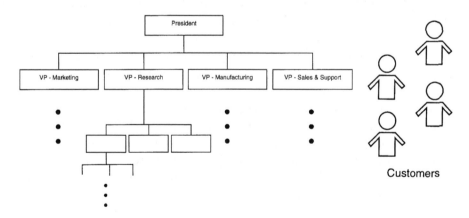

Figure 7.2 Customers added to the traditional organization chart. Note that since most of the management in a traditional organization is done up and down the organization, customers should logically appear at either the top or the bottom of the chart. But neither promotes broadband communications between the organization and the customer. Process management emphasizes the horizontal linkages across functions and promotes broadband communication with customers.

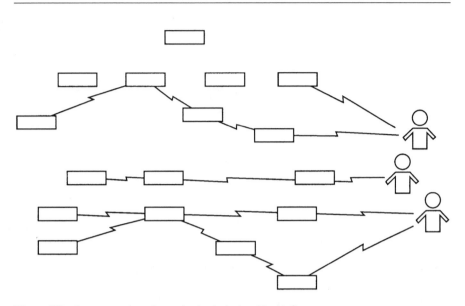

Figure 7.3 A process-oriented organization is depicted in this figure.

oriented enterprise requires understanding what the customers want and delivering that. There are (hopefully) more customers than bosses, so this is easier said than done.

Process management does not obviate the need for hierarchical management. On the contrary, it requires special skills and makes management more challenging. Further, process management should not dilute the importance of skill in performing functions. Functional excellence is essential and enterprises will continue to have functional reporting structures.

A second example, based on choices presented in Chapter 2, contrasts process management with other approaches and concerns databases, once again examining the results of data clean-up and process improvement. Suppose that data in a particular database, of great importance to the enterprise, are of sufficiently low quality that some corrective action is required. For the sake of the example, assume that the database consists of current customers' names and addresses. Two approaches to correct the inadequacies are under consideration.

The first approach is a variant of error detection and correction (discussed in Chapter 2) in which:

1. A team will be assembled.
2. This team will telephone each customer in the database and verify names and addresses.

3. All inaccurate data will be discarded and the new, correct names and addresses entered into the database.

The second approach is process control and improvement. In this approach:

1. All processes that can enter and/or change customer name and address information will be identified.

2. These processes will be put into a state of statistical control (as described in Chapter 10).

3. The quality levels of data entering the database will then be compared with requirements and deficient processes will be improved.

Both methods have advantages and disadvantages, as shown in Table 7.1. Most important, the future quality level of data in the database is predictable for both approaches. Figure 7.4 depicts these predicted quality levels. The contrast is stark. The clean-up approach works well in the short term but, because processes that create data are untouched, quality gains are lost. The process control and improvement approach, on the other hand, shows modest gains in the short term but quality levels continually improve and are sustained.

It is not necessarily wrong to clean up the data; short-term considerations may necessitate quick clean-up. But short-term considerations are often of less real concern than they appear to be. Considering only the short term can lead healthy enterprises into in a situation where database clean-ups are continually

	Feature	Clean-Up Approach	Process Approach
Short-Term	cost	high	low
	improvement to data	high	low
	improvement to process	none	medium
Long-Term	cost	high	low
	improvement to data	low	high
	improvement to process	none	high

Table 7.1 Positive and Negative Features of the Clean-Up and Process Approaches to Improving Data Quality

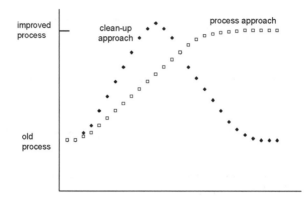

Figure 7.4   Shown are predicted data quality levels in a database under two improvement scenarios.

needed.[3] Furthermore, it is possible to combine some of the best features of both approaches to meet both short- and long-term considerations.

7.2   Future Performance of Processes

The purpose of the remainder of this chapter is to describe process management in some detail. The overarching theme is focus on the *future performance of the process*. As a general rule, this will involve:

1.   Establishing a process owner and management team;
2.   Describing the process qualitatively, and understanding customers and their requirements;
3.   Establishing a measurement system;
4.   Establishing process control and checking conformance to requirements;
5.   Identifying improvement opportunities;
6.   Selecting opportunities to pursue and setting objectives regarding each;
7.   Making and sustaining improvements.

---

3.   I conjecture that managers in many large enterprises are comfortable with database clean-up exercises. They can be learned and done well in many cases and enterprises may reward the short-term benefits, which are readily apparent. The endless cycle of database clean-up is simply viewed as a cost of doing business.

Before proceeding with a description of each step, some comments are in order. First, the steps in process management described here are from AT&T's *Process Management and Improvement Guidelines* [2, 3]. Other descriptions of process management differ in detail, but the essence is the same.

Second, to a large degree, process management is an all-or-nothing affair. These guidelines absolutely will not work if management, for example, sends key members of the enterprise out to understand customer requirements and then decides that customers do not really know what they want.

Third, it takes time to learn and gain experience in properly applying process management. Over the last several years, many industries have gained this experience in manufacturing. To begin implementing process management enterprise-wide, it is best to make a few attempts in organizations that are receptive to new ideas and on some relatively small-scale processes. As successes are achieved, interest from other areas will follow.

Finally, process management is probably most threatening, on its surface and in its early phases, to middle management. Those above and below in the management hierarchy are urged to be especially patient yet persistent with the much beleaguered group.

7.2.1   Step 1: Establish a Process Owner and Management Team

No management task will be carried out if clear roles and responsibilities are not established. Therefore, the first and most important step is establishing a *process owner* (or *information chain*). The operable word is *owner*. According to *Webster's Ninth New Collegiate Dictionary* [4] to own is "to have or hold as property: possess." Compare with *manage*, defined as "to handle or direct." Owning connotes much stronger commitment than managing, a greater degree of involvement, and much greater responsibility. So it is with the process owner, who is more than simply the process manager. The process owner must assume responsibility for the process. Ownership cannot be assigned; real ownership must be taken, in much the same way that an individual takes possession of a car, house, or any other personal possession.

Just as wanting to own a car is not sufficient to own one, wanting to own a process does not make a person a process owner. In addition to self-assumed responsibility for process performance, the process owner must have the authority, including necessary resources, to change it.[4] Similarly, just as one cannot

---

4.   Middle managers must often relinquish control. This is the root cause for middle management anxiety over process management.

buy a home without a willing seller, a certain degree of support is required of the process owner's management. Thus, three elements—assumed responsibility, authority, and support—are required.[5]

The major responsibilities of the process owner are to establish an environment in which process management can succeed and for seeing that success follows. Since most information chains span functional areas, it is often appropriate for the process owner to establish a *process management team* consisting of members of each relevant functional area. This team ensures that:

- Subsequent steps of the process management cycle are completed;
- Suboptimization is not occurring (i.e., improvements made to one step in the process are not made at the expense of others);
- Cross-functional improvement opportunities are identified and made, and, in particular, existing barriers between functional organizations are overcome.

Process management teams are frequently essential for success on information chains. Typical chains are large, complicated, interact with other processes, span many functional organizations, and often involve many locations. The ever-expanding capacity of communications networks is promoting decentralization. It may be impossible for the process owner to carry out responsibilities without a process management team.

In some organizations, the process management team itself, not the process owner, owns the process. This has merit—if common process management team commitment can be obtained, real power may result. But there are dangers. Process ownership often requires hard decisions and some teams are not good at making hard decisions. The best approach balances these considerations. Day in and day out, the process owner behaves like any other member of the process management team. This builds powerful shared commitment. But at certain times, the process owner must assume greater authority and make hard deci-

---

5. In every enterprise there are great stories about the way some determined, rugged individual accomplished some magnificent feat on behalf of the enterprise, in spite of overwhelming odds—lack of authority, funds, and so forth. Careful examination of those stories usually reveals that, for some reason or another, the individual(s) concerned took ownership for something. Such stories prove that process owners can occasionally succeed without support and authority. But the number who fail is large and many who succeed advise others to take such ownership reluctantly. If an enterprise wishes to have process owners succeed, it must provide authority and support.

sions. It is then incumbent on the process owner to justify or at least explain that decision as best as he or she can. Members of the team must occasionally accept a decision with which they do not agree.

A second issue that only the process owner can address is fear on the part of those who work within the process. Process management is often threatening to people, to their jobs, and to their sense of self-worth. The process owner should expect this fear and deal with it openly. Lessening fear requires integrity—probably the number one job requirement.

A third important issue for the process manager is making sure that everyone who works within the information chain understands who the customers of the process are, the customers' requirements, and their role in meeting those requirements. Said somewhat differently, the process owner's role is to see that the "voice of the customer" [5] is heard throughout the information chain and translated into action (step 2). Teaching others about the process can be a shared responsibility of the process management team.

Finally, establishing and communicating a value system so that everyone understands the importance of the customer and their roles in the context of the end-to-end process, is extremely important.

7.2.2 Step 2: Describe the Process and Understand Customer Needs

The process management team's first job (after having formed itself) is to develop a rudimentary understanding of the information chain it is supposed to manage. This includes understanding who the customers are and what they want and what the chain is supposed to do and what it actually does. Then the process management team must make sure that everyone understands his or her role in meeting customer needs. Deliverables include:

- A clear, consistent set of customer requirements for the entire information chain;
- Qualitative descriptions of the information chain, including major processes and subprocesses and their interrelationships;
- A mapping of customer requirements into technical specifications on those processes and subprocesses;
- A communications package that in one way or another informs people of overall customer requirements and their role in meeting them.

Three models have proven useful in accomplishing these tasks:

1. <u>1.</u>   The *customer-supplier model,* which describes who the customers are and their needs; suppliers and their inputs; and the outputs of the information chain;
2. <u>2.</u>   A *flowchart,* which describes sequences of work activities;
3. <u>3.</u>   The *functions of information processing (FIP) model,* which describes processes in terms of information flows.

Each serves a slightly different purpose. The customer-supplier model focuses externally on the customers and their requirements. The flowchart focuses both externally and internally. It places greater emphasis on how added value is delivered to the customer and where inputs enter the process. The FIP representation is internally focused. It concentrates on technical details of how information is developed, modified, and communicated within the chain.

Taken together, these three representations form a trilogy, building on and supplementing one another. The three descriptions need not be developed together, though after a little practice it is often easy to produce them as a set. These details are summarized in Table 7.2.

A generic customer-supplier model is displayed in Figure 7.5. The customer-supplier model features communications channels between the process management team and customers and suppliers for requirements and feedback. The voice of the customer is heard through these communication channels. The customer-supplier model is usually sufficient to understand overall customer requirements, but overall requirements do not usually provide enough detail to

Representation	Focus	Purposes
Customer-Supplier Model	External to the Process	1. Determine customers 2. Determine customer requirements 3. Determine suppliers 4. Determine requirements
Flowchart	Value-added steps	1. Show where inputs occur 2. Show where value is added
FIP	Internal to the Process	1. Show how data/information is developed

Table 7.2   Pertinent Features of the Customer-Supplier Model, Flowcharting, and the FIP Method

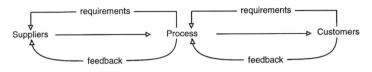

Figure 7.5 This is the customer-supplier model, adapted from reference [2].

let individuals know exactly what they must do. For one thing, customers usually state their requirements in nontechnical language and most work is technical. For another, customers state their requirements of the overall information chain, not individual processes.[6] Therefore, there is a need to translate soft, high-level customer requirements into technical process-specific specifications, including specifications for suppliers. This subject is discussed in Chapter 9. (See also reference [6] for a good discussion on developing user requirements for information systems.)

Figure 7.6 illustrates a standard set of flowcharting symbols. While a standard symbol set is not essential, confusion can result if no standard is adopted.

Because many readers are likely already familiar with the customer-supplier model and flowcharting, and good references are available, no more will be said

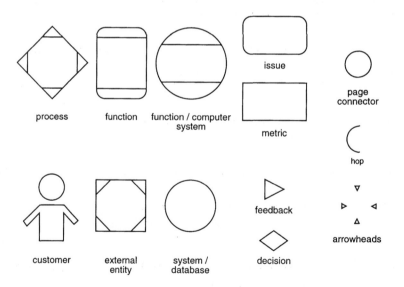

Figure 7.6 A hypothetical flowchart illustrating a standard set of symbols is depicted in this figure.

---

6. External customers probably will not even be aware of the information chain. The chain may produce products and services in addition to data and information.

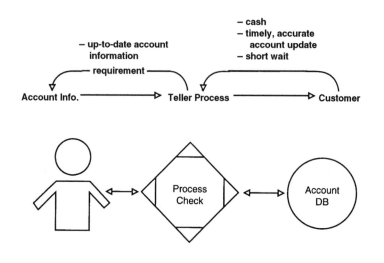

Figure 7.7 This illustrates the completed customer-supplier model, flowchart, and FIP diagram for a hypothetical check-cashing process.

about them here. FIP is apt to be new to most readers and is discussed fully in Chapter 8.

Figure 7.7 shows how the three representations complement each other, using a simple example about cashing and depositing a check.

7.2.3   Step 3: Establish a Measurement System

Once customer needs are understood, the process described, and specifications determined, a system of measurements to gauge whether or not customer needs are being met is put in place. Measurements provide hard evidence of process performance. Without them, the process management team can only rely on intuition and anecdotes. Measurements do not replace customer opinion as the final arbiter of quality. Instead, they are a vehicle to help ensure that customer satisfaction is high.

Good measurement systems satisfy the following needs.

- They inform the chain owner and management team about how well the chain, as a whole, is meeting customer needs.
- They inform the chain owner and lower-level process owners how well each process is meeting its specifications.
- They signal short-term problems of immediate concern.
- They provide a basis for establishing statistical control (Section 7.2.4 and Chapter 10) and improving performance.
- The overall system is simple and efficient.

These criteria are difficult to satisfy and so it is not surprising that good measurement systems are difficult to install and implement. Advice for doing so is provided in Chapter 11.

7.2.4   Step 4: Establish Statistical Control and Check Conformance to Requirements

We noted earlier that the process owner is concerned not just with current performance, but with the future performance of the information chain he or she manages—for example, at the end of one month, the process owner would like to take satisfaction not just in having met customer requirements that month, but also in feeling comfortable that requirements will be met next month. Statistical quality control (SQC) provides a basis for making such judgments. SQC will be discussed more fully in Chapter 10. The key idea is that one can confidently predict that a *stable process* will perform, within limits, as it has in the recent past. So it is important, in step 4, to make the information chain stable or put it in a state of *statistical control*. Of course, a stable process may not meet customer requirements, so it is also important to check conformance. Figure 7.8 illustrates the three most important cases and the actions taken by the process owner.

- A process that is out of control. It is impossible to predict whether this process will meet requirements in the future or not. It must be put into a state of control.
- A process in a state of control that does not meet requirements. It must be improved.

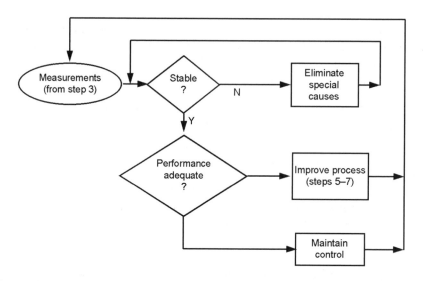

Figure 7.8 Process management team actions are based on whether or not a process is in control and whether or not requirements are met.

- A process in a state of control that does meet requirements. While all processes are candidates for improvement, it is only necessary to sustain control until requirements change.

The process management team also uses statistical control to sustain improvements made in step 7.

7.2.5 Step 5: Identify Improvement Opportunities

Many opportunities for improvement will surface in steps 1–4, and there is temptation to work on them. After all, it is more fun and more rewarding to improve processes than it is to describe them and establish control. However, it is difficult to pursue more than a few improvement opportunities at a time, as doing so consumes resources. Further, it is dangerous to do so, as some improvements may be made at the expense of other parts of the process. Therefore, the discipline of developing a complete list of opportunities and carefully selecting those to pursue pays dividends. This discipline is the point of steps 5 and 6.

To develop a complete list of improvement opportunities, the process management team should consider the following sources.

- Customer needs (from step 2). Often the information chain does not meet them.

- Descriptions of the information chain (also from step 2). Some steps may add no value, and eliminating these are good candidates for improvement opportunities. Chapter 8 describes a number of specific things to look for to identify these steps.

- Parts of the process that are in control, but not meeting requirements (from step 4).

- Interfaces between processes. A merit of a functional organization is that subprocesses frequently work well when performed within a single organization. However, the interfaces between subprocesses are often weak. A good interface provides for adequate communication and clear delineation of responsibility.

- New technologies. While automating a process that does not work well is unlikely to lead to good results, new technologies often provide better ways to do things.

7.2.6   Step 6: Select Opportunities

As noted in the previous section, actually making improvements is hard work. Improvements are made through projects: focused, carefully managed efforts adequately staffed and funded. Novice process management teams should pursue only a few projects at a time. In addition, it is advisable to begin with small-scale projects to gain experience with the methods of improvement, to build confidence, and to create success stories. Nothing kills process management faster than failed improvements.

On the other hand, of course, the whole idea of process management is to make real improvements. Thus, important projects must be tackled before too long. Nothing energizes process management more than a big success, visible to those working within the process, their management, and their colleagues. The process management team should also try to involve as many people as possible. Choosing improvement projects involves many considerations, and there is no prescription for doing so.

One final note: The process management team, upon selecting an improvement project, should set quantitative goals for the improvement team. Like all goal setting, this is a combination of science and art. In some enterprise cultures, "stretch" goals are viewed as challenges and accepted. In others, a sequence of reasonable, easily achievable short-term goals is preferred. The main point is that clear agreement between the process management team and the improvement team on what is to be achieved is essential.

7.2.7   Step 7: Make and Sustain Improvements

The part of quality that most people consider the most fun is process improvement. Although improvement is fun, discipline must be maintained. Following a few guidelines maximizes the probability that an improvement project will succeed, that it will lead to overall process improvement and increased customer satisfaction, and that the improvement will be sustained.

The process management team has done all the work of steps 1–6, and new improvement teams are chartered to make actual improvements. In some cases the process management team may charter itself. The process management team's responsibilities are:

1. Organize the improvement team. Name a team leader first, as the team leader and the process management team often work together to choose the rest of the team. The team should have people with expert knowledge of the portion of the process to be improved, data analysis skills, and quality training. In some cases, a *team facilitator* is included.

2. Provide resources. This includes staff time, capital equipment, and training.

3. Provide direction. The goals developed in step 6 should be assigned to the improvement team as its mission.

4. Monitor progress and support the team. Help with implementation as required. For example, the team may need support with widespread implementation.

5. Continue to manage the overall process. Coordinate the activities of parallel improvement teams and return to the steps above as appropriate. Most importantly, when the improvement team's work is done, update the process descriptions developed in step 2 and establish control at the new levels of performance achieved in step 4.

   Figure 7.9 illustrates these responsibilities. A long period of time may have elapsed since the process management team was formed, customers were identified, and so forth. It may be necessary to reform the process management team. These relationships are also noted in Figure 7.9. Note that Figure 7.9 shows a cycle of ongoing activities. When fully implemented, process management is an eternal cycle.

6. Recognize and reward the accomplishments of the improvement team.

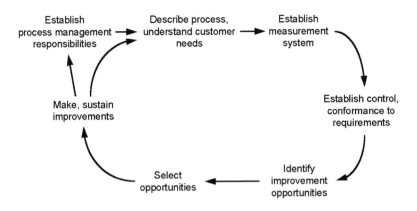

Figure 7.9   The process management cycle illustrates the process management team's responsibilities.

The responsibility of the improvement team is to change the process to improve it, as suggested by the process management team. As with everything in quality, disciplined adherence to a few well-established principles is important. Much has been written both about the dynamics of such teams [7] and about how they should proceed [8]. The critical points are as follows.

1.   Organize as a team. While the process management team can ensure that the improvement team has the right technical skill mix, only the team members can decide that the team's goals supersede all others. Each individual has to realize that the reason there is a team is to achieve something over and above what individuals can achieve. Similarly, the team must realize that it is made up of individuals, each with his or her own legitimate desires, needs, and interests. The team should work dynamically to take best advantage of individual skills, create synergies between those skill sets, establish rules (such as "meetings begin on time") to help minimize problems, and deal with conflict openly, honestly, and fairly.

2.   Determine the root causes of problems. The process management team will probably have given the improvement team a change that is too high level to be actionable. For example, the opportunity goal may be something like: "Improve the interface between subprocesses A and B so that we can deliver data to our customer two days faster." Note that such a statement gives no indication as to what is "broken" or otherwise preventing faster delivery of data. The goal of this step is to determine what is really wrong. Pareto charts,

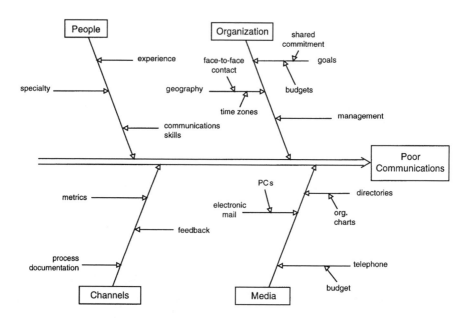

Figure 7.10   A cause-and-effect diagram, illustrating potential root causes of poor communication between two organizations.

cause-and-effect diagrams [9] (illustrated in Figure 7.10), interviews with others involved in the relevant steps, and special studies can be used to determine root causes.

3. Develop and try solutions.

4. Implement solutions.

5. Provide for "holding the gains." Nothing is more frustrating than developing and implementing a solution that works and then having improvements lost through lack of management attention. While establishing control is a process management team responsibility, the improvement team is responsible for making sure the measurements to be used are in place. Frequently, the improvement team's solution requires a new measurement. If so, it should be devised and added to the measurement system of step 3. Solutions that cannot be measured should be avoided.

Ensure that the process management team fully understands the implications of the team's work. Often, improvement teams notice other significant improvement opportunities during the course of their work. Similarly, they may notice dangers to holding the gains or previously unknown problems in the process. The quality im-

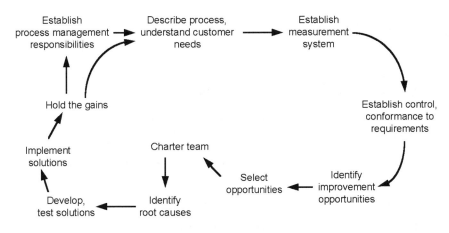

Figure 7.11   These are the steps in quality improvement and their relationship to the process management cycle.

provement team is responsible for informing the process management team about such things.

Figure 7.11 illustrates the steps the improvement team takes, as well as the relationship of these steps to the process management cycle.

7.3   Summary

Process management helps an organization hear the voice of the customer and manage its functions to deliver added value to the customer. The heart of process management is the process *owner*. Process ownership is characterized by responsibility for process performance and by authority to change the process. Frequently, large cross-functional processes require a process management team to support the process owner.

Process management is achieved via a sequence of highly interactive steps in which the information chain is described and measured; control and conformance to requirements is established; and improvement opportunities are identified, selected, and pursued. Improvements are made one at a time using chartered improvement teams.

Process management is cyclic. When improvements are made, the original process changes and must be redescribed. The improved process may also require new measures. Customer requirements also evolve. Thus, the steps are continuously repeated.

REFERENCES

[1]   Chandler, A. D., Jr., *The Visible Hand: The Management Revolution in American Business*, Cambridge, MA: Belknap Press, 1977.

[2]   *Process Management and Improvement Guidelines, Issue 1.1*, AT&T, Select Code 500-049, 1988.

[3]   *PQMI: Tips, Experiences and Lessons Learned*, AT&T, Select Code 500-446, 1990.

[4]   *Webster's Ninth New Collegiate Dictionary*, New York: Merriam Webster, 1991.

[5]   Davis, S. M., *Future Perfect*, Reading, MA: Addison-Wesley, 1987.

[6]   Fidel, R., *Database Design for Information Retrieval*, New York: John Wiley & Sons, 1987.

[7]   Scholtes, P. R., *The Team Handbook*, Madison, WI: Joiner Associates, 1988.

[8]   Juran, J. M., *Managerial Breakthrough*, New York: McGraw-Hill, 1964.

[9]   Ishikawa, K., *Guide to Quality Control*, 2d ed., Tokyo: Asian Productivity Organization, 1982.

Chapter **8**

Process Representation and the Functions of Information Processing Approach

*"If you do what you've always done,
you'll get what you always got."*
—Paul Strassman

8.1 Introduction

Process representation is motivated by the need to understand what is actually happening in a process.[1] But what is happening is generally complicated, and a complete description is infeasible. A partial solution is to develop simple models

---

1. Pat Janenko [1] is responsible for much of the work of developing the functions of the information processing approach.

of the process to capture some aspect of the process in some way. The customer-supplier model is one such model. It emphasizes high-level descriptions of added value from suppliers, value added by the process, added value delivered to customers, and communication channels. Flowcharting techniques allow us to build sequence-of-work-activities models of processes. Such models are of great value in understanding the flow of work, organizational responsibility, and so forth. As these techniques are both widely known and discussed elsewhere [2–4], they are not reviewed here.

The focus is on developing an "information model" of an information chain using the *functions of information processing* technique. The information model complements the customer-supplier and sequence-of-work-activities models. The latter two models have proven highly effective for describing manufacturing processes and are just as useful for information chains. The information model considers data as they are created, moved, stored, and so forth. All three models are not always needed. The information model is particularly effective for:

- Highlighting certain high-level features of information chains that other models do not capture well;
- Suggesting critical measures of process quality;
- Aiding detailed process improvements;
- Designing new processes.

In some respects, the information model is similar to a data flow diagram [5, 6]. The differences stem from their purposes: data flow diagrams help analysts design *information systems*, information models help process owners describe information chains.

This chapter is organized as follows: First, we present the basic ideas behind the functions of information processing (FIP) technique. Next, we describe the development of information models in terms of FIP charts. The FIP chart often suggests process measures and is effective in identifying improvement opportunities in step 5 of the process management cycle. We discuss these measurement and improvement opportunities in detail, using the process of updating an employee's address (after he or she moves, say) in two databases as an example.

8.2 Basic Ideas

All processes start with raw material, manipulate it, and produce output.[2] For an information chain, this raw material is generally source or input data, which

---

2.   The functions of information approach has its roots in reference [7].

itself may be the output of an earlier process. The process acts to transform the input into the output data that are (usually) stored in a database.

The essence of the FIP approach is to model the information chain as it transforms input data into output data. Thus, the focus is on the dynamic aspects of the process in terms of data. The dynamic functions that FIP techniques utilize are as follows.

Function	Purpose
Associate	To compare, group, match, or sort
Filter	To change content To change format To copy
Prompt	To start or stop a process To trigger action
Queue	To delay processing
Regulate	To decide among alternatives To inspect
Store	To put aside for possible later use
Transmit	To send or deliver

At their most basic level, FIP descriptions are of the form

$$\text{Data set A} \quad \text{FIP} \quad \text{Data set B} \quad = \quad \text{Data set C}$$

While the specific translation of this equation depends on the data sets and FIP involved, the equation is often read as "data set A is transformed, using data set B, into data set C." Generally, the essence of the FIP technique is to create an information model of the information chain using as many data sets and FIPs as necessary. An information model can be thought of as a series of equations of the general form shown in this equation. For convenience, the data sets on the left-hand side of the equation are called input information products (IIP) and those on the right are called output information products (OIP).

This equation makes it clear that the quality of the output data depends on the quality of the input and the quality of the FIPs. Not surprisingly, this suggests that the most direct way to improve the quality of the outputs is to improve the quality of the performance of the FIPs and suppliers of the inputs.

Note the simple structure of the English translation of the equation. Most information models have simple English-language translations. In the analogy, information products serve the role of nouns, and FIPs serve the role of active verbs. Thus, information products are subjects and objects and FIPs are the dynamic actions on them. This correspondence often helps make FIP techniques a natural language for people to use to describe processes.

8.3   The Information Model/ The FIP Chart

An expanded version of the previous equation provides the information model of the process. The model is expressed in the form of an FIP chart: a matrix giving the FIPs and IIPs involved in each step of the process. The rows and columns of the matrix are as follows.

·Step	1	2	3	.	.	.
FIP						
Process Instruction						
IIPs						
OIPs						
Physical Devices						
Organization/Person						

The columns denote steps, although some sophistication is needed for parallel processes and rework. These are discussed later in the chapter. Of the six rows, FIP, IIP, and OIP have already been briefly described; more complete explanations as well as descriptions of the other rows follow. Finally, not all rows are needed for every step.

8.3.1   The FIP Row

As noted previously, each FIP corresponds to one of the major ways data can be modified, transformed, transmitted, and so forth. In their purest senses, each FIP works in a very specific way (although, of course, things are not always so pure in practice).

Associate matches, compares, sorts, and groups data. A typical example occurs when data from two or more sources are needed to complete some task. As records from the various sources arrive, the appropriate records are matched with one another.

Filter acts to change the data in form or content. Thus, adding two numbers together is an example of a filter, as is the use of any computer-programmed algorithm. The creation of new values is also a filter. Finally, copying an information product is a filter.

Prompt is a signal to start, continue, or stop the information chain. All processes begin and end with a prompt.

Queue is a delay in the process. When an information product is set aside for later use, further on in the process, the queue function is used. Queue time is often a large fraction of the end-to-end process cycle time. One well-known example of a queue is your mailbox. After the mail arrives, it sits in a queue until you process it further (i.e., until you read it).

Regulate makes decisions among alternative paths for further processing. An example occurs when the process is to proceed along path A when some data value equals 0 and along path B when the data value equals 1. An inspection (such as an editing routine) is also a regulate function.

Store sends an information product to a storage device. Storage is often one result of a process or an intermediate step. Storage of data in a database is an example of the store function.

Transmit sends an information product from one place to another. No new data are created, nor are data destroyed. These data do not change form, and data values are not altered. Postal delivery and computer-to-computer file transfers are examples.

Determining the best FIP is usually straightforward. It is a simple matter of isolating the action verb in the step and determining which FIP works best. A dictionary of verbs and associated FIPs is given in reference [1].

As with any language, syntax governs the use of FIPs. The syntax specifies which FIPs can follow any other and which need a prompt between them. Table 8.1 specifies the allowable combinations. In addition, a prompt is needed to initiate and terminate the process.

8.3.2   The Process Instruction Row

The FIP is used to state which of seven basic functions is occurring. Specific detail is not provided by FIPs; the process instruction row provides the needed

FIP	Associate	Filter	Prompt	Queue	Regulate	Store	Transmit
			Allowable Following FIPs				
Associate		x	x				
Filter			x	x	x	x	
Prompt	x	x	x	x	x	x	x
Queue	x	x	x	x	x	x	x
Regulate	x	x	x	x	x	x	x
Store			x				
Transmit		x	x	x			

Table 8.1   Summary of certain rules of syntax in the use of the FIP technique. An "x" indicates that the columnar FIP may follow the row FIP.

detail, usually in English. The process instruction row also frequently gives the action verb used to determine the FIP. Example process instructions, with their associated FIPs, follow.

Process Instruction	FIP
Save new record in database	Store
Perform edit suite	Regulate
Match records from data sources A and B	Associate
Begin processing new order	Prompt
Delay further work until 3/15	Queue
Reformat record in accordance with user specifications	Filter
Mail bill to client	Transmit

8.3.3   The IIPs/OIPs Rows

In these rows, any information products are noted. A special class of IIPs is called embedded information products. These are information products, such as organizational methods and procedures, job aids, and so forth, and are not output. Such products exist only to ensure proper functioning of the process, playing a critical role as they systematize good or bad practice. Embedded information products should be noted as in IIP row.

8.3.4   The Physical Devices Row

Any physical devices, such as databases (electronic or otherwise), communications equipment, and so forth, should be noted in this row.

8.3.5   The Person/Organization Row

The last row of the chart specifies who or what performs the action described by the FIP. In many cases, a single person performs the FIP; in other cases it is an organization. In some cases, the FIP is performed by a computer program. In such cases, the name of the program should be specified.

8.3.6   An Example—an Employee Move

A familiar example involves the process set in motion when employees move. Assume for simplicity that the employees' work location (department, etc.) remains unchanged. The purpose of the process (which we'll call the "new address process") is to update the company's databases containing employee addresses. It is a very simple example, but it illustrates all the points needed for modeling a large information chain. In the example, two such databases are maintained: one by the department secretary, the other by the enterprise's human resources organization. We present the information model in terms of a completed FIP chart and describe the modeling of each step.

Step	1	2	3	4	5
FIP	Prompt	Transmit	Prompt	Queue	Filter
Process Instruction	Secretary learns that employee has moved	Secretary gives new address form to employee	Secretary instructs employee to complete form	Form sits on employee's desk	Employee completes form
IIP	Grapevine	New address form	Form, Instructions	Form	Form
OIP					Completed form
Physical Devices					
Person/ Organization	Secretary	Secretary	Secretary	Secretary	Employee

Step 1.   The action that triggers the need for the process is the department secretary learning that an employee has moved. Note that when the employee moves, both databases in the example are no longer correct. But the employee moving does not necessarily get the process started. The FIP is the "prompt."

Step 2.   Once the secretary learns that the employee has moved, he or she gives the employee a new address form (a transmit). This blank form is an IIP.

Step 3.   The secretary also prompts (an FIP) the employee to fill out the form. If the form is not self-explanatory, the secretary may also provide the employee with an instruction sheet, which is an embedded information product.

Step 4.   The form will likely sit on the employee's desk. Processing has been delayed (queue FIP).

Step 5.   The employee completes the form. A new output information product (the completed form) has been created, so filter is the proper FIP.

Step	6	7	8	9	10
FIP	Transmit	Queue	Prompt	Regulate	Prompt
Process Instruction	Employee returns form to department secretary	Form sits on secretary's desk	Secretary is reminded to update databases based on form	Secretary reviews form	Form okay
IIP(s)			Secretary's time organizer	Completed form	
OIP(s)	Completed form			Completed form	
Physical Devices					
Person/ Organization	Employee		Secretary	Secretary	

Step 6.   The employee returns the form to the secretary (a transmit FIP).

Step 7.   The form now waits in queue on the secretary's desk.

Step 8.   A prompt, in this case the secretary's time organizer, gets processing started again. The time organizer is an embedded information product.

Step 9.   The completed form is reviewed by the secretary. This step is likely a very informal one—the secretary may review the form to determine its readability and perhaps also to determine if the new values are sensible.

Step 10.   If the form is okay, processing will continue. We will return to the example later to describe what happens if the form is not okay.

Step	11	12	13	14	15
FIP	Associate	Filter	Store	Prompt	Queue
Process Instruction	Find old employee record in department database	Change department records based on form	Store new address	Form ready to be sent to resource department	Wait
IIP(s)	Form	Employee record			
OIP(s)	Employee record	Updated record			
Physical Devices	Department database	Department database	Department database		
Person/ Organization	Secretary DB software	Secretary	Secretary		

Step 11.   The secretary now locates the relevant employee in the department database. For the sake of the example, we will assume that database is a flat file on a personal computer. From the point of view of the data, this step is an associate FIP—two pieces of data (the two realizations of the employee's name) are being matched.

Step 12.   The data in the department database are now changed to reflect the correct values. This is a filter FIP.

Step 13.   Storage is achieved when the "save" command is issued. The official department database should now reflect the correct address. Of course, if processing has in some way been compromised, this may not be the case.

Step 14.   The process now calls for the new address form to be faxed to the human resources department (a prompt).

Step 15.   Processing is delayed (a queue) until the secretary gets around to faxing the form.

Step	16	17	18	19	20
FIP	Transmit	Prompt	Regulate	Prompt	Queue
Process Instruction	Fax form to human resources	Form ready for processing in personnel	Check form	Form okay	Form put in keypunch operator worklist
IIP(s)	Form		Form		Form, Worklist
OIP(s)	Faxed form		Form		
Physical Devices	Facsimile machine				
Person/ Organization	Secretary, HR Clerk		Data processing supervisor		

Step 16.   Faxing the form to the human resources organization is a transmit FIP.

Steps 17–24 are similar in purpose to steps 8–13; the former update the corporate database, the latter the department's database. Updating the corporate database is slightly more complicated, as a data processing supervisor and keypunch operator are required to perform the role of the secretary.

Step 17.   Exactly analogous to step 8.

Step 18.   Analogous to step 9, except performed by a data processing supervisor.

Step 19.   Analogous to step 10.

Step 20.   The process at human resources is slightly more complicated. The completed form is put onto a keypunch operator's worklist. It remains in queue until . . .

Step	21	22	23	24	25
FIP	Prompt	Filter	Queue	Store	Prompt
Process Instruction	This form next	Contents input into personnel database update file	Wait	Database updated from update file	Process complete
IIP(s)	Worklist	Form, Input screen			
OIP(s)		Updated record			
Physical Devices		Terminal		Corporate database	
Person/ Organization		Keypunch operator		Database software	

Step 21.   . . . it reaches the top of the worklist.

Step 22.   Step 22 is analogous to step 11, but the database environments are different. In particular, the clerk does not have direct access to the corporate database in human resources; instead, the data from the new address form are put in a personnel database update file. This is a filter FIP.

Step 23.   Since the update file is processed only at night, the new values wait in queue.

Step 24.   The database software now updates the official corporate record for this employee and stores the new record.

Step 25.   The process is complete.

8.4   Enhancements to the Basic Information Model

As described so far, there are several shortcomings to the information model. These include:

- The relatively poor readability of the FIP chart (as compared to a flowchart, for example);

- The fact that only processes of a sequential nature have been considered.

This section addresses these shortcomings.

8.4.1   Pictorial Representation

Flowchart symbols and conventions can be employed in association with the FIP chart. Figure 8.1 provides a set of conventions for associating the flowchart symbols of Figure 7.6 in Chapter 7 with the functions used in FIP (with a couple of additions). The key ideas are as follows.

- Group FIPs into flowchart functions or subprocesses as needed. For example, it often is useful to combine prompts with the actions that follow. A good rule of thumb is to employ one flowchart function each time a new information product is created or a new person or organization becomes involved.

- The line with the arrowhead is translated "goes to." A single slash in such a line means transmit; two slashes mean transmit and filter. An "x" in a line is a queue, and slashes and x's may be combined as needed. A line with an arrowhead terminating in a database means store—such a line may also include a single slash and/or an x.

Using the conventions of Figure 8.1, the pictorial representation for the new address process appears in Figure 8.2. Such a picture is often a useful supplement to the FIP chart.

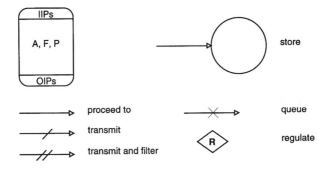

Figure 8.1   Standard flowchart symbols are adapted for FIP.

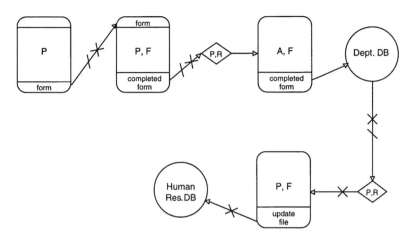

Figure 8.2   A pictorial representation of the new address process is shown.

8.4.2   Exception, Alternative, and Parallel Processes

The new address process is simplistic because processing could only follow one path. Obviously, most important data-intensive processes are more sophisticated than that. It is straightforward to apply the FIP technique in more general situations.

To do so, first create an information model of the process as it works when no errors are present, or consider the process how it works most often. Then consider exceptions to the process, as well as alternative and parallel portions and describe them in the same way.

Exception processes frequently follow a regulate FIP. Typically, the regulate function sends the information along the main path if some test is passed and along another if the test is failed. For example, if, in FIP 9, the secretary determines that the change of address form is incorrectly filled out, then he or she may send it back to the employee. In effect, the secretary initiates a feedback loop, as shown in Figure 8.3. Alternatively, the secretary may consult with the employee and make corrections (Figure 8.4).

As Figures 8.3 and 8.4 show, steps in exception processes are incremented with lower-case letters (i.e., 9a, 9b, etc.). Such inspection and rework are the most frequently encountered types of exception process. In effect, the information product is not allowed beyond the regulate function until it passes the standard that the regulate function effects. In such cases, the exception process

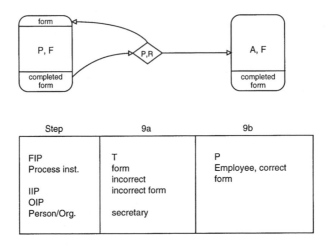

Step	9a	9b
FIP	T	P
Process inst.	form	Employee, correct
	incorrect	form
IIP	incorrect form	
OIP		
Person/Org.	secretary	

Figure 8.3   The information model, including pictorial representation and FIP chart for a portion of the new address process. Here the secretary has rejected the new address form and returned it to the employee for rework.

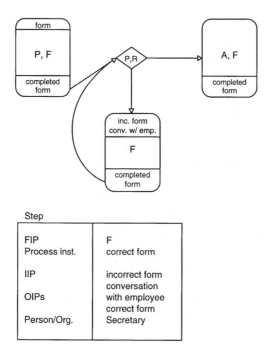

Step	
FIP	F
Process inst.	correct form
IIP	incorrect form
	conversation
OIPs	with employee
	correct form
Person/Org.	Secretary

Figure 8.4   The information model, including pictorial representation and FIP chart for a second way the rejected new address form could be corrected. Here the secretary makes changes to the form after consultation with the employee.

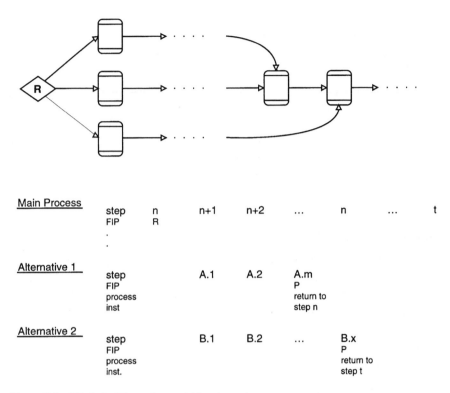

Figure 8.5   This is the information model for alternative processes.

may link up with the main process at the regulate or any previous FIP. An exception process may also return to the main process at any step.

Alternative processing is also often the result of a regulate FIP. Alternatives result, for example, when a standard interface to a customer defines the first several steps in the process and then different types of orders enter alternative subprocesses. Such alternatives may relink later in the process. Because of this, careful numbering of the alternatives is important. There are many ways to do this: One way is to label each alternative with a capital letter (A, B, C) and number steps sequentially (1, 2, 3). When the alternatives rejoin the main process, numbering continues from where the regulate FIP that initiated the alternatives left off. Note that not all alternatives need return to the same point in the main process (see Figure 8.5).

Portions of processes that proceed in parallel are represented, drawn, and numbered in the same way as alternative processes. However, parallel processes rarely stem from regulate functions, in contrast to alternative processes.

8.5 Measurement and Improvement Opportunities

The information model, in the form of the FIP chart and pictorial representations, often immediately suggests critical measurement and improvement opportunities. Issues associated with measurement are considered more fully in Chapter 11. These issues are important: It is easy to underestimate the traps and difficulties in implementing measurements. As discussed in Chapter 7, it is best to work through each step of the process management cycle, rather than pursuing improvements at the process description step.

8.5.1 Accuracy

Data values or their representations (i.e., information products) can only change (be created, etc.) by filter FIPs. Thus, an important measurement is whether they (data values and representations) change for other FIPs. Determining whether changes occur as they should is complicated and is discussed in Chapter 11.

8.5.2 Timeliness

Experience has shown that the total time that it takes to complete a process (i.e., cycle time) is often dominated by queue, transmit, and prompt FIPs, which makes these FIPs good candidates for measurement of timeliness. Measurement is straightforward: The "duration" of the FIP is simply the complete time minus (–) the initiate time.

8.5.3 Cues for Improvement

Queues. As previously noted, queue time often comprises a substantial fraction of overall process-cycle time. Queues function to balance workloads, keeping the work force busy by ensuring that there is always work to be done. Interestingly, queues may also make it easier to hide defects. Queues do not add any value from the customer's perspective (there are some situations, such as the customer having no use for an information product before a specified date, where this is not strictly true). Further, there is reason to believe that reduced cycle time will be of greater competitive importance in the future [8] (in design and manufacturing cycle time has been a critical competitive determinant for some time). Eliminating queues or at least minimizing queue time to the greatest extent possible is clearly an important way to improve cycle time. Queues can sometimes be moved to improve overall process performance. This subject requires detailed measurement and is reserved for Chapter 11.

Transmit. Transmit FIPs can also often be sped up. As an example, mail can often be replaced by facsimile transmission. Note that the form of the information product often dictates the types of transmission possible. Facsimile is useful when the information product is paper. In many cases a computer-to-computer file transfer may be quicker, more accurate, and save time elsewhere in the process. For example, the process may include inputing the information product into a PC, printing it, faxing the printed document, and re-entering the information into a second PC. Replacing the facsimile with a computer-to-computer transfer saves only a few seconds of transmission time, but much time elsewhere. This example is particularly germane to the new address process example.

In general, computing and communications technology can be employed to speed up many queues and transmits.

Regulate. The question to ask with regulate functions is why is this step needed? Sometimes, regulates add value, such as when they initiate alternative or parallel processing. Other times—as when regulate FIPs model an information product inspection—they do not add value. One should strive to minimize inspection and rework when deciding which steps are necessary.

Store. In and of itself, a store usually is not a good cue for improvement. However, stores often have hidden queues and/or transmits, and points made earlier about these functions apply.

Filter. For filter FIPs, accuracy is generally more important than timeliness. Accuracy is difficult to measure for individual steps, so the data-tracking technique, described in Chapter 11, should be used.

Combinations of FIPs or the entire information model may suggest further improvement opportunities. For example, there may be opportunities for parallel processing. In the new address process, a completed new address form precedes updating the department records database, which in turn precedes updating the human resources database. Note that updating the human resources database does not require that the department records database be current. Thus, processes leading to the updates for these two databases may proceed in parallel, as illustrated in Figure 8.6.

Some sequencing of steps is generally required. In particular, some information products are required for production of information products further downstream. Allowing for such requirements, parallel processing can be pursued vigorously.

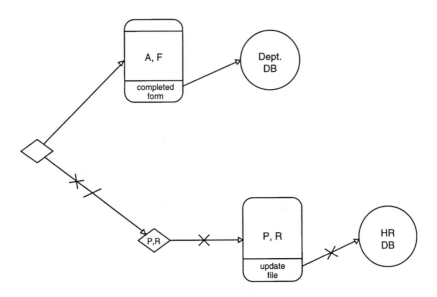

Figure 8.6   A redesigned information model for the new address process. The redesign takes advantage of parallel processing to improve overall cycle time.

8.6 Summary

This chapter has focused on the functions of information processing approach to process description, the second step of the process management cycle. Alternative approaches to process representation, such as flowcharting and the customer-supplier model, involve different points of view of the process. FIP views the process from the point of view of information and is complementary to the customer-supplier model and flowchart.

FIP is used to develop an information model of the process and features seven basic functions—associate, filter, prompt, queue, regulate, store, and transmit—all of which act on information products to produce new ones. A relatively simple syntax specifies how functions may be combined. The model is captured in an FIP chart and in simple pictorial representations.

The information model often suggests many improvement opportunities, although, of course, the process owner should proceed through all steps of the process management cycle before acting on these opportunities. Much of the focus of this chapter has been on overall cycle time, and two major opportunities have been identified.

- Time in queues and transmits can be minimized through use of more advanced technology. More mundane techniques to minimize queue time are also effective.
- Parallel processing can reduce cycle time.

Measurement and improvement of accuracy are discussed in Chapter 11. Data-tracking techniques can also be used to measure cycle time.

REFERENCES

[1]   *Process Representation: The FIP Technique*, AT&T, Select Code 500-488, 1992.

[2]   *PQMI: Tips, Experiences and Lessons Learned*, AT&T, Select Code 500-446, 1990.

[3]   Gane, C., and T. Sarson, *Structured Systems Analysis: Tools and Techniques*, Englewood Cliffs, NJ: Prentice Hall, 1979.

[4]   Yourdon, E., *Modern Structured Analysis*, Englewood Cliffs, NJ: Prentice Hall, 1989.

[5]   Licker, P. S., *Fundamentals of Systems Analysis with Application Design*, Boston: Boyd & Fraser, 1987.

[6]   DeMarco, T., *Structured Analysis and System Specification*, Englewood Cliffs, NJ: Prentice Hall, 1979.

[7]   Miller, J. G., *Living Systems*, New York: McGraw-Hill, 1978.

[8]   Davis, S. M., *Future Perfect*, Reading, MA: Addison-Wesley, 1987.

Chapter 9

Data Quality Requirements

"If you don't know where you're going,
you might end up somewhere else."
—Yogi Berra

9.1 Introduction

The focus of this chapter is on data quality requirements, continuing the discussion from Chapter 8 on step 2 of the process management cycle. Procedures are provided for developing requirements specific to each process of an information chain and its suppliers. The ideas described throughout stem from Quality Function Deployment (QFD). First, we consider an existing information chain and give a detailed procedure for mapping customer requirements to each process, focusing on processes that create data values. We then turn our attention to the design of new information chains and information systems. Here, a customer is any person or organization that uses data. Customers may be internal or external to the enterprise.

Developing requirements is one of the most difficult jobs in the delivery of any product or service. There are dozens of reasons that this is so, and two are especially worthy of note. First, requirements are most often developed in an environment characterized by a lack of knowledge. Customers often have poor knowledge of what they really want, the technology on which leading-edge products and services is based is constantly changing, and competitors' plans and market demands are hard to predict. It is difficult to arrive at good requirements in the face of all the unknowns and variables. Second, good requirements are difficult to develop because a wide range of skills is needed to do so. For example, one must be able to identify and talk to potential users in their language, translate those requirements into the technical language associated with delivery of the product or service (in this case, the information chain), and resolve conflicts that are certain to arise. This range of skills is rare.

9.2   Quality Function Deployment

QFD is a general-purpose tool for translating subjective user requirements into objective technical specifications [1, 2]. This is accomplished through an increasingly detailed series of matrices, the elements of which describe important relationships between user requirements and features and processes associated with the product or service. These relationships may include, for example:

- The impact of features on customer satisfaction (on a high, medium, or low scale) for each requirement;
- A translation of each customer requirement into technical feature specifications;
- A further translation of each customer requirement and technical feature specifications into technical process specifications.

A generic, two-dimensional QFD matrix[1] is shown as Figure 9.1. Column and row descriptions define variables to be related in the body of the matrix. And the elements in the body describe the relationship of interest for the particular (row, column) pair. For example, the row variables may be features; the column variables, requirements; and the relationship, the importance of features in meeting requirements. It is usual to build such two-dimensional

---

1.   QFD can accommodate multidimensional matrices. Here we concentrate on two dimensions only.

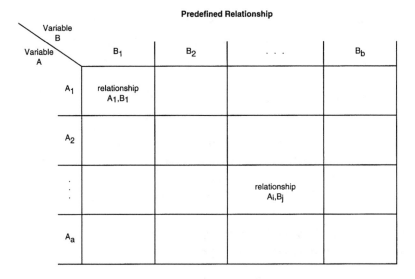

Figure 9.1 A generic, two-dimensional QFD matrix. Rows and columns represent variables, and the entries of the matrix define a predefined relationship between these two variables.

matrices on top of one another, creating (in Hauser and Clausing's terms) a "house of quality [2]."

QFD has proven effective in the design of products in many industries. In addition, QFD-like matrices have been applied to service industries such as telecommunications [3]. This chapter describes sequences of matrices that define useful relationships for existing information chains and for the design of new ones. We will not make use of the house of quality, preferring instead the matrix approach.

9.3 Data Quality Requirements for an Existing Information Chain

In this section, we will assume that an information chain already exists. The goal is to translate the voice of the customer into the language of the process. In other words, the idea is to develop from overall user requirements specific technical requirements for data quality and then performance specifications for the processes that create data.

The method for doing so consists of five steps.

1. Understand what customers want in their terms.

2. Develop a single set of consistent user requirements.
3. Translate user requirements into data quality requirements.
4. Map each data quality requirement into one or more performance requirements.
5. Establish individual process performance and supplier requirements.

Each step is discussed in detail and illustrated below using the new address process described in Chapter 8. This process is extremely simple compared to most information chains. But it is large enough to illustrate the most important features of the use of QFD to develop useful data quality requirements.

9.3.1 Step 1: Understand Customers' Requirements

Customers[2] can have an astonishing range of data quality requirements. Most want the "data to be right." They may also want "all of them to be there by the first of the month," "these data to match those data," to access needed data "within 2 seconds," data protected from "those who shouldn't get them," and data presented to them in the "most appealing way." Different customers may have different priorities, even conflicting needs—for example, one customer may want the data, in whatever shape, as soon as possible, while another has stringent completeness requirements.

Obtaining requirements is usually accomplished via interviews, focus groups, prototype demonstrations, and so forth. Obtaining good customer requirements is hard work. There are no good tricks—active listening in one form or another is essential. It is very important that the customer's actual requirements, subjective though they may be, are documented. These words are the "voice of the customer," to be understood by everyone working on the information chain.

9.3.2 Step 2: Develop a Set of Consistent Customer Requirements

As noted, customer requirements come from many sources and may appear to conflict. Many may not even bear on data. Thus, the second step is to develop a set of consistent data quality requirements. To do so, first develop the so-called

---

2. Information chains usually have many customers along the way.

"Impact Matrix." The Impact Matrix has five rows and N columns. Label the rows "data model," "data values," "presentation," "information systems," and "other." Each column corresponds to a requirement. In the body of the matrix, rate the importance of the requirement (column) to the row category—for example, an access time requirement bears on "information systems," an accuracy requirement bears on "data values," and so forth. It is usually sufficient to rate relevance on a "high," "medium," "low," or "not applicable" scale. Figure 9.2 depicts Impact Matrix for the new address process.

Next, parcel requirements to responsible parties. It is clear that the owner of the information chain should be responsible for requirements that are relevant to data values, and a manager of the enterprise's IT organization should be responsible for those that bear on systems. The two will probably split responsibility for requirements relevant to data models and presentation, and they should determine who is responsible for the other category.

The matrix in Figure 9.2 depicts another use of QFD. In this case, all requirements are of "low" impact to data presentation. It seems unlikely that customers will not care how data are presented to them, so the requirements may be incomplete. This should be reviewed with customers (of course, this figure intentionally includes only a subset of requirements).

Impact Matrix 1

	customer group 1		customer group 2		customer group 3	
Area \ Customer requirement	New Address must be "in system" within 2 weeks	Employee code must match HR records	New address should be submitted by the 10th day of the month after move	New address must be correct, including 9-digit zip code	HR and department records must agree	Only authorized people may access data records
Data Model	L	H	L	H	M	L
Data Values	H	H	H	H	M	L
Presentation	L	L	L	L	L	L
Information System	H	M	M	L	L	H
Other	L	L	L	L	L	L

Figure 9.2 Figures 9.2–9.6 refer to the new address process presented in Figure 8.2. This figure presents the Impact Matrix for a subset of user requirements.

Impact Matrix

Customer requirement / quality dimension	New Address must be submitted within 2 weeks	Employee code must match HR records	New address should be submitted by the 10th day of the month after move	New address must be correct, including 9-digit zip code	HR and department records must agree
Accuracy	L	M	L	H	M
Completeness	L	L	H	L	L
Consistency	L	H	L	L	L
Currency	H	L	H	L	L

Figure 9.3 The Impact Matrix for data values is displayed in this figure.

As a result of this exercise, the information chain owner will have responsibility for a reduced set of M requirements. The four dimensions of quality for data values are accuracy, completeness, consistency, and currency (these are discussed in detail in Chapter 13). The next step is to develop a $4 \times M$ Impact Matrix, with rows corresponding to the four quality dimensions of data values and columns corresponding to the remaining requirements. In our example, $M = 5$. Figure 9.3 depicts this second Impact Matrix.

Next, work across each row. Requirements that are rated "high" (or "high" or "medium") are summarized into a few "most stringent requirements." The idea is that meeting these (relatively) few requirements will lead to all customer requirements being met. An important philosophy is being represented here. Simply put, the philosophy is that owners of information chains must meet all customer requirements simultaneously. The alternative is to create sets of data specific to each customer. This in turn increases the management burden, increases cost, and causes all other benefits of separating data from application to be lost.[3] Figure 9.4 illustrates the summarization of five requirements into four for the new address process.

---

3.   In contrast, it is good practice to give data to customers in their preferred format. Technically, this is called "data presentation."

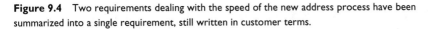

New address must be submitted within 2 weeks. ⊕ New address must be submitted by 10th of the month after move. = New address must be submitted within 10 days.

Employee code should match HR records

New address must be correct including 9-digit zip

HR and department records must agree

Figure 9.4 Two requirements dealing with the speed of the new address process have been summarized into a single requirement, still written in customer terms.

9.3.3 Step 3: Translate Customer Requirements into Technical Language

At this point we have a set of R data quality requirements. Each is relevant to the process and the entire set is internally consistent. Requirements are still in the customers' languages. The next step is to translate this language into the technical language of the information chain. This is done via a "Translation Matrix." The Translation Matrix is $R \times 2$, a row for each requirement and a column each for the requirement in users' and technical language.

The continuation of the example is shown as Figure 9.5.

Translation Matrix

User requirement	Technical requirement
New address must be submitted within 10 days	The new address process is initiated the day of an employee move. It is to be completed within six work days.
The employee code must match records in Human Resources	The process uses the employee code field as a primary key. This field should match existing records.
New address must be correct, including 9-digit zip	99% accuracy in all fields is required
HR and department records must agree	Data values should be entered into the HR and department databases

Figure 9.5 The Translation Matrix for the new address process is depicted in this figure.

9.3.4 Step 4: Map Data Quality Requirements into Individual Performance Requirements

The fourth step is to map the technical requirements into requirements on processes and suppliers. The process Performance Matrix features k columns, one for each process, and R rows, one per technical requirement.

Figure 9.6 gives this matrix for our example. In this example, the information chain is self-contained; there are no suppliers. If suppliers were critical, a column for each would be added to the process Performance Matrix. Note that in the example, the processes correspond to the aggregated FIPs from Figure 8.2. Depending on the detail needed, it may have been appropriate to use a high-level flowchart on the complete set of FIPs. A useful alternative is to first develop a process Performance Matrix at a higher level (as in Figure 9.6), and then further translate the resultant requirements to lower levels. This is done the same way that the process performance matrix is created.

In cases where a technical requirement is translated into two or more performance specifications,[4] this mapping can be a bit more involved than has

Process Performance Matrix

	1- secretary gives form to employee	2- employee completes and returns form	3- secretary reviews, corrections made	4- secretary updates dept. records	5- secretary transmits to HR	6- HR updates its DB
1- complete within 6 workdays	day of move	within 2 days	within 1 day	within 1 day	within 1 day	within 1 day
2- primary key match		100% correct	No errors	No errors	No errors	No errors
3- 99% Accuracy		best of employee's knowledge	form must be 100% accurate	99% Accuracy		99% Accuracy
4- HR/dept. records agree						

Figure 9.6 The process Performance Matrix for the new address process. Each requirement has been budgeted to processes, with the exception of requirement 4. No subprocess bears on this requirement—so it seems unlikely it will be met.

---

4.   We use the term "specification" for individual technical requirements at the process level.

Process Impact Matrix

	1- secretary gives form to employee	2- employee completes and returns form	3- secretary reviews, corrections made	4- secretary updates dept. records	5- secretary transmits to HR	6- HR updates its DB
1- complete within 6 workdays	H	H	H	H	H	H
2- primary key match	NA	H	M	M	M	M
3- 99% Accuracy	NA	H	H	H	M	H
4- HR/dept. records agree	NA	L	L	L	L	L

Figure 9.7   This is the process Impact Matrix for the new address process.

been indicated. It is not enough that individual performance specifications correspond to satisfaction of the technical requirement. For example, suppose that a technical requirement is 99% accuracy for some fields, that two independent processes can impact the specification, and that the performance requirement for each process is 99% accurate. The overall accuracy will be $.99 \times .99 = .98$ and the technical requirement will not be met. There is a need to ensure that the performance requirements, when taken in toto, lead to satisfaction of the requirement. In the above example, 99.5% accuracy for each process is needed to meet the technical requirement of 99% accuracy.

Determining technical specifications in such situations is often quite involved. In effect, a so-called requirement budget is associated with the requirement and it can be spent on any process. For the completion time requirement, the requirement is 6 days. And there are any number of ways to spend the time. In such situations, it is often useful to develop a third Impact Matrix prior to constructing the process Performance Matrix. This matrix will also be of R rows and k columns and the entries simply rate the potential impact of the process on the requirement. This matrix assists in budgeting by pointing to processes where it (the budget) must be applied. Figure 9.7 gives this process Impact Matrix for our example.

Finally, as part of this step, ensure that the requirement budgets have not been overspent.

9.3.5   Step 5: Establish Performance Specifications for Processes

The result of step 4 is a matrix consisting of individual performance specifications. Each row provides performance specifications for a single process. To ensure that they are as useful as possible, it is a good idea to review these requirements as a set and make necessary additions, deletions, and/or simplifications. This can be accomplished by adding a row to the process Performance Matrix and accumulating the requirements in each row into most stringent requirements. This accumulation is much the same as in step 1 for customer requirements. In practice, one need only populate this row if a new requirement results. Figure 9.8 gives the process Performance Matrix, so augmented, for the example process.

9.3.6   Summary Remarks

Clearly, a high-quality information chain is one that meets customer needs. But the voice of the customer may be subjective, confusing, and even contradictory. The series of steps presented here are designed to help the process owner understand customer requirements and then parcel them out correctly. The

	1- secretary gives form to employee	2- employee completes and returns form	3- secretary reviews, corrections made	4- secretary updates dept. records	5- secretary transmits to HR	6- HR updates its DB
1- complete within 6 workdays	day of move	within 2 days	within 1 day	within 1 day	within 1 day	within 1 day
2- primary key match		100% correct	No errors	No errors	No errors	No errors
3- 99% Accuracy		best of employee's knowledge	form must be 100% accurate	99% Accuracy		99% Accuracy
4- HR/dept. records agree						
			Form must be 100% Accurate			

Figure 9.8   Requirements for process 3 can be simplified somewhat. This is done by accumulating the relevant rows of the process Performance Matrix into a final row.

result is technical specifications on each process. Taken in total, meeting the specifications will lead to satisfying the requirements. Note the following sequence of steps.

1. First, customer requirements are understood *in the customers' terms*.
2. Second, a consistent set of data quality requirements is developed.
3. Data quality requirements are then *translated* into technical requirements.
4. Each technical requirement is taken apart by budgeting the requirement to relevant processes of the information chain. This produces *performance specifications* on each process.
5. Finally, performance specifications are accumulated to give the overall specifications for each process.

9.4 Data Quality Requirements at the Design Stage

9.4.1 Background and Motivation

Information systems designers tend to design systems without regard to the processes that will use them, and process designers tend to design processes with little regard for the capabilities of the information systems the process will use.[5]

Given its importance, the distinction between *process* and *system* is worth a short discussion. A process is a sequence of activities that create, move, transform, and store data. Information systems consist of database management systems, including hardware and software; applications software; physical devices such as terminals; local area networks; and human interfaces to this technology. Thus, systems are the technology, and processes are the means by which that technology is used. Note that processes explicitly involve human beings. Information systems recognize and interface with human beings, but do not include them.

Process design is not more important than information system design; good practice in the design of new information systems explicitly recognizes that the way that systems are to be used is a key factor in their design. However, it is clear

---

5. I owe this description of the situation to C. J. Fox of James Madison University.

that the design of processes has been subordinated to the design of systems. Failure to design processes and systems in concert has contributed to poor data quality.

Instead, we argue that process and system design should be placed on an equal footing. Ideally, process design and information system design should take place in parallel and in close concert with one another. Unfortunately, this is easier said than done. While thousands of information systems have been developed and implemented, *designing* information systems has not been reduced to practice. One reason is that technology continues to explode, and merely keeping up is a huge task. Similarly, the technology underlying information systems is fascinating—and taking full advantage of that technology has distracted attention from the processes they are to support. Another important point is that the emergence of information systems has promised great power for improved white-collar productivity. In many enterprises, organizations with a specific charter to manage these new systems has emerged. It is interesting to note that the new information systems have not led to the promised improvements in white-collar productivity [4].

The body of knowledge on how to design information chains, or even what constitutes a good process design, is far from complete, and the integration of systems- and process-oriented techniques has not yet begun. An information system may support any number of chains, and a chain may make use of many information systems. Thus, the job is difficult, but it should not be ignored.

9.4.2   The Complete Job—the Entire Data Life Cycle

As if the situation described above is not bad enough, it gets even worse. Understanding user data quality requirements is obviously necessary if they are to be met. Because successful completion of many activities may be needed to meet them, translating user requirements into requirements on processes and systems that impact data quality is needed. The situation is qualitatively the same as with a single information chain, although, of course, it is much larger. But mapping user requirements to processes is not sufficient. The situation is further exacerbated by the fact that customers come up with new ways to use data years after these processes are developed. In particular, a given set of data may be developed to meet the needs of some well-defined application. Successful use of data breeds new applications for that data and in time a second or third application may arise. These new applications, which need be only peripherally related to the first, will have new data quality requirements. It will be extremely expensive and often impossible to correct inadequacies in the original set of data or otherwise adapt it to meet the new needs. The only solution is to make explicit provisions for data quality throughout its life cycle at the design stage. In particular, those who develop information systems, those who populate them with data, those who maintain data—indeed anyone who uses data—must not only understand current user requirements, but also predict how those requirements will evolve over the anticipated lifetime of the data and understand what they can do to impact satisfaction of those requirements. We will fully describe activities of the data life cycle in Chapter 12.

9.4.3   The Methodology Applied at the Design Stage

As before, the basic idea is to move from customer requirements to technical requirements to specifications on processes, using matrices that describe key relationships between customer requirements and activities that bear on satisfaction. We will work through the five-step methodology introduced earlier for existing processes, extending and modifying it as the situation demands. As before, the first step is to understand customer needs. (See reference [5] for a good discussion on the development of user requirements at this stage.)

The first modifications are to the Impact Matrix. Two requirements have been explicitly added, both motivated by potentially long data lifetimes. The first recognizes that the information system under design will probably outlive initial user requirements. Thus, this requirement explicitly notes the *anticipated lifetime of the information system* and any added customer requirements that result. The second requirement is motivated by the observation that data will probably also outlive the new information system. Thus, the second requirement explicitly notes the *anticipated lifetime of the data* and any added quality requirements that result. This second added row obviously provides more stringent requirements than the first. But the first set is less speculative and thus serves an important purpose. See Figure 9.9.

The Impact Matrix is populated as before. However, the purpose of this Impact Matrix is somewhat different. In particular, at the design stage it is not appropriate to decide that certain requirements are irrelevant. It is important to ensure that requirements do not fall through the cracks. Therefore, each column should contain at least one high rating. Similarly, one should check that each row contains at least one high rating. If not, it is appropriate to reconsider the completeness of the requirements (examples of such omissions were already noted in Figures 9.3 and 9.6).

The second series of modifications is made to the process Performance Matrix, now called the Systems/Process Matrix. The obvious way to populate

Req	1	2	. . .	N	IS lifetime	data lifetime
Data model						
Data values						
Presentation						
Information system						
Other						

Figure 9.9   This is the general shape of the Impact Matrix at the design stage.

it is to budget each technical requirement among activities rated to be of high (or perhaps high or medium) impact. But this matrix also offers opportunities to integrate process and system requirements.

Two opportunities are particularly relevant. First, the needs of a process owner to measure process performance in many cases can be more easily accommodated at the design stage. For example, the data tracking technique, fully described in Chapter 11, can more easily be implemented at this point. Data tracking helps ensure that data values are accurate. Recognizing and planning for the management of that process at the design stage can yield powerful benefits.

The second opportunity is to integrate system and process capabilities in meeting some user requirements. For example, an accuracy requirement can be addressed, using a suite of edits as part of the system, through process-oriented measurement and control, or both. Clearly, the latter option offers the greatest advantage. Similarly, a cycle-time requirement can be met both by enhancing systems performance and by designing processes so work can be conducted more efficiently (see Chapters 8 and 11).

9.5   Summary

This chapter has presented a framework for systematically moving from customer requirements to technical requirements and to specifications on processes. The framework was extended to the design stage so the joint design of processes and systems could follow. Explicit provisions for long data lifetimes have been made.

The framework features three matrices—the Impact, Translation, and process Performance (or Systems/Process) Matrices—and three operations: translation, budgeting, and accumulation.

Taken together, the three matrices and the approach presented here put user data quality requirements in a usable form and make them explicit. In particular, customer requirements, which generally are quite subjective, have been translated into objective technical specifications for all the information chains and for the processes that make up these chains. This approach and these matrices provide several advantages for existing processes and information chains.

- They complete step 2 of the process management cycle. In particular, they translate the voice of the customer throughout the information chain.

- At the same time, they ensure that requirements are carefully budgeted, helping ensure that they are met.

- They help ensure that user requirements don't "fall through the cracks."

- They help ensure that customer requirements are complete. For example, if no requirement is associated with data accuracy, it may be that a requirement is missing.

- What is developed is useful throughout the process management cycle.

At the design stage, other advantages include:

- They help make explicit the roles information chains and information systems play in data quality. To illustrate this point, consider the completeness of a view and the accuracy of a value. If a needed attribute is not included as part of the data model, then applications that depend on that attribute will be disabled. Similarly, if values are obtained in error, then applications that use that data can be adversely impacted. And no later activity can make up for these defects. Even sophisticated "integrity checks" in modern information systems cannot detect most inaccuracies in data, let alone correct them. These issues are exacerbated by long data lifetimes and underscore the need for joint information system and process design.

- They explicitly recognize the potential for long data lifetimes.

- They provide a powerful methodology for designing information systems to ensure that high-quality data will result.
- The machinery also permits the designer to revisit requirements after one or more processes have been completed. This capability also permits the designer to conduct more sophisticated analyses of potential ways to meet requirements.

REFERENCES

[1]   Sullivan, L. P., "Quality Function Deployment," *Quality Progress*, Vol. 19, No. 6, June 1986, pp. 39–50.

[2]   Hauser, J. R., and D. Clausing, "The House of Quality," *Harvard Business Review*, Vol. 66, No. 3, May–June 1988, pp. 63–73.

[3]   Richters, J. S., and C. A. Dvorak, "A Framework for Defining the Quality of Communications Services," *IEEE Communications*, Vol. 26, No. 10, October 1988, pp. 17–23.

[4]   McCarroll, T., "What New Age," *Time Magazine*, Vol. 138, No. 6, August 12, 1991, pp. 44–46.

[5]   Fidel, R., *Database Design for Information Retrieval*, New York: John Wiley & Sons, 1987.

Chapter **10**

Statistical Quality Control

"Change is my theme. You gods, whose power has wrought,
All transformations, aid the poet's thought,
And make my song's unbroken sequence flow
From earth's beginnings to the days we know."
—Ovid

10.1 Introduction

Step 3 of the process management cycle involves defining and implementing a measurement system, and step 4 involves establishing statistical control and checking conformance to requirements. Taken together, these are probably the most misunderstood (and sometimes reviled) aspects of quality management. This is unfortunate because the well-known saying "that which doesn't get measured, doesn't get managed" really is true. In this chapter and the next, we'll tackle these subjects. We first consider statistical quality control (step 4) and then measurement systems (step 3), because measurement systems for information chains should support statistical control.

Statistical quality control (SQC) was invented by W. A. Shewhart [1, 2] in the 1920s. During the 1930s and 1940s, the basic ideas of SQC were extensively implemented in manufacturing, where they are now well established. SQC is of fundamental importance both in forming the quality foundations for managing manufacturing processes and in providing the technical horsepower to do so. It also plays a critical role for quality of data and information. As described earlier, information chains and dynamic processes create the values that populate databases. For such chains and processes, SQC can provide the same gains it has enabled in manufacturing. We do not yet have enough experience to distill the application of SQC to information chains into recipes. Therefore, in this chapter the basic ideas are carefully reviewed[1] to give the reader means for experimenting with SQC and adapting it to meet his or her needs. Much of the discussion in this chapter is an example most readers will find familiar. SQC was featured in the case study of Chapter 5.

The first and most important basic idea is the *purpose* of statistical control. The purpose of statistical control is to predict the future performance of a process. Simple as this statement may appear, it is of great philosophical and practical importance. In particular, the focus on prediction contrasts with competing goals, such as explanation of past performance. This is not to say that explaining past performance is not valid and useful or that SQC cannot be used in explanation (as we will see, the past has a role in making valid predictions). But the proper focus of SQC is the future.

Predictions such as the following are desired: "The process under consideration will perform within stated limits unless it is changed or affected by some special cause."[2] Such predictions are of vital importance to those who manage processes. For example:

- The process owner can compare a prediction with requirements. If predicted performance is less than required performance, changes to the process are needed.

---

1.   Over the last 50 years many technical advances based on Shewhart's ideas have occurred, and sophisticated techniques now exist. This chapter does not present the more sophisticated techniques, since they are not used in the remainder of the book, although a list of references is provided.

2.   Shewhart originally used the term "assignable cause" and it is used in much of the SQC literature.

- If process performance for a given time period is not within stated limits, the owner can be reasonably certain that a special cause has occurred and take actions to eliminate it. This will have the effect of once again making future performance predictable.

The logic of SQC is that valid predictions can be made when the recent past and current process performance shows "stability" (or when the process is "in control"). Loosely, stability means that the past and current performance exhibit no evidence of special causes in variation—the stated limits hold for the recent past. A key element of quality control is elimination of any special causes that do appear.

Implementing this logic is hard because processes naturally exhibit variation, some of which cannot be eliminated. Many sources of variation stem from so-called "common causes" inherent to the process (in contrast, special causes are those not inherent to the process). For any given level of performance, it can be difficult to tell whether the performance is the result of special or common causes. Thus, the stated limits (from the prediction above) must balance two considerations.

- They should identify situations where there is high likelihood that the variation is due to the presence of a special cause or causes.

- They should not identify situations where there is high likelihood that the variation is due to common causes.

The stated limits should indicate, for the recent past and present, the presence of special causes. The mathematics of statistical quality control aim to determine these limits.

To conclude this introduction, we briefly review the logic of SQC.

1. The goal is to predict process performance.

2. Prediction is possible when evidence suggests that the process is stable.

3. Process stability can be judged by studying the process's current and past performance. Stability is achieved by eliminating special causes.

4. When there is sufficient evidence of process stability despite common sources of process variation, predictions that a process will perform within mathematically derived limits are valid.

The preceding discussion is "top-down." SQC can also be described from a "bottom-up" perspective.

1. Processes exhibit variation. Some of the variation is due to sources common to the process (i.e., sources that are always present) and some to special sources (i.e., sources external to the process).

2. Stable processes are those for which no special sources of variation are in evidence. Stability can be achieved and maintained by identifying and eliminating special causes.

3. For stable processes it is possible to predict future process performance, within limits. These limits can be derived mathematically.

The remainder of this chapter expands on these points, from the bottom-up perspective.

The discussion in this chapter is somewhat abstract. As noted, a good understanding of the underlying priciples is critical to real-world implementation of SQC on information chains. Information chains are sufficiently different from manufacturing processes that straightforward application of SQC methods may not yield satisfactory results. Further, understanding the underlying philosophy enables the reader to tailor the methods to his or her specific circumstances. The chapter also includes an exercise to help the reader appreciate the philosophy and the necessary mathematics for developing limits in common situations.

10.2 Variation

The most important purpose of SQC is to determine what can be predicted about process performance in the face of variation. The concept of variation is sometimes misunderstood. The following discussion and exercise are aimed at helping the reader gain an intuitive understanding of variation. For a given population (of people, other living things, manufactured products, etc.), variation measures the degree to which individuals differ. Some measures of variation include the standard deviation, the variance, and the range. Simple observation of the world around us suggests that the world is highly variable. People are of different sizes and abilities; not every ear of corn—including those from the same field—tastes the same; even the best manufacturing process producing the simplest product occasionally produces defects. More pertinent to information chains, data are sometimes entered incorrectly, computer programs are sometimes in error (they can even manipulate some data correctly and other data incorrectly), and so forth.

Thus, observation suggests that variation is inherent to nature and human activity. Careful efforts can reduce variation in many cases, but variation can be reduced only so much. We should expect variation to be an important feature of information chains as well. Indeed, inherent variation can plague data and information to a greater degree than it does manufacturing. See reference [3] for a fascinating discussion of many aspects of imprecision in data.

While variation can be intellectually understood, at least to some degree, it is useful to acquire a "feel" for it. To do so, pick something you do each day and record the value of some associated attribute. A good example is commuting time. Make up any rules you like (when you leave and arrive), measure the result each day (in any units you like—we'll return to measurement issues in Chapter 11), and record the results. Plot the results as you get them on graph paper. Try not to interpret the results until you have about 20 measurements. Look at the plot. My commuting times are in Table 10.1 and plotted in Figure 10.1. While you may be able to identify some unusual points (perhaps due to a traffic jam or a flat tire), chances are your plot will look much like mine, with seemingly random variation.

10.2.1   Sources of Variation

Sometimes, some observed variation can be attributed to a particular source. For example, consider the commuting time plot in Figure 10.2. Point 13 seems unusual. Often some known unusual event contributes to unusual points. For example, a flat tire is the cause of point 13.

In SQC, two general categories of variation are of interest. These include those due to:

- Special causes;
- Common causes.

A flat tire is an example of a special cause. The remainder of the variation in Figure 10.2 is haphazard and due to common causes. For example, the number of red lights hit can affect how long a trip takes.

Sources of variation are important because the actions one must take to minimize their impact are different. Consider the actions one could take based

	To Work			To Home		
	Arrive	**Leave**	**Commute Time**	**Arrive**	**Leave**	**Commute Time**
Week 1						
Monday	8:21	7:57	24	5:24	5:02	22
Tuesday	8:18	7:53	25	5:32	5:07	25
Wednesday	8:19	7:53	26	5:32	5:07	25
Thursday	8:22	7:59	23	5:30	5:05	25
Friday	8:25	8:01	24	5:21	5:00	21
Week 2						
Monday	8:12	7:50	22	5:36	5:10	26
Tuesday	8:15	7:53	22	5:30	5:07	23
Wednesday	8:14	7:50	24	5:37	5:10	27
Thursday	8:24	7:56	28	5:26	5:04	22
Friday	8:22	7:57	25	5:30	5:07	23
Week 3						
Monday	8:19	7:53	26	5:23	5:01	24
Tuesday	8:20	7:54	26	5:23	5:03	20
Wednesday	8:18	7:56	22	5:26	5:00	26
Thursday	8:21	7:59	22	5:35	5:10	25
Friday	8:20	8:00	20	5:28	5:06	22
Week 4						
Monday	8:14	7:49	25	5:31	5:06	25
Tuesday	8:24	8:02	22	5:34	5:08	26
Wednesday	8:19	7:55	24	5:30	5:10	20
Thursday	8:16	7:52	24	5:34	5:09	25
Friday	8:18	7:55	23	5:29	5:03	26

Table 10.1 Commute Time Data

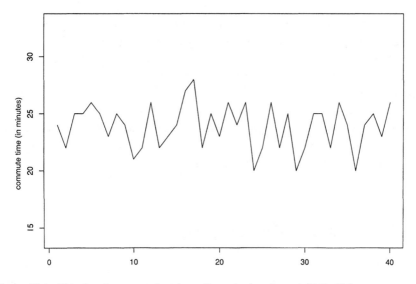

Figure 10.1   This plot of commute time data reflects the data shown in Table 10.1.

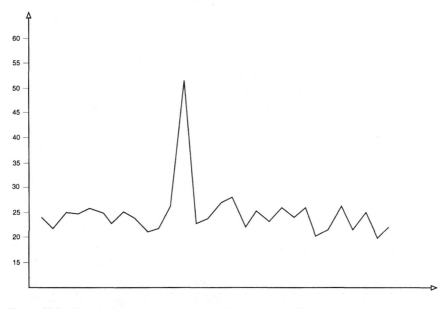

Figure 10.2   Hypothetical commute time data, indicating an unstable situation.

on Figure 10.2. One addresses special causes by trying to eliminate them. In the case of a flat tire, one may decide to inspect one's tires routinely and replace tires of poor quality before they become flat. In contrast, one addresses common causes by changing the process. For example, one could change a route to one with fewer traffic lights.

Two common mistakes are to treat special causes as common causes and vice versa. Changing the process does not address special causes, since they are external to the process. Nor can common causes be removed by treating them as though they were external to the process.

10.3   Stable Processes

Plots such as those shown in Figures 10.1 and 10.2 convey a great deal of interesting information about the past, but the purpose of SQC is not to explain the past—it is to predict the future. In SQC, questions such as "how long should I allow to get to work?" are of interest, while questions such as "how long on average did it take to get to work last week?" are of less importance. Of course, these two questions are related to one another. For example, the average time it took to get to work last week may be a good estimate of the time it will take in the future, but more may be required. Figure 10.3 presents three cases, with the same average commute time for the last two weeks. In case a, most people would feel comfortable inferring that it will take about 24 minutes to get to work tomorrow. In contrast, few would feel comfortable making this prediction in case c. Case b lies somewhere in between. Stable processes are those not impacted by special causes of variation. They are processes such as case a. Note that the process is still variable, but the variation is small. Most important, there is no evidence of a special cause. The prediction that it will take between 22 and 26 minutes to get to work tomorrow is very much justified.

At this point readers may wish to look at their plots and form an opinion as to stability. The final judgment of stability should *not* be based on opinion, but rather on the control limits described shortly. If the process is stable, it is still necessary to assess whether performance is adequate. If not, improved performance can result only if the process is changed. Note the logic here: Because the process is stable, we predict that it will continue to perform as it has. If performance is not adequate, change is needed. If the process is not stable, then special sources of variation should be identified and eliminated.

This logic is graphically represented in Figure 10.4.

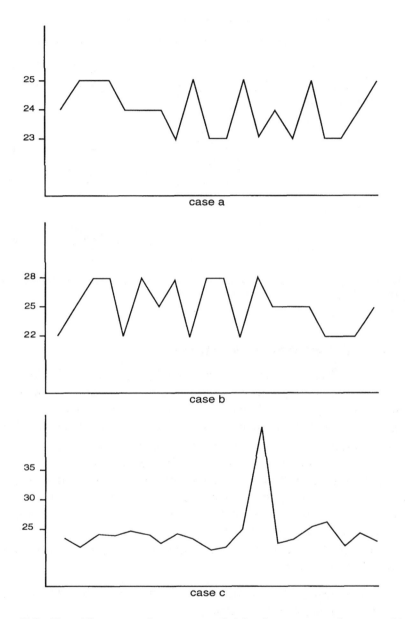

Figure 10.3 Three different cases of commute time. Each has the same average, but one would draw different conclusions about stability.

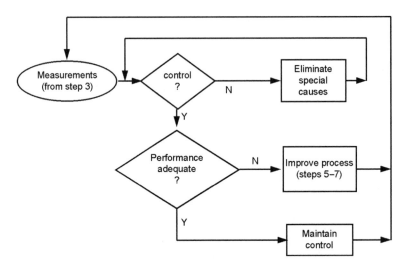

Figure 10.4   This flowchart gives the appropriate actions for the process owner to take based on the stability of the process and conformance to requirements.

10.3.1   Judgment of Stability

As Figure 10.4 illustrates, the judgment of stability plays a key role in establishing and maintaining statistical quality control, improving quality and, by implication, managing processes. Since all processes possess inherent variability, however, it is impossible to state with absolute certainty that an observed result is due to a given cause. As an example, if a tossed coin comes up heads 20 times in a row, most people immediately suspect that the coin is not fair or that some other, perhaps unknown, mechanism is at work. It is possible that a fair coin tossed fairly can come up heads that many times in a row. Rare though it is (it should occur about once in two million tosses of 20 fair coins), such a result can be obtained without a special cause.

Errors in judgment of stability are inevitable. The goal is to minimize the impact of these two types of error:

- Judging a process to be stable when it is not (i.e., incorrectly judging that there are no special causes);

- Judging a process to be unstable or out of control when it is stable (i.e., incorrectly judging that a special cause is present when it is not).

Statistical theory is used to balance these considerations.

The second point is that since processes possess different amounts of inherent variation, the judgment of stability should be based on observed variation in process performance after accounting for special causes. Statistical theory also helps estimate inherent process variability and quantify observed variability.

10.4   Control Limits: Statistical Theory and Methods of SQC

10.4.1   The Underlying Theory

Consider an infinite sequence of variables Y_t, $t = 1,2, \ldots$ Shewhart's idea was that a judgment of stability is justified when the observed portion of this sequence, $Y_i, \ldots, Y_k$, is a random sample from a random variable Y. More specifically, if $Y_1, \ldots, Y_{k-1}$ represents the observed past, Y_k the observed present, and $Y_1, \ldots, Y_k$ is random, then a firm basis for predicting the unobserved future, $Y_{k+1}, Y_{k+2}, \ldots$, exists. Unfortunately, one cannot test whether a sequence is random. Shewhart proposed, based on both mathematical and practical considerations, that "3σ limits" be used as operational surrogates. Here σ denotes the standard deviation of Y. More specifically, an observation outside limits given by

$$(\text{variable mean} - 3\sigma \, , \text{ variable mean} + 3\sigma)$$

is taken as evidence of instability or, equivalently, of the presence of a special cause.

It is often possible to quantify the probabilities of errors in judgment of stability. When Y has a normal distribution (see Figure 10.5) and the process is stable, then the probability of an incorrect assessment is less than three in a thousand.

$$P\,[Y_i > \text{Mean} + 3\sigma] + P\,[Y_i < \text{Mean} - 3\sigma]$$
$$\sim .00135 + .00135$$
$$= .0027$$

Shewhart's theoretical and practical insights have stood the test of time. While numerous technical advances have been made, his logic and the 3σ limits

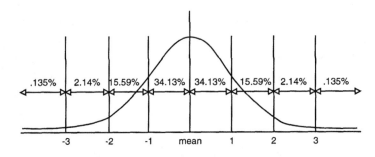

Figure 10.5 The normal distribution of Y is shown.

are at the heart of all methods. The general form of control charts is shown in Figure 10.6 and features the following notation.

- Center Line (CL) mark = (estimate of variable mean)
- Upper Control Limit (UCL) = (estimate of variable mean + 3σ)
- Lower Control Limit (LCL) = (estimate of variable mean – 3σ)

This theory and these formulae comprise much of the foundation of all control charts. They are used to make judgments about the stability of a process and to predict its behavior, as follows.

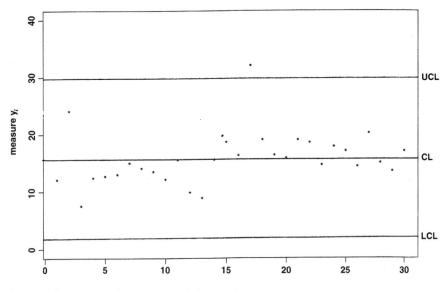

Figure 10.6 The general form of control charts is shown.

- A sequence of observations (at least 25) within the LCL and UCL is good evidence of a stable process. If one or more points lie outside these limits, there is good evidence that a special cause of variation exists. Thus, observation 17 in Figure 10.6 should be investigated to find such a cause.

- When stability has been achieved, it is predictable that future performance, Y_{k+1}, Y_{k+2}, ..., will be within the LCL and UCL and that the mean and variation (standard deviation) will remain about the same, unless the process is changed or some unexpected special cause occurs.

The next section focuses on specific limits based on the nature of Y.

10.4.2   Formulae

The purposes of this section are to suggest what variables need to be controlled and to give the formulae for some common situations. The references at the end of this chapter give the rationale and formulae for more complex situations.

So far we have kept mathematical notation to a minimum. Unfortunately, this is no longer possible. Given the long and successful history of SQC, it is not surprising that a standard notation has developed and is in common use—we shall adhere to it herein.

The essence of each case is to determine, based on the specifics of the variable Y, how to estimate the unknown variable mean and standard deviation (i.e., σ). We first consider two simple cases, then list several other cases and explain why the simplest treatment is insufficient. Finally, we give all formulae needed in the remainder of this book and return to our commute time example.

Case 1. Y_t represents the proportion defective, in a sample of n individual units, each either good or bad. For example, Y_t could be the proportion of a sample of $n = 100$ records that fail a set of edits. Suppose such a sample is available for $k = 25$ days.

In the standard notation,

$$Y_t = p$$
$$\text{estimate of variable mean} = \bar{p} = \sum p / k$$
$$\text{estimate of } \sigma = \sqrt{\frac{\bar{p}(1-\bar{p})}{n}}$$

Thus,

$$CL = \overline{p}$$

$$UCL = \overline{p} + 3\sqrt{\frac{\overline{p}(1-\overline{p})}{n}}$$

$$LCL = \overline{p} - 3\sqrt{\frac{\overline{p}(1-\overline{p})}{n}}$$

It frequently happens that the LCL is less than zero. It is then omitted from the control chart. Figure 10.6, with CL, UCL, and LCL interpreted as above, is called a p-chart.

Case 2. Y_t represents the average of a sample of n ($n \geq 2$) individual units. In the standard notation $(X_1, \ldots, X_n)$ denotes this sample,

$$Y_t = \overline{X} = \sum_{i=1}^{n} X_i / n$$

$$CL = \overline{\overline{X}} = \sum \overline{X} / k$$

$$\overline{s} = \sum s / k$$

$$s = \left[\sum_{i=1}^{n} \left(X_i - \overline{X} \right)^2 / n-1 \right]^{1/2}$$

$$UCL = \overline{\overline{X}} + A_3 \overline{s}$$

$$LCL = \overline{\overline{X}} - A_3 \overline{s}$$

In the above formulae, A_3 is an adjustment factor, which takes two considerations into account.

- It multiplies by 3 (for 3σ limits);
- It makes s a better estimate of σ.

A_3 and a number of adjustment factors used for other cases are given in Table 10.2. A control chart featuring the above CL and limits is called an $\overline{X}$ (X-bar) chart. It is generally paired with an S- or R-chart, to be introduced shortly.

The above two cases are frequently encountered. However, there are many other ways that Y_t could have occurred.

Case 3. Y_t could be a single observation, as in our commute time example.

| Observations in Sample, n | Chart for averages | | | Chart for standard deviations | | | | | | Chart for ranges | | | | | | |
| | Factors for control limits | | | Factors for central line | | Factors for control limits | | | | Factors for central line | | | Factors for control limits | | | |
	A	A_2	A_3	c_4	$1/c_4$	B_3	B_4	B_5	B_6	d_2	$1/d_2$	d_3	D_1	D_2	D_3	D_4
2	2.121	1.880	2.659	0.7979	1.2533	0	3.267	0	2.606	1.128	0.8865	0.853	0	3.686	0	3.267
3	1.732	1.023	1.954	0.8862	1.1284	0	2.568	0	2.276	1.693	0.5907	0.888	0	4.358	0	2.574
4	1.500	0.729	1.628	0.9213	1.0854	0	2.266	0	2.088	2.059	0.4857	0.880	0	4.698	0	2.282
5	1.342	0.577	1.427	0.9400	1.0638	0	2.089	0	1.964	2.326	0.4299	0.864	0	4.918	0	2.114
6	1.225	0.483	1.287	0.9515	1.0510	0.030	1.970	0.029	1.874	2.534	0.3946	0.848	0	5.078	0	2.004
7	1.134	0.419	1.182	0.9594	1.0423	0.118	1.882	0.113	1.806	2.704	0.3698	0.833	0.204	5.204	0.076	1.924
8	1.061	0.373	1.099	0.9650	1.0363	0.185	1.815	0.179	1.751	2.847	0.3512	0.820	0.388	5.306	0.136	1.864
9	1.000	0.337	1.032	0.9693	1.0317	0.239	1.761	0.232	1.707	2.970	0.3367	0.808	0.547	5.393	0.184	1.816
10	0.949	0.308	0.975	0.9727	1.0281	0.284	1.716	0.276	1.669	3.078	0.3249	0.797	0.687	5.469	0.223	1.777
11	0.905	0.285	0.927	0.9754	1.0252	0.321	1.679	0.313	1.637	3.173	0.3152	0.787	0.811	5.535	0.256	1.744
12	0.866	0.266	0.886	0.9776	1.0229	0.354	1.646	0.346	1.610	3.258	0.3069	0.778	0.922	5.594	0.283	1.717
13	0.832	0.249	0.850	0.9794	1.0210	0.382	1.618	0.374	1.585	3.336	0.2998	0.770	1.025	5.647	0.307	1.693
14	0.802	0.235	0.817	0.9810	1.0194	0.406	1.594	0.399	1.563	3.407	0.2935	0.763	1.118	5.696	0.328	1.672
15	0.775	0.223	0.789	0.9823	1.0180	0.428	1.572	0.421	1.544	3.472	0.2880	0.756	1.203	5.741	0.347	1.653
16	0.750	0.212	0.763	0.9835	1.0168	0.448	1.552	0.440	1.526	3.532	0.2831	0.750	1.282	5.782	0.363	1.637
17	0.728	0.203	0.739	0.9845	1.0157	0.466	1.534	0.458	1.511	3.588	0.2787	0.744	1.356	5.820	0.378	1.622
18	0.707	0.194	0.718	0.9854	1.0148	0.482	1.518	0.475	1.496	3.640	0.2747	0.739	1.424	5.856	0.391	1.608
19	0.688	0.187	0.698	0.9862	1.0140	0.497	1.503	0.490	1.483	3.689	0.2711	0.734	1.487	5.891	0.403	1.597
20	0.671	0.180	0.680	0.9869	1.0133	0.510	1.490	0.504	1.470	3.735	0.2677	0.729	1.549	5.921	0.415	1.585
21	0.655	0.173	0.663	0.9876	1.0126	0.523	1.477	0.516	1.459	3.778	0.2647	0.724	1.605	5.951	0.425	1.575
22	0.640	0.167	0.647	0.9882	1.0119	0.534	1.466	0.528	1.448	3.819	0.2618	0.720	1.659	5.979	0.434	1.566
23	0.626	0.162	0.633	0.9887	1.0114	0.545	1.455	0.539	1.438	3.858	0.2592	0.716	1.710	6.006	0.443	1.557
24	0.612	0.157	0.619	0.9892	1.0109	0.555	1.445	0.549	1.429	3.895	0.2567	0.712	1.759	6.031	0.451	1.548
25	0.600	0.153	0.606	0.9896	1.0105	0.565	1.435	0.559	1.420	3.931	0.2544	0.708	1.806	6.056	0.459	1.541

*The above table is a copy of Table 27 in *ASTM Manual on Presentation of Data and Control Chart Analysis* (1976). ASTM Publication STP15D, American Society for Testing and Materials, Philadelphia, pp. 134–135. Used with permission.

Notes: For $n > 25$, $A = 3/\sqrt{n}$, $A_3 = 3/c_4\sqrt{n}$, $c_4 \simeq 4(n - 1)/(4n - 3)$; $B_3 = 1 - 3/c_4\sqrt{2(n - 1)}$; $B_4 = 1 + 3/c_4\sqrt{2(n - 1)}$,

$$B_5 = c_4 - 3/\sqrt{2(n - 1)}, \quad B_6 = c_4 + 3/\sqrt{2(n - 1)}$$

Table 10.2 Constants Used in SQC

Case 4. Y_t could be the count rather than the proportions of defectives.

Case 5. Y_t could count the number of defects rather than simply the number of defectives. This is pertinent when an item can have two or more defects. For example, a record could fail multiple edits.

Other cases can also be identified.

As noted, a number of technical shortcomings are clear.

1. There is a tacit assumption that the amount of inherent process variation is constant. Specifically, the above formulae consider only the mean, ignoring other features that may be of interest. This assumption is counter to the goal of statistical quality control, which is to detect such changes—not assume them away—so that predictability can be established. Fortunately, stability in process variation can be examined in much the same way as stability for the process mean. Further, experience and statistical reasoning confirm that establishing stability on the process mean and variation are sufficient.

2. The formula for calculating the standard deviation for the $\overline{X}$-chart is cumbersome. This shortcoming can be addressed using well-established relationships between standard deviations and ranges (i.e., $\max_i X_i - \min_i X_i$), which are much easier to compute. With the advent of personal computing, this concern is being mitigated.

3. It may be desirable to have indicators of process instability other than exceeding 3σ limits. For example, if process performance exceeded the Center Line 10 times in a row, even though the UCL was not exceeded, performance might not be predictable. "Zone tests" have been developed to provide these signals.

4. The cases considered assume the sample size n is constant. This assumption can be relaxed by weighting estimates based on corresponding sample sizes.

The creation of control limits has become quite sophisticated.[3] A complete discussion of all available methods is beyond the scope of this chapter and beyond the needs of this book. Here we show how points 1 and 2 above are

---

3. In fact, several points beyond these have also been raised. The science of control includes techniques useful for detecting small shifts in process performance, for incorporating standards, for predicting the fraction of outgoing product that will meet specifications, for understanding process capability, and so forth. See the references for discussions of these subjects.

incorporated into our basic framework for cases 1–3 and provide some hints on interpreting control charts, including zone tests.

Case 1. (Y_t is the proportion defective.) The process standard deviation is a function of the process mean:

$$\sigma = \sqrt{p(1-p)/n}.$$

Thus, the p-chart does not assume that the process variation is constant and is also adequate for investigating the stability of process variation.

Case 2. ($\overline{Y}_t$ is the average of a sample of n units.) The user has two choices depending on whether he or she wishes to use standard deviations or ranges to study process variation. When standard deviations are used, $\overline{X}$- and S-charts are based on the following:

$\overline{X}$-chart: $\text{CL} = \overline{X}$

$\text{UCL} = \overline{X} + A_3\bar{s}$

$\text{LCL} = \overline{X} + A_3\bar{s}$

S-chart: $\text{CL} = \bar{s}$

$\text{UCL} = B_4\bar{s}$

$\text{LCL} = B_3\bar{s}$

When ranges are used, $\overline{X}$- and R-charts are based on the following:

$\overline{X}$-chart: $\text{CL} = \overline{X}$

$\text{UCL} = \overline{X} + A_2R$

$\text{LCL} = \overline{X} - A_2R$

R-chart: $\text{CL} = \overline{R}$

$\text{UCL} = D_4\overline{R}$

$\text{LCL} = D_3\overline{R}$

The constants A_2, B_3, B_4, D_3, and D_4 are, like A_3, standard notation for adjustment factors and can be found in Table 10.2.

As their name implies, $\overline{X}$- and S- and $\overline{X}$- and R-charts are generally paired, as shown in Figure 10.7. Many practitioners prefer the $\overline{X}$- and R-chart due to simplicity of calculation. As will be more fully discussed in Chapter 11, putting a control chart as near its process as possible increases its utility. Simplicity in calculation may be an aid in doing so.

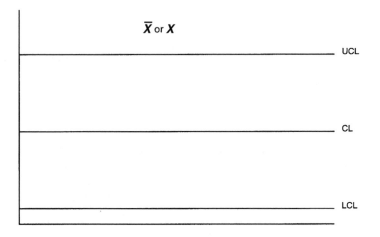

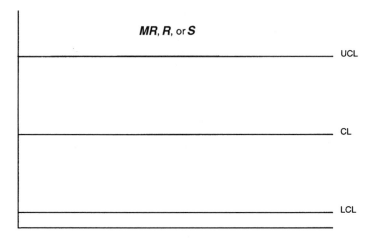

Figure 10.7   This is the general form of $\overline{X}$-, S-, $\overline{X}$-, R-, and $\overline{X}$-, MR-charts.

Case 3. (Y_t is a single observation.) In the standard notation $Y = X$. The so-called "moving range," the absolute value of the difference between the present and last value, is used to develop an estimate of σ. The formulae are:

X-chart:

$$\mathrm{CL} = \overline{X} = \sum X / k$$
$$\mathrm{UCL} = \overline{X} + 2.66 M\overline{R}$$
$$\mathrm{LCL} = \overline{X} - 2.66 M\overline{R}$$

MR-chart: $$CL = M\overline{R} = \sum MR / (k-1)$$
$$UCL = 3.27 M\overline{R}$$
$$LCL = 0$$

Figure 10.8 is the X-, MR-chart for the traveling time data of Table 10.1 and Figure 10.1. Readers may wish to construct their own X-, MR-chart with their own data.

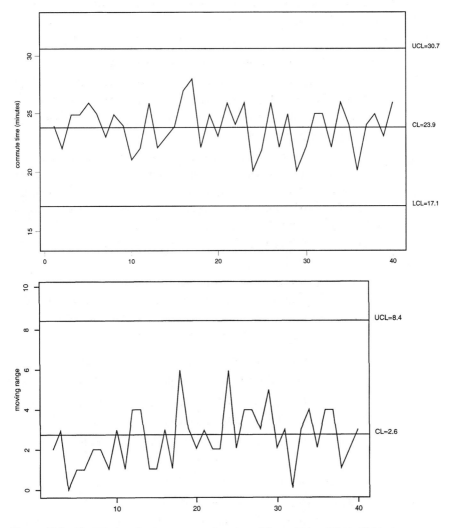

Figure 10.8 X-, MR-chart for the commute time data of Figure 10.1 and Table 10.1 is shown.

10.5 Interpreting Control Charts

Like most analyses, interpretation of control charts is part art and part science. Similarly, finding and eliminating special causes is much like detective work. The following points are "helpful hints," rather than hard and fast rules.

1. A judgment of stability requires about 25 points. A judgment of instability can sometimes be made with fewer points. However, eliminating special causes and improving a stable but inadequate process require different types of actions.

2. Start by interpreting the MR-, R-, or S-chart. The X- or $\overline{X}$-chart is easier to interpret when process variation is stable.

3. When the process is stable, a histogram of observed points will look much like the normal density (Figure 10.5). In particular, most points will be near the Center Line, with a decreasing number closer to either Control Limit.

4. It is beneficial to know as much as possible about the process and the measurements themselves. Interpreting control charts is not simply an analytic exercise. Those who work with a process have much domain knowledge and immediately know the root cause of an out-of-control situation. Further, operators frequently have great ideas for making improvements. These pointers also apply when implementing control charts.

5. Look for patterns other than violation of 3σ limits. Zone tests are frequently of great utility. The idea behind zone tests is that not all special causes put points beyond 3σ limits. The following zone tests are also taken as indicators of special causes.

  • The two out of three rule: Two consecutive, or two out of three consecutive points beyond either 2σ limit.
  • The four out of five rule: Four consecutive, or four out of five points beyond either 1σ limit.
  • The eight in a row rule: Eight points on the same side of the Center Line.

The zone tests are illustrated in Figure 10.9.

6. After the root cause(s) of out-of-control situations has been eliminated, it is appropriate to recalculate control limits, ignoring out-of-

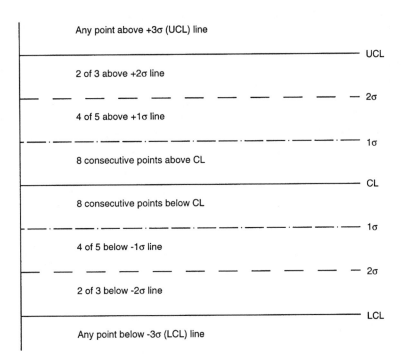

Figure 10.9 These zone tests are discussed in point 5.

control points. This will tighten limits and may lead to identification of further special causes.

7. There may be other indicators of lack of stability. Figures 10.10 through 10.12 illustrate three situations observed from time to time. Each uses hypothetical commute time data to illustrate indicators of lack of stability. Consider Figure 10.10a. Note that points tend to alternate, over the Center Line, under the Center Line, over, under, and so forth. In Figures 10.10b and 10.10c, the morning and afternoon commute times have been split from one another. These plots indicate that Figure 10.10a actually consisted of two stable processes—a stable morning commute process and a stable afternoon commute process. This interpretation is more dramatically displayed in Figures 10.10d–f, of moving ranges. Such a situation is referred to as a *mixture* because two stable processes with different means have been mixed together.

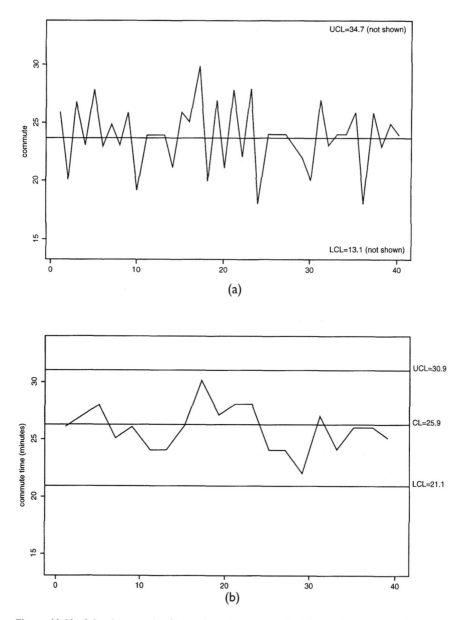

Figure 10.10a & b An example of a mixture using commute time data. In Figure 10.10a, all data are plotted together. In Figures 10.10b and 10.10c, data for the morning and afternoon are plotted separately. Figures 10.10d, 10.10e, and 10.10f are plots of the respective moving ranges. While there are no indicators of instability, variation is greatly reduced when the data are split into morning and afternoon groups. This is evidenced on plots of both the data and the moving ranges.

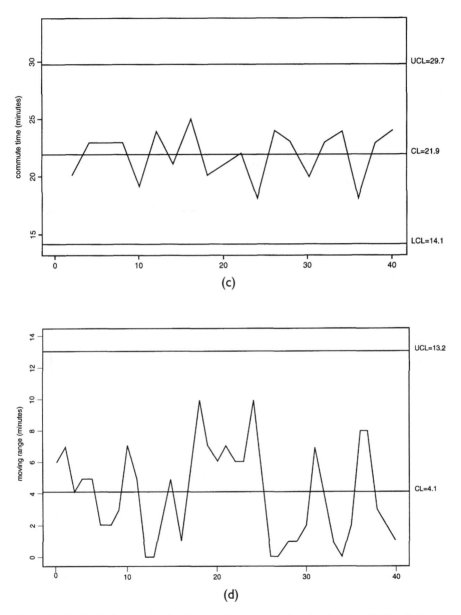

Figure 10.10c & d   An example of a mixture using commute time data. In Figure 10.10a, all data are plotted together. In Figures 10.10b and 10.10c, data for the morning and afternoon are plotted separately. Figures 10.10d, 10.10e, and 10.10f are plots of the respective moving ranges. While there are no indicators of instability, variation is greatly reduced when the data are split into morning and afternoon groups. This is evidenced on plots of both the data and the moving ranges.

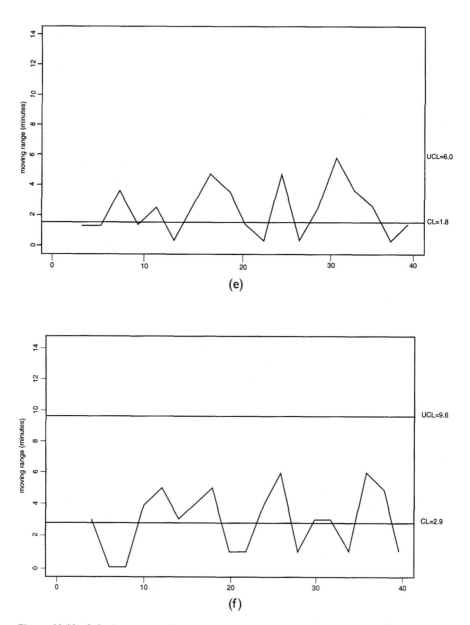

Figure 10.10e & f   An example of a mixture using commute time data. In Figure 10.10a, all data are plotted together. In Figures 10.10b and 10.10c, data for the morning and afternoon are plotted separately. Figures 10.10d, 10.10e, and 10.10f are plots of the respective moving ranges. While there are no indicators of instability, variation is greatly reduced when the data are split into morning and afternoon groups. This is evidenced on plots of both the data and the moving ranges.

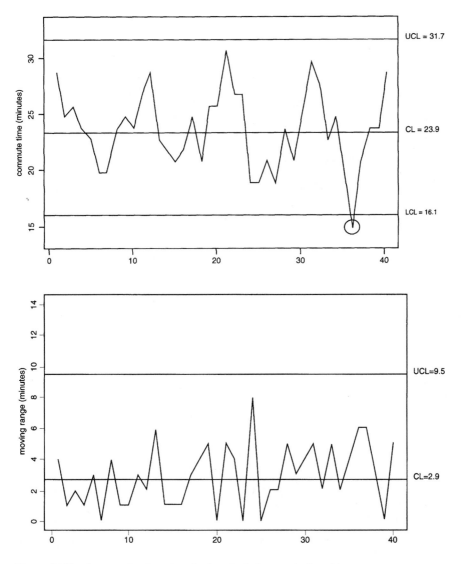

Figure 10.11 An example of a cycle, using hypothetical commute time data.

Figure 10.11 shows a *cycle*. Here the cycle shows differences in commute time associated with different days of the week. More generally, cycles indicate complicated mixing variables.

It is misleading to think of mixtures and cycles as indicating a lack of stability. What they suggest is that the mechanisms underlying the process, and hence judgments of stability, are more complicated.

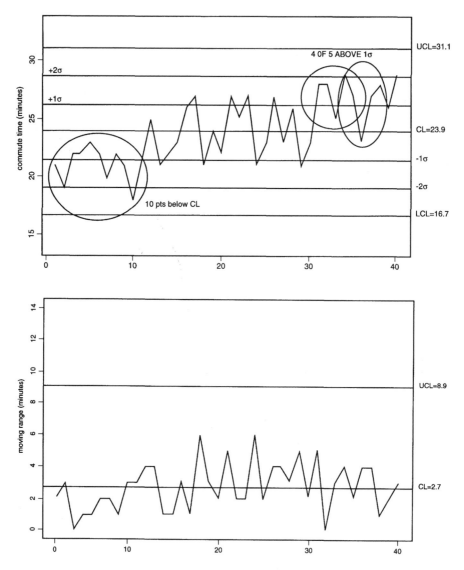

Figure 10.12 An example of a trend, using hypothetical commute time data. Note that zone tests are failed at both ends of the plot.

Figure 10.12 illustrates a *trend*. Trends are usually easy to identify. Points at either end of the control chart are often beyond limits, zone tests may fail, and there is a distinct difference in performance between the first and last points. Trends often reflect gradual changes to the process; sometimes these trends reflect improved performance. The root causes should be understood and

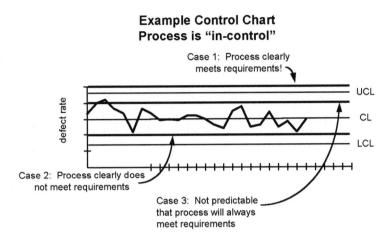

Figure 10.13   This process is in-control—whether its performance is adequate depends on customer requirements.

captured. Other times a trend reflects steadily decaying performance, and root causes should be determined and the trend arrested.

10.6   Conformance to Requirements

Once control is established, future performance of the information chain is predictable. The next question is, "Is the predicted quality level acceptable?" This answer depends on the relationship between relevant requirements or specifications. The possible scenarios are presented in Figure 10.13.

10.7   Summary

This chapter has focused on the reasoning underlying SQC. The specific need that SQC addresses is prediction about the performance of a process. The theory of statistical control provides:

- A condition, termed process stability, under which prediction is justified;
- Ways to help achieve stability;
- The desired predictions.

10.8   Notes on References

Many good SQC references are available. The following are a few good ones, with apologies to authors not listed.

Shewhart [1, 2] and Duncan [4] provide rich discussions of statistical theory. The *Statistical Quality Control Handbook* [5] and *Analyzing Business Process Data: The Looking Glass* [6] are aimed at manufacturing and business processes, respectively. These references are directed at operators of processes and give numerous examples explaining precisely how to implement SQC in these settings. Grant and Leavenworth [7]; Wadsworth, Stephens, and Godfrey [8]; and Ott [9] are good texts that also provide statistical background. Juran [10] is a classic of quality management, with a good section on statistical control. Two topics beyond those presented here may be of interest to many readers. First, the concept of process capability has proven useful as a means of comparing performance of a process with requirements and with other processes. Most of the references cited above discuss process capability. In addition, *Continuing Process Control and Process Capability Improvement* [11] is an excellent reference on applications. Caby [12] extends concepts of process capability to categorical data. CUSUM (Cumulative Sum) control charts are gaining favor where it is desired to detect small shifts in process performance. These and other more advanced procedures are discussed in Ryan [13] and Montgomery [14].

REFERENCES

[1]   Shewhart, W. A., *Statistical Method from the Viewpoint of Quality Control*, Washington, DC: Graduate School of the Department of Agriculture, 1939.

[2]   Shewhart, W. A., *Economic Control of Quality of Manufactured Product*, New York: D. Van Nostrand, 1931.

[3]   Kent, W., *Data and Reality*, Amsterdam: Elsevier Science Publishers, 1978.

[4]   Duncan, A. J., *Quality Control and Industrial Statistics*, rev. ed., Homewood, IL: Richard D. Irwin, Inc., 1959.

[5]   *Statistical Quality Control Handbook*, Western Electric, Select Code 700-444, 1956.

[6]   *Analyzing Business Process Data: The Looking Glass*, AT&T, 1990.

[7]   Grant, E. L., and R. S. Leavenworth, *Statistical Quality Control*, 6th ed., New York: McGraw-Hill, 1988.

[8]   Wadsworth, H. M., K. S. Stephens, and A. B. Godfrey, *Modern Methods for Quality Control and Improvement*, New York: John Wiley & Sons, 1986.

[9]   Ott, E. R., *Process Quality Control, Troubleshooting and Interpretation of Data*, New York: McGraw-Hill, 1975.

[10]   Juran, J. M. (ed.), *Juran's Quality Control Handbook*, 4th ed., New York: McGraw-Hill, 1988.

[11]   *Continuing Process Control and Process Capability Improvement*, Dearborn, MI: Ford Motor Company, 1987.

[12]   Caby, E. C., "Process Capability for Categorical Data," unpublished manuscript.

[13]   Ryan, T. P., *Statistical Methods for Quality Improvement*, New York: John Wiley & Sons, 1989.

[14]   Montgomery, D. C., *Introduction to Statistical Quality Control*, New York: John Wiley & Sons, 1985.

Chapter **11**

Measurement Systems, Data Tracking, and Process Improvement

"I'd lie for you. And that's the truth."
—Meatloaf

11.1 Introduction

This chapter is about making measurements on information chains, understanding what the measurements really mean, and using the measurements to establish statistical control and identify improvement opportunities. Establishing the measurement system is the third step of the process management cycle. As noted in Chapter 10, we chose to discuss measurement after discussing statistical control because we want the measurement system to support control. Identifying improvement opportunities is the fifth step. Then, selecting the opportunities to pursue (step 6) and making and sustaining improvements (step 7) complete a round of the process management cycle. The examples used in this chapter are based on real data. We'll show both an out-of-control situation and an in-control situation where user requirements are not met.

Our focus in this chapter is on a particular measurement protocol called *data tracking*.[1] Other types of measurements, such as failed edits and data-related customer complaints, are also valid and useful. But data tracking is particularly important because it provides in-process measurement and so supports higher accuracy levels.

Throughout this book we have noted that the ways data are distinct from other assets makes application of the process management cycle more difficult. The principal difficulty with measurement is that data do not have physical properties, such as weight, size, or impedance. In many cases, subjective opinions about data aren't even valid. On the other hand, data and the information chains that produce them are highly redundant and this redundancy is the key to measurement. Data tracking takes advantage of redundancy to give measures of accuracy and consistency. It can also be used to measure process-cycle time, a factor of ever-increasing importance. Thus, this chapter describes the *logic* and *how to* of developing and applying a measurement system based on the data-tracking technique.

11.2   Measurement Systems

Perhaps no subject is more confusing or more important to sustainable quality improvement than the roles and how tos of measurement systems. It is universally accepted that metrics, be they financial, social, or quality, can drive behavior. But at least two traps should be recognized.

- Selecting inappropriate measures, which motivate inappropriate behavior;
- Managing the measurement system instead of the processes that are being measured.

---

1.   Young Huh [1] and Bob Pautke [2] helped invent and implement the first several data-tracking systems. Young is now with Lucent Technologies, the AT&T spin-off that designs and manufactures telecommunications systems and equipment. Bob is now with AT&T Laboratories. Errol Caby of AT&T Laboratories helped formalize data tracking [3]. Pat Baker and Steve Borbash of AT&T and Arnold Lent of AT&T Laboratories contributed to the formulation of measurement systems presented here.

These traps are substantial.[2] A frequently cited example is focusing on quarterly profits to the detriment of an enterprise's ability to compete over the long run. Unfortunately, the danger in *not* instituting measurement systems is even greater. Measurement is the only way of knowing what an information chain (or system, function, etc.) is producing.

At the same time, no measurement system can be perfect, and no measurement system can possibly provide all the information that will ever be needed.[3] Thus, measurement systems do not obviate the need for management. The best that can be hoped for is that the measurement system will provide a factual foundation for managerial decisions (the managerial actions dictated by statistical process control and process management require great judgment, for example). There will always be essential features that are not and cannot be measured. In such circumstances, the process owner's intuition and knowledge play a critical role. Measurement systems contribute even in such circumstances by removing some (but not all) uncertainties and helping the process owners shape their thinking.

In Chapter 7 a number of characteristics of good measurement systems are noted. Here we focus on components of measurement systems relevant to a particular information chain (as distinct from an overall enterprise measurement system). At the information-chain level, a measurement system consists of four integrated components.

- Performance requirements on the chain: Performance requirements stem from customer requirements (step 2) and are coupled with the process owner's responsibility to manage and improve the process;
- Determination of "what to measure";
- A measurement device and a protocol for using it;
- Summaries of process performance: Summaries are compared with requirements and appropriate actions taken.

Such measurement systems are aimed at meeting the day-in and day-out *operational* needs in managing a process. As noted in Chapter 7, there are higher level *tactical* and *strategic* needs that operational-level measurements feed.

Each component of measurement systems should be targeted at a small set of practical goals. Information chains may have hundreds of individual facets;

---

2. These traps are exacerbated when the measurement system is computerized. After all, if the information is in the computer, it must be right.

3. Deming says "the most important figures are unknown and unknowable."

measurement systems that encompass too many facets are expensive, burden-
some, and hard to manage. A good rule of thumb is that the measurement system
should include features that are critical to customer satisfaction and process
efficiency—and relatively little else.

Measurement systems, like the chains they measure, must be dynamic.
There is a synergistic relation between the information chain and the measurement system; measurements may suggest opportunities to improve a process,
sometimes through the incorporation of higher technology. A higher technology process may require a higher technology measurement system. Similarly, as
a chain evolves, new or different features may require emphasis. These should
be reflected in changes to the measurement system.

In the remainder of this chapter, we discuss these four components of
measurement systems for information chains in greater detail. The information
chain illustrated via flowchart in Figure 11.1 is used as an example. This chain
is a composite of several large processes on which the methods of this chapter
have been successfully implemented. Each of the points illustrated using this
composite process is based on actual experience, although the measured quality
levels have been changed.

Our example chain features two databases (labeled DB A and DB B, respectively) and five processes. Figure 11.2 illustrates the fields that are created and
appear in each process. The goals of the measurement system will be to measure,
control, and improve the accuracy of data entering DB A, the consistency of
fields common to DBs A and B, and the cycle time of the process feeding DB A.
It may be useful at this point for the reader to construct a specific example similar
to the hypothetical one of Figures 11.1 and 11.2. The example can feature two
databases, as does the employee address process of Chapter 8, or a single

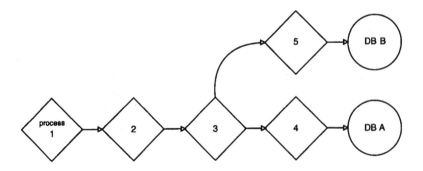

Figure 11.1 This hypothetical process is used throughout the chapter to illustrate the main points.
Two databases, labeled DB A and DB B, respectively, and five processes, numbered 1–5, are featured.

field \ Process DB	1	2	3	4	5	DB A	DB B
a	created	✔	✔	✔	✔	✔	✔
b	created	✔	✔	✔	✔	✔	✔
c		created	✔	✔	✔	✔	✔
d		created	✔	✔	✔	✔	✔
e			created	✔	✔	✔	✔
f				created		✔	
g				created	created	✔	✔
h					created		✔

Figure 11.2 The fields that are created and appear throughout the hypothetical process. The "✓" indicates the presence of the field.

database. Example processes used to provide access (telephone) service to business customers were described in Chapter 5. In these cases, the data fields of Figure 11.2 correspond to employee and circuit data fields.

11.3 Process Requirements

Process requirements are an essential part of a measurement system because they are the link to customer satisfaction. Measurement systems on information chains should be designed to support requirements of the following nature.

1. The chain should be put and maintained in a state of statistical control.
2. The chain should produce no more than a stated level of defects.
3. The chain should be improved continuously and meet future performance levels.

It is important to note the fundamental roles played by statistical control. First, statistical control makes quality levels of both the database and processes predictable. The need for predictability and its value was discussed extensively in Chapter 10. Second, once control is established, quality levels can be compared with requirements. Third, statistical control provides the foundation for improvement activities.

11.4   What to Measure

Figures 11.1 and 11.2 simplify considerably the real situation in many enterprises. The enterprise may have hundreds of data fields traversing dozens of major information chains. One critical activity is developing a relatively simple model, such as provided by Figures 11.1 and 11.2, of what to measure. The issues include:

- What processes should be measured?
- What fields should be included?
- What measures are most important?

If the first two steps of the process management cycle have been successful, addressing these issues is much simpler. In particular, the answer to each question stems from understanding critical customer needs and the information chain.

Another useful basis for determining what to measure is past experiences in cleaning up the database. For each class of database errors, potential error sources often can be identified. These error-process combinations can help answer the questions about what to measure.

There is utility in making conservative selections, at least initially. It is better to work with only a few (rather than all) processes, a few (rather than more) fields, and a very few measures to start.[4] As experience is gained, the measurement system can be extended.

---

4. This advice is based on the shared experiences of many practitioners. I have yet to hear of anyone claim to have implemented a measurement system (the first time anyway) without many frustrations. The number of things that can and do go wrong is staggering. Keeping it simple to start with does not alleviate all the frustrations, but it will help keep the number of failures to a minimum.

11.5   The Measuring Device and Protocol: Data Tracking

11.5.1   Philosophy

The application of quality techniques and in particular statistical process control in manufacturing (e.g., on assembly processes) is well known. One samples the output of each step of an assembly operation, tests whether each sampled item meets requirements, and summarizes the results on a graph. After several samples are obtained, control limits are calculated and control charts created. This sequence of steps is illustrated in Figure 11.3.[5]

The ability to measure performance in-process is critical to this application. Similar in-process measurement, as has been described previously, is not feasible for data. As has been discussed, one can edit data to check formats and simple logical requirements, but one cannot easily determine whether a given data value is correct. To do so requires comparing data values against some (usually real-world) standard. This can be extremely expensive and time consuming. Thus, it is not particularly useful to independently sample each step of an information chain.

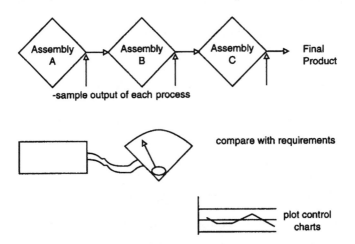

Figure 11.3   These are the steps in making measurements and plotting results when objective measurement is possible, such as in manufacturing.

---

5.   This paragraph, nor any part of this book, does not imply that manufacturing processes are simpler than information chains.

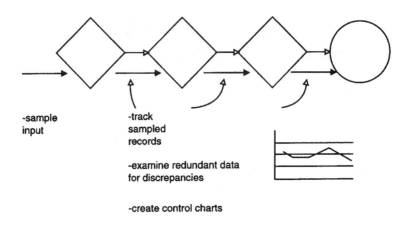

-sample
input

-track
sampled
records

-examine redundant data
for discrepancies

-create control charts

Figure 11.4 A pictorial description of the steps in data tracking is illustrated.

The essence of data tracking is to sample records as they enter the first process and track them through each subsequent process until they enter the database. Changes in records as they progress are used to develop record-specific standards of correctness. In effect, the data's redundancy is used to develop a surrogate for objective measurement. The general scheme is illustrated in Figure 11.4.

As will be discussed fully in the next section, sampled records are labeled so they may be tracked. Such labeling and tracking is not uncommon in science. For example, banding enables workers to track birds.

Key steps in applying data tracking are as follows.

1. Take a random sample of records entering the first process. Label each sampled record for later identification.

2. Track sampled records as they progress through each process and into the database. Write out the contents of each sampled record as it exits each process. Also note the time of entry and exit.

3. Identify defects and errors produced by the chain and its constituent processes. Also determine components of the cycle time.

4. At appropriate intervals, summarize the progress of sampled records. Develop relevant plots and summaries to verify conformance to requirements and analyze changes or errors to re-establish control and suggest process improvements (this step comprises the fourth component of the measurement system).

11.5.2   Step 1: Sampling

Sampling is used because it has many advantages over complete inspection [4]. Many information chains processes are continuous in the sense that records enter the first process singly and more or less continuously. In this case, sampling should be performed continuously. If the process is a batch process, a random sample from each batch may be appropriate.

In either case, continuous or batch, records are randomly selected. The purpose of random selection is to avoid biases that might result if the sample were selected in any other way. For example, there may be correlations from one record to the next.

One way of ensuring randomness is as follows.

1. Determine the overall sampling rate, r, and let each record have the same probability r of being sampled. For example, $r = .15$ corresponds to randomly selecting 15% of the records entering the information chain.

2. For each record i entering the initial process:

   a. Generate a random number x_i, uniformly distributed over $[0,1]$.

   b. If $x_i < r$, then select the record; if not, do not select the record.

Note that $r = 1$ corresponds to complete, 100% sampling and $r = 0$ to no sampling, effectively turning off data tracking.

Some of the more subtle features of measurement systems involve the interrelationships of the four components. Selection of the sampling rate is one good example. Many factors influence the sampling rate, including cost and the summaries that are needed. More explicitly, the sampling rate, r, depends on the following factors.

- Sample size, n: How many records are needed to create the desired summaries (i.e., records/sample interval)?
- Sample frequency, f: How often should results be summarized (i.e., how many sample intervals/month)?
- Total volume, v: How frequently do records enter the process (i.e., records/month)?

If n, f, and v are known, the sampling rate may be computed using $r = \dfrac{n \cdot f}{v}$.

11.5.3   Step 2: Tracking

Once sampled, the records are marked (or tagged) so they can be tracked through the chain and into the database. This marking can be accomplished in either of the following ways.

- Unique identifying field: If there is a data field, or a set of data fields, that uniquely identifies each record (i.e., a primary key), it may be used for retrieving sampled records. To use this method, the values of this data field for the sampled records are stored for subsequent referencing. This method requires no change to the data structure.

- Tag field: A special data field may be added to each record as a tag that identifies the record as selected or not. This method allows for easy identification of selected records through the process. However, it requires a change of the data structure to include the tag field.

In either case, it is important that people who work within the information chain are not able to distinguish sampled from unsampled records. This is to avoid the possibility that sampled records are given special attention.

As the sampled records progress from one process to the next, their data values are recorded, along with the date and time of process entry and exit. If the record is to complete the process at a prespecified time, the due time is also recorded. An example of the resultant information is presented in Figure 11.5.

11.5.4   Step 3: Identify Errors and Calculate Process Cycle Times

Sampled records such as those shown in Figure 11.5 are used to quantify accuracy, consistency, and cycle time. For accuracy, the emphasis is on changes in data fields as records progress into a single database (DB A in our example). For consistency, the emphasis is on changes in data fields as processes diverge into separate databases (DBs A and B in our example). Conceptually, the analyses for accuracy and consistency are quite similar. For cycle time, we use the date and time information.

We first consider accuracy and consistency. Changes to fields are illustrated in Figure 11.5. Changes are categorized into the following three types.

- *Normalizational*: Changes made, such as insertion or deletion of delimiters, spaces, and so forth, to meet different format criteria of different computers or other systems in various processes. An example of a normalizational change is shown in Figure 11.5 in field *a*, process 2.

	1	2	3	4	5	DB A	DB B
a	-DHBC-	-DHBC-	-DHBC-	-DHBC-	-DHBC-	-DHBC-	-DHBC-
b	408727	408727	408831	408831	408831	408831	408831
c		SRBEX	A	A	A	A	A
d			DEC	DEC	DEC	DEC	DEC
e			H23A	F17B	H23A	F17B	H23A
f			$23.25		$23.25		
g				N	Y	N	Y
h					bf		bf
entry	2/24 10:00	2/24 12:15	3/1 12:00	3/5 8:00	3/10 8:00	3/6 0:13	3/12 0:30
exit	2/24 10:45	2/24 17:00	3/2 12:00	3/5 10:15	3/10 17:00		
due		2/24 17:00	3/1 17:00	3/5 17:00	3/9 17:00	3/6 8:00	3/10 8:00

Figure 11.5   An example of a tracked record is illustrated.

The human eye immediately detects that the values assigned to field *a* by processes 1 and 2 are the same. Thus, this kind of change is a change in *presentation* only.

- *Translational*: Changes due to the use of different languages throughout the information chain. An example of a translational change is shown in Figure 11.5 in data field *c* at process 3. Such changes are also in presentation only. The key distinction between normalizational and translational changes is that the human eye recognizes normalizational changes, but not translational.

- *Spurious-operational*: Changes introducing an incorrect value. Examples of spurious-operational changes are shown in Figure 11.5 in data fields *b*, *e*, and *g*. It is not possible at this point to know what caused the incorrect value (that is the job of subsequent analyses). When a spurious-operational change appears, it may have occurred because an error occurred in that process or to correct an error produced by an earlier process. In either case, a spurious-operational change indicates an error in the information chain.

Three types of analyses involving entry, exit, and due dates/times are of interest. Let S_i (for start), C_i (for complete), and D_i (for due) denote the entry, exit, and due date/times, respectively, for process i for a particular record (for databases a slight modification is necessary—let D_A denote the time the record is due to enter the database and C_A denote its actual entry time). The first analysis of interest is based on timeliness of completion of processes:

$$T_i = C_i - D_i$$

The second is based on the length of time required to complete the process:

$$L_i = C_i - S_i$$

The third analysis of interest is based on queue time:

$$Q_i = S_i - C_{i-1}$$

In the example of Figure 11.5, process 4 took 2 hours and 15 minutes to complete (i.e., L_4 = 2 hrs., 15 min.), it was completed 6 hours and 45 minutes ahead of schedule (i.e., T_4 = –6 hrs., 45 min.), and this record waited in queue for 2 days and 16 hours prior to the initiation of process 4 (i.e., Q_4 = 2 days, 16 hrs.).

11.5.5   Step 4: Summarize Results

In this section, we discuss analyses and summary plots that have proven useful. These analyses are based on standard quality control and improvement techniques and are tightly coupled with the process owner's actions. The following section also illustrates:

- The sorts of decisions that a process owner is to make;
- How an opportunity for improvement is identified;
- Some generic process improvements.

Accuracy

For accuracy and consistency the collected data can be analyzed at three levels of detail, as follows.

- The "metrics" level, where the goal is to determine the overall performance of the information chain.
- The "localization" level, where the goal is to determine processes (more precisely, pairs of processes) and field combinations that present the greatest problems.

- The "control" level, where the goal is to establish statistical control and provide the basis for improvement.

Information from higher level analyses is used to determine what lower level analyses are needed and all analyses are aimed at helping the process owner determine what actions to take.

In this section, we focus on processes 1–4 and DB A. We will step through the three-layered analysis plan (metrics, localization, control) noted above.

Figure 11.6 is an example of a useful plot at the metrics level. In this plot, the average numbers of all three types of changes for the entire process—normalizational, translational, and spurious operational—are plotted against time. The root causes for normalizational and translational changes are known—vary-

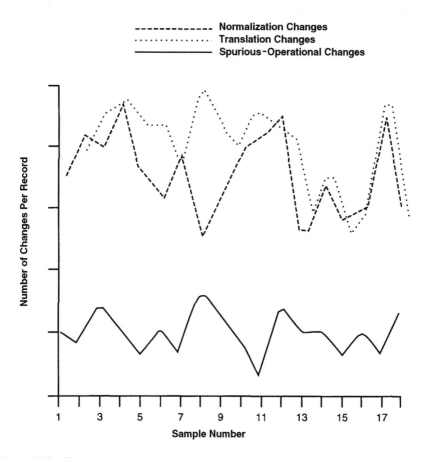

Figure 11.6 The average number of each type of change per record is plotted against time for the hypothetical process.

ing formats and languages across processes. Opinion varies on the seriousness of such changes; the situation illustrates the kinds of choices that a process owner is forced to make. On the one hand, it is hard to see how varying formats provide any real value to customers. Further, adjusting formats or making translations adds time and expense to both software development and processing and provides opportunities for errors. On the other hand, there may be good reasons for the use of different computer systems and different languages and formats. In the short run, the resources needed to eliminate these changes may not be available.

No clear prescription exists for the process owner. My own feeling is that the process owner should consider both short- and long-term improvement options. In the short term, the process owner may wish to use *data dictionaries* to make allowable changes explicit. This will have the salutary effect of minimizing other errors caused by changing formats and languages. In the long term, consideration should be given to common languages and formats as current computer equipment is retired.

We now concentrate on the spurious-operational changes. Moving to the localization stage of the analysis, the goal is to determine which process/field combinations offer the greatest opportunity for improvement. There are many ways to proceed. One way is to plot the proportion of records experiencing spurious-operational changes for each data field on a pareto chart. (A pareto

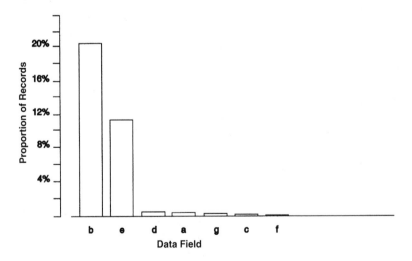

Figure 11.7 A pareto chart shows the proportion of spurious-operational changes for each field of the hypothetical example.

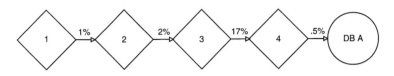

Figure 11.8 Process-overview-of-differences chart for field *b* is shown here..

chart is a bar chart in which the categories of the *x*-axis are ordered by frequency or percentage. The frequencies or percentages are plotted on the *y*-axis, i.e., the heights of the bars.) Figure 11.7 is a pareto chart, and it shows that the greatest opportunities for improvement lie with fields *b* and *e*. We will continue the description of the analysis with field *b*.

One could also plot the percent of fields spuriously changed between subsequent processes for this field, which can be done with a pareto chart as well. There is also utility in plotting these numbers directly on the flowchart. The resultant chart, Figure 11.8, is referred to as a process-overview-of-differences chart. Figure 11.8 shows that the majority of changes occur between processes 3 and 4.

In the control level of analysis, p-charts (discussed in Chapter 10) are made for process/field combinations of interest. Figure 11.9 is a p-chart for field *b* changes between processes 3 and 4.

The pair exhibit a high average proportion defective and many points out of control. In accord with the reasoning in Chapter 10, the process owner should seek a special cause of variation.

Before proceeding, a note about a difficulty in constructing control charts is in order. Because records wind their way through the chain at different speeds, care is needed in selecting records to be included at each time period on control charts. In particular, it is important that only records that actually proceed through a process during the relevant time period be included in the sample for that period. The situation and solution are illustrated in Figure 11.10.

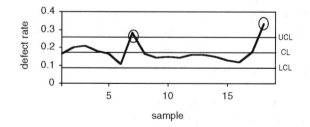

Figure 11.9 p-chart for field *b*, between processes 3 and 4, is hsown here..

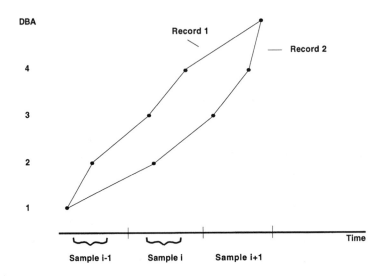

Figure 11.10   It is important to associate the proper records with each sample in plotting control charts. The simple rule is to select records that have progressed through a process in any given time period.

Consistency

The analysis for detecting inconsistencies between DBs A and B proceeds much the same as for accuracy. At the metrics level, the total numbers of discrepancies between records as they enter databases in each of the normalizational, translational, and spurious-operational categories are plotted against time. As this plot has the same axes as Figure 11.6, it is not repeated.

Focusing on the spurious-operational changes, a pareto chart (Figure 11.11) shows that the majority of inconsistencies occur in fields e and g. The process-overview-of-differences charts for these fields are shown in Figures 11.12 and 11.13.

First, consider field e. A great many changes occur between processes 3 and 4 and virtually none elsewhere. Further, field e was cited earlier as exhibiting accuracy problems. This suggests that consistency is not the root problem. Rather, the problem appears to be similar to that of field b, discussed in the preceding section. The problem with field e should be addressed as an accuracy issue.

The situation for field g is not so clear. Figure 11.14 is the p-chart for field g spurious-operational differences between processes 4 and 5. This figure suggests that field g is in control, although the defect rate is high: No special causes of variation seem to be present. The apparently random behavior of this

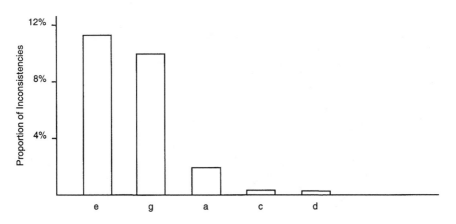

Figure 11.11 A pareto chart of inconsistencies between DBs A and B is shown.

process suggests that this defect level is inherent to the process, as it is currently defined. The process will have to be changed to improve.

Process owners are faced with another critical decision: They must decide whether the observed defect rate on field *g* warrants improvement. That decision should be based in part on process requirements. Figure 11.15 features the control chart of Figure 11.14 with three possible placements of a requirement line.

For the sake of discussion, assume that the quality level reflected in Figure 11.14 corresponds to case 2 (this seems the most likely case—after all, the defect rate is 11%). To determine improvement opportunities, further detailed knowl-

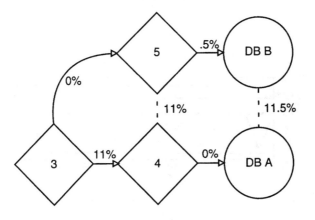

Figure 11.12 A process-overview-of-differences chart for the portions of the hypothetical process that involve consistency, field **e**.

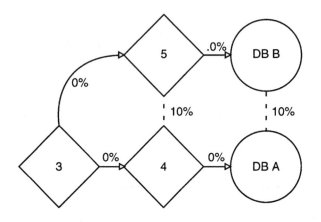

Figure 11.13 A process-overview-of-differences chart for the portions of the hypothetical process that involve consistency, field **g**.

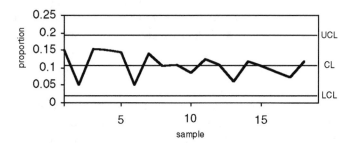

Figure 11.14 p-chart, field **g** spurious-operational differences between processes 4 and 5.

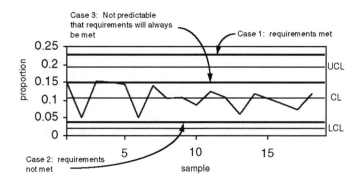

Figure 11.15 Possible relationships of requirements to process performance plotted on the control chart. Appropriate actions for the process owner are noted in the text.

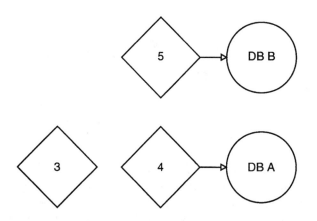

Figure 11.16 A more detailed flowchart for field **g**. Note that field **g** is independently determined in processes 4 and 5, with no communications.

edge of the process in the neighborhood of the source is required. (The FIP techniques of Chapter 8 are useful in this regard.) In our example, field *g* illustrates a fairly common situation, and all that is needed is a more careful flowchart. Figure 11.16 is drawn to show field *g* changes only. Figure 11.16 shows two independent processes feeding DBs A and B, respectively. Field *g* is independently determined by both processes 4 and 5. As a result, whether the two field *g*'s match is random, resulting in the behavior as noted in Figure 11.14. The process owner must close the discontinuity to eliminate this source of inconsistencies.

Two Subtleties

This section explains a subtle distinction between accuracy and consistency and shows how data tracking can be used to improve accuracy of processes involving transaction-based systems.

Since the analyses of data accuracy and data consistency are so similar, it is natural to wonder what makes accuracy and consistency distinct. After all, one compares records in exactly the same ways, and the comparisons used for accuracy are nothing more than subprocess consistency checks.

The distinction between the accuracy and consistency problems is only in goals—one accurate database versus two or more consistent databases. Direct comparison works for accuracy only because information chains are redundant. Thus, accuracy of data is akin to consistency of its constituent processes.

One other subtlety may be important for transaction-based systems. The information chains associated with such systems may look much like Figure

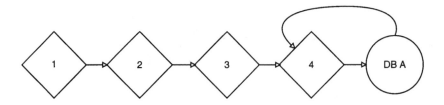

Figure 11.17   An example flowchart for a transaction-based process is illustrated.

11.17, which is similar to Figure 11.1, but with many repeats of process 4 and updates of DB A. Data tracking also works on such chains. Records are tracked into DB A as before and tracked continuously thereafter. Consider as an example Figure 11.17 with the fields of Figure 11.2 and a new field i. In the expanded process 4, a new field e is created and field i is incremented by field e (i.e., the new value in field i equals the old value in field i plus the value in field e).

To continue the example, in a given time interval the values could be as shown in Figure 11.18. Spurious-operational changes now correspond to transaction errors. Thus, in Figure 11.18, though field i is incorrect seven times, there is only one spurious-operational change. Analysis of such changes proceeds along the lines previously discussed.

Cycle Time/Currency

The analyses of entry and exit times for processes are a bit more sophisticated, although still based on standard techniques of quality control and improvement. A number of new details about the process are needed for the analyses to make sense. The analyses are not particularly sensitive to details (meaning that if the details were changed, the thrust of the analyses would not change). In this section we consider processes 1–4 and DB A. In addition, we assume that:

- Entering a record into DB A corresponds to delivery of some value-added service to a customer. In particular, D_A corresponds to the time the service is promised and C_A to the time the service is delivered.

- Based on D_A, other processes are scheduled. That is, D_1, D_2, D_3, and D_4 are determined so that D_A may be achieved.

- The customer is free to cancel the order or order something different up until D_A.

Figure 11.19 is a redrawing of Figure 11.1, emphasizing the aspects of the chain that are important in analyzing currency.

	field *e*	field *i*
initially		17.05
transaction 1	3.06	20.11
2	17.46	37.57
3	-12.19	49.76
4	-16.37	33.39
5	14.16	49.55
6	-1.12	48.43
7	12.19	60.62
8	27.06	87.68
9	-19.59	68.09

Figure 11.18 A tracked record for the transaction-based system. There is one transaction error, hence one spurious-operational change.

The first analysis involves T_A, which is the time the service is delivered minus the time it is promised (so $T_A > 0$ implies late delivery). The $\overline{X}$ and S (or $\overline{X}$ and R) control chart is used to begin the analysis (see Figure 11.20). Since $T_A > 0$ corresponds to late service delivery, the UCL on the $\overline{X}$-chart should be comfortably below zero. In effect, the process requirement is $T_A \leq 0$ (a business decision that service is delivered significantly early generates a slightly different requirement). Another effective plot is of the distribution of T_A shown in Figure 11.21, which is used to estimate the percentage of orders not delivered as promised.

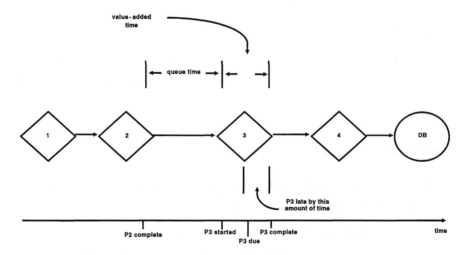

Figure 11.19 A redrawing of the hypothetical process of Figure 11.1, emphasizing features of interest in cycle-time analyses.

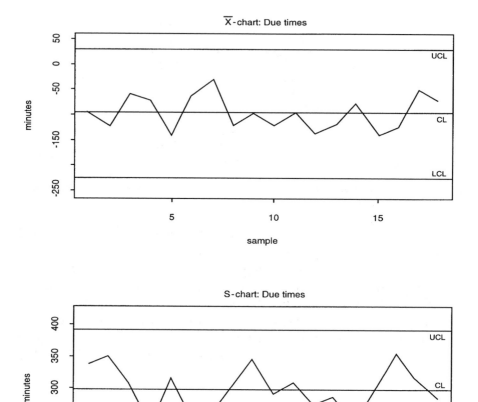

Figure 11.20 $\overline{X}$- and S-charts for service delivery are shown.

If service is frequently late (i.e., $T_A > 0$), the process owner may have to consider several possibilities, including:

- One or more processes may have problems.

- The process may not be capable of delivering service on time. In a similar vein, some processes may not be capable of finishing on time.

- Customers change their orders so frequently that too much rework of already completed processes is needed.

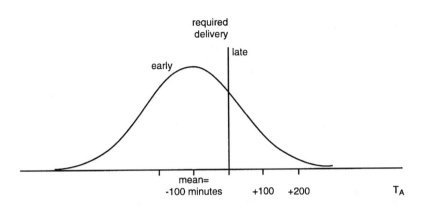

Figure 11.21   The statistical density of T_A. This plot shows that 37% of orders are being delivered later than promised.

The following paragraphs outline how to detect and correct these problems.

To determine whether the problem lies with one or more processes, make $\overline{X}$- and S-charts similar to Figure 11.20 for each of T_1 through T_4. Analysis of special and common causes proceeds as usual.

Analysis of whether the information chain is capable of delivering the service on time is based on how long it takes to complete the processes. For example, if on average $L_1 = 1$ day, $L_2 = 1/2$ day, $L_3 = 2$ days, and $L_4 = 1$ day, then the chain is not capable of delivering the service in 2 days. (Note that a "special-attention" process, in which orders are flagged for immediate attention and separate handling, may be in place. But that process is not the process examined here.) The time frame in which an information chain is capable of delivering service is based on the distribution of the sums of the times required to complete each process. The distributions of L_1 through L_4 are presented in Figure 11.22. These distributions are assumed to be independent (if they are not independent, some straightforward adjustments are required) and the distribution of their sum is also shown in Figure 11.22. We call the 99th percentile of the summed distribution the delivery capability interval. Due dates negotiated with customers should allow for at least this interval.

Issues involving customers changing their orders are more subtle. On the one hand, customers certainly have the right to change their minds. On the other hand, substantial rework can result when they do and there may be too little time for the process to be completed. But experience suggests that the opposite is more often true: Promised and actual delivery intervals often far exceed the process delivery capability interval, by up to an order of magnitude. This is because the time spent in queue far exceeds time spent in value-added activity. For example, customers may be promised delivery in 30 days, while their orders

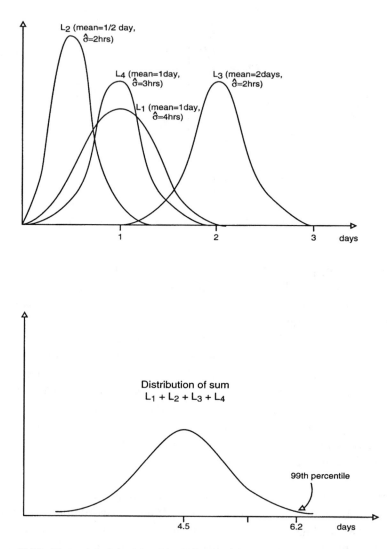

Figure 11.22   The statistical densities of L_1, L_2, L_3, L_4, and their sum. This plot assumes an 8-hour work day. The 99th percentile of the sum is called the process delivery capability interval.

take only 5 to 7 days of work. The other 23 to 25 days is spent in queue somewhere in the information chain.

This situation suggests a different schedule, accommodating customers yet minimizing the impact of order changes. For example, the order processing can be scheduled as shown in Figure 11.23. As much queue time as possible is

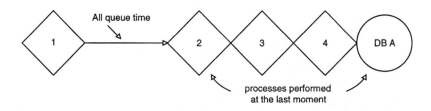

Figure 11.23 Scheduling all the anticipated queue time as early in the process as possible accommodates customers changing their minds, while minimizing impact.

scheduled between processes 1 and 2, and the value-added work of processes 2, 3, and 4 is scheduled for the last moment. Customers may still change their orders, but the impact of changes is minimal.

This solution can be extended. If no queue time is allowed, then service can be delivered to the customer (with high probability) at the process capability interval. In the 30-day example, eliminating the entire 25 days may not be immediately practical, but eliminating 15 to 20 days is often easy. Thus, what is currently promised in 30 days could be delivered in 14 days (6 value-added days + 8 queue days) with only small changes.

A word of caution: All of the time between the completion of one activity and the start of the next may not be queue time—some may be transmission time. Differences in transmission speeds may affect the process delivery capability interval (consider the differences between regular mail, overnight mail, facsimile service, and real-time data communication). We have tacitly assumed that transmission time is built into each process and that the interprocess time is all queue time. Speeding up transmission time using modern technology is another process improvement opportunity.

The second remark is that queue time serves one function: It buffers work to smooth out workloads. But experience with Just-In-Time manufacturing [5] also suggests that buffers act to hide defects. In manufacturing, eliminating queues has had the added benefit of improving quality because defects are easier to see.

11.6 Implementation

There are many ways to implement data tracking and conduct the needed analyses. In this section we discuss a modular implementation of the technique.

The needed modules include:

- A sampler/labeler. This module selects tracked records and, depending on the tracking mechanism, either puts the correct value into the tag field or updates a list of sampled records.
- A filter. This module recognizes sampled records, captures their contents, and time stamps their activities. Filters are placed at the beginning and end of processes.
- A secondary store. This module keeps track of samples and the data from each sample as captured by filters, associates common records from the various processes together, and stores them for subsequent analysis.
- A communications module. This module sends the contents of captured records to the secondary store.
- A data massager. This module manipulates sampled data by recognizing normalizational and other changes and calculating queue, completion, and late times.
- An analysis module. This module is equivalent to a good statistical software package, able to produce the graphs and analyses described herein.

The decision as to how to configure these modules depends on the degree of process automation, the sample size, and so forth. One architecture, called the *decentralized image-capturing (DCI) system*, is described. The DCI can be applied when:

- Tag field marking, as described above, is feasible.
- Each process is at least partially computerized.

Most important information chains already meet these criteria and, if current trends in office automation continue, all will meet them soon.

The essence of the DCI is to build the necessary modules as close to each process as possible. As Figure 11.24 illustrates,

- The sampler/labeler can be built into the first process.
- Filters can be built into each subsequent process.
- Communications modules can be built into each process (including the first).
- The secondary storage location, calculator, and the analysis module are colocated, as close as possible to the process owner.

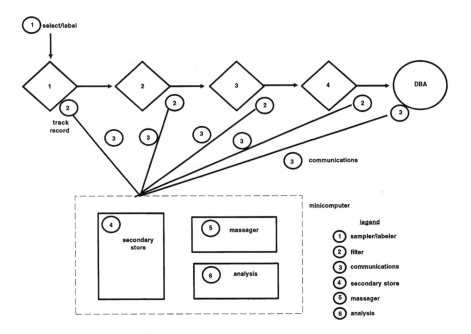

Figure 11.24   This is one potential architecture for implementing data tracking.

11.7   Summary

In this chapter we introduced the concept of a measurement system for information chains. A measurement system consists of four interrelated components.

- Requirements;
- Items or characteristics to be measured;
- A measurement instrument and a set of rules for using it;
- Appropriate summaries.

Requirements provide the link to customers and are the translation of the voice of the customer into quantifiable performance. Requirements heavily influence what is to be measured. Summaries aim at providing the process owner the information needed to establish statistical control and identify improvement opportunities.

Data tracking is the measurement instrument of choice when the goals are to control and improve data accuracy, data consistency, and process-cycle times. The basic ideas behind data tracking are to capture and use the data redundancy inherent in the process and to time stamp key events. Sampling is used to keep measurement expense low. For accuracy and consistency, a straightforward three-tiered analysis strategy quantifies overall process quality, pinpoints trouble spots, and provides control charts. Action by the process owner is based on these summaries.

Analysis of cycle-time data is more involved. The initial focus should be on whether service is delivered to customers on time. Plots of statistical densities and control charts are used.

The discussion throughout highlights generic improvement opportunities. These include:

- A communications channel is needed to ensure data consistency.
- Common computer languages and formats eliminate opportunities for error.
- Data dictionaries can help minimize errors.
- Information chains can be scheduled to minimize rework caused by customer changes.

Finally, depending on the degree of automation and other factors, there are many ways to implement measurement systems.

REFERENCES

[1]   Huh, Y. U., F. R. Keller, T. C. Redman, and A. R. Watkins, "Data Quality," *Information and Software Technology*, Vol. 32, No. 8, 1990, pp. 559–564.

[2]   Pautke, R. W., and T. C. Redman, "Techniques to Improve Quality of Data in Large Databases," *Proc. of Statistics Canada Symposium 90: Data Quality*, pp. 319–333.

[3]   *Improving Data Accuracy: The Data Tracking Technique*, AT&T, Select Code 500-489, 1992.

[4]   Cochran, W. G., *Sampling Techniques*, 3rd ed., New York: John Wiley & Sons, 1977.

[5]   Schonberger, R. J., *Japanese Manufacturing Techniques*, New York: The Free Press, 1982.

Part III: For Information Professionals

Chapter 12

Just What Is (or Are) Data?

"The modern age has a false sense of superiority because of the great mass of data at its disposal, but the valid criterion of distinction is rather the extent to which man knows how to master the material at his command."
—Goethe

12.1 Introduction

We now turn our attention to topics of special interest to information professionals.[1] This chapter explores various concepts of data—where they come and go, what they are, and the properties that are pertinent to managing them as business assets—especially their quality. The next chapter focuses on defining the most important dimensions of data quality. A number of these subjects have

---

1. Anany V. Levitin and Christopher J. Fox are responsible for many of the ideas presented in this chapter [1–5].

been noted earlier. In these chapters they are treated in greater detail. Still, neither chapter represents the final word on any subject. First, philosophical debates among competing definitions of data and information (and their even more esoteric brethren, knowledge and wisdom) have raged for centuries. Second, and in contrast, the application of modern quality principles to data is relatively recent. Complicating matters still further is the range of everyday uses of the terms. Consider the term "data."

One hears comments such as the following [4].

1. "The data on this graph prove my point."
2. "The newest data point is six."
3. "See! Here are the data we need."
4. "I can't get the data out of the database."
5. "When you see data like this, you know it is time to do something drastic!"
6. "The data misled us because they were wrong."

Some of these uses treat data as tangible measurements, as in comments 1 and 2. In other uses, the term seems less tangible—more as a motivator for action—as in comments 3 and 5. Some uses (comment 2) treat data as abstract or conceptual; others deal with data representations, as in comments 1 and 4. In some cases data are treated as factual, while in others, such as comment 6, the data need not be correct.

Our goal in these two chapters is not to resolve, or even join, the debates. Instead, we'll review and synthesize a number of perspectives that have proven useful in helping leaders and information professionals improve data quality.

Our first perspective considers the dynamic nature of data. Throughout, we've alluded to three separate activities—data creation, data storage, and data use. We'll explore the dynamic nature of data further in terms of a model of the data life cycle. This model is especially important because it elucidates the activities (i.e., business processes) that impact data quality. As also noted throughout, the key to quality improvement is improving the performance of these activities.

Next, we'll look at competing definitions of data. As noted, we have no interest in joining the debate as to which definition is superior. It seems instead that each approach aims to advance some discipline or other, so none is inherently superior. Our purpose is to advance data quality, so we select the one that is most natural from that standpoint.

Next, we discuss properties of data pertinent to managing them as business assets. As was noted in Chapter 4, there is little dispute that data and information should be managed as business assets. But a management science for data and information has not yet been developed. Properties of data are a first step. We also discuss implications for data quality.

We then present a simple model of data at the enterprise level. Finally, we will review competing approaches to defining "information."

Chapter 13 builds on this chapter by defining specific dimensions of data quality.

Before proceeding, a further comment on why Chapters 12 and 13 are needed is in order. The first decades after the invention of the computer were spectacularly successful, with little regard to definition. Indeed, Mealy [6] started his pioneering paper with the following: We do not, it seems, have a very clear and commonly agreed upon set of notions about data—either what they are, how they should be cared for, or their relation to the design of programming languages and operating systems.

Ten years later, Kent, in the preface to *Data and Reality* [7], repeated the lament, despite the fact that thousands of database systems had been deployed successfully. New ideas in data modeling [8, 9] including modeling using objects [10, 11] and attempts to integrate database theory, programming languages, and artificial intelligence [12, 13] motivate the need to address fundamental issues.

Interestingly, quality issues have not yet played an important role in the design and implementation of information systems. Perhaps promoters of the new technologies have had their hands full in solving pressing technical issues. Today, quality issues are becoming increasingly important for many reasons—the most important of which, as discussed in Chapter 1, is the fact that current quality levels are so low.

12.2 The Data Life Cycle

We have noted repeatedly that efforts at quality improvement should be focused on information chains and business processes that create data. This section introduces a general model of the data life cycle that elucidates the principal data-impacting activities—from data creation, through storage and use, to possible destruction. This model is simple but general in its applicability and provides a foundation for a deeper understanding of what data are.

12.2.1 Preliminaries

Our proposed model will have data storage as the middle activity. Most processes and/or systems that touch data make use of storage at some point or another. One can classify systems according to the role played by storage. If storing data is an ultimate goal, then the system is said to be of the *acquisition type*. If the system typically starts with access of already stored data, it is said to be of the *usage type*. Finally, most systems and processes both acquire and use data and are referred to as the *combined type*. We can further distinguish between two kinds of combined-type systems: the so-called *rigid* (or *store-and-forward*) and *flexible* kinds. A message-processing system is an example of a store-and-forward system, in which data acquisition and data usage strictly alternate. Most database management systems are of the flexible type. Here acquisition and usage need not strictly alternate.

Typically, processes involving data are repetitive. Therefore, it is more appropriate to refer to acquisition, usage, and combined *cycles*. The four types and kinds of systems described are pictured in Figures 12.1 through 12.4. Of course, these figures simplify reality considerably. Usually a single database will support several such cycles. And the distinction between acquisition and usage is not always clear-cut. Consider, for example, a process that accesses data from one database, processes them in some way, and stores the resultant data in a second database. From the point of view of the first database, the process is of the usage type; from the point of view of the second, it is of the acquisition type. A second example is a telephone directory. For the enterprise producing an annual issue, the acquisition cycle is a model of (most of) the enterprise. But

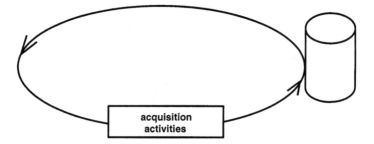

Figure 12.1   The acquisition cycle is illustrated in this figure.

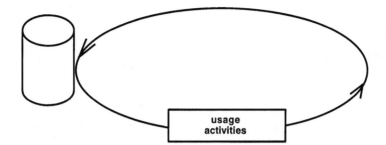

Figure 12.2 The usage cycle is illustrated in this figure.

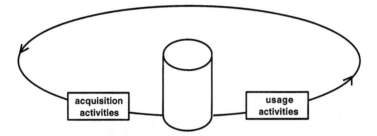

Figure 12.3 The combined cycle of the "rigid" kind is illustrated in this figure.

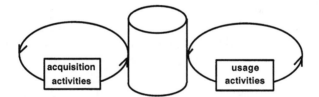

Figure 12.4 The combined cycle of the "flexible" kind is illustrated in this figure.

consumers aren't much interested in that perspective. From their perspective, the usage cycle is most important. And, of course, there is a larger perspective in which the entire process (creating and using the telephone directory) is a combined cycle of the flexible kind.

We now expand on acquisition and usage activities.

12.2.2 Acquisition Cycle

The principal activities common to data acquisition include the following (see Figure 12.5).

Figure 12.5   This figure illustrates a model of the data acquisition cycle.

1. **Define a view.** According to the prevailing approach to data modeling, specification of a view is a required first step in dealing with data. A view defines the "part of the real world" to be captured in the data. One or more entity classes have to be specified, each defined by a set of attributes. As an example, an entity class `EMPLOYEE` can be defined by attributes such as `Employee Number`, `Name`, `Sex`, `Date-Of-Birth`, `Address`, `Department`, and so forth. For each attribute, a domain of possible values must be specified. We discuss the view in more detail when the term "data" is defined.

2. **Implement the view.** A view is merely a set of definitions. Thus, it must be implemented. This step should take into account restrictions and/or limitations imposed by the storage medium and by the data management system. As an example, a company with 10 employees may require nothing more than a paper spreadsheet for storing basic data. View implementation amounts to nothing more than specifying the order in which the attributes are listed on the spreadsheet. On the other hand, `EMPLOYEE` may be one of several entity classes of interest to a large enterprise, which will store the data as part of a larger electronic database. In such cases, implementing the view is much more involved. First, a so-called normalization of the view may be required.[2] Second, the normalized view must be stated in the data definition language provided by the DBMS. Such a definition is often referred to as a *schema*. The schema is stored in a computer and used by the DBMS.

3. **Obtain values.** This step deals with acquiring specific values for the attributes of individual instances of the defined entity classes. Conceptually this activity is straightforward, but its importance has been underestimated by both theoreticians and practitioners. A list (incomplete) of the ways data values may be obtained includes measurement, surveys, observation, and copying from another source.

---

2.   See Kent [14] for a short, clear explanation of the concept of normalization.

This list illustrates the diversity this activity involves and suggests potential difficulties, as well as the impact on data quality. Typical business processes and information chains, such as billing, order realization, human resources management, finance, and so forth, are all "obtain values" processes. Neglect of this activity lies at the root of many data quality issues. The interested reader is referred to reference [15] for a general set of rules to guide data collection.

4. **Update records.** Here, data are stored in or on some medium. We use the term "update" in its broad sense, to include addition of a new record, deletion, and modification of existing records. There are three aspects of storage technology that make data quality of special importance. First, the sheer amount of data stored in today's systems—with no letup in capability in sight—makes data quality particularly important. Users will continue to have access to more data and especially more unfamiliar data. They can be more easily victimized by such data. Second, modern database systems allow several users to access data almost simultaneously, leading to synchronization problems. And third, advances in computer architectures and communications have led to distributed systems where the data reside in several computer systems in different locations. Maintaining data quality in such a complex environment is extremely difficult.

Almost all the complexities of the life-cycle model can be illustrated with surprisingly simple examples. We conclude the discussion of the acquisition with a familiar example: an individual's calendar. Here the calendar is the storage medium and the activities of the model lead to entries.

First, "define a view." Embedded in the structure of the calendar is the concept that time is structured into days, weeks, hours, and so forth. For the sake of the example, further define an entity class MEETINGS and attributes Who, Where, Start Time, and End Time (we leave it to the interested reader to develop careful definitions).

Second, "implement the view." This is accomplished by creating or obtaining a blank calendar. There are any number of implementations of calendars (and, of course, there are media for storing meeting data other than calendars). Note that at this point, the calendar is blank.

Third, "obtain data values." Ongoing processes such as conversations with customers and colleagues lead to creation of entities (meetings) and values of attributes. Anyone whose secretary has access to his or her calendar knows the

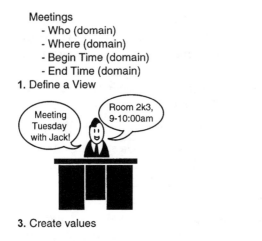

Figure 12.6 The activities of the acquisition cycle as applied to a "calendar of meetings."

complications that multiple processes for defining meetings engender for the calendar.

Finally, meeting data are stored on the calendar, changes are noted, and so forth. As with multiple processes, multiple physical calendars lead to any number of problems with the calendar. Even such mundane decisions as whether a pen or pencil is used can affect the utility of the calendar.

These activities are depicted in Figure 12.6. Note the diversity of activity. Earlier we noted that the information management community seems largely to have ignored the "obtain values" activity. It does seem to have done a reasonably good job on the others. The example illustrates this hypothesis. A seemingly infinite variety of calendars and books describing how to use these activities are readily available. Much less help is available to the ongoing processes that generate meetings and put the meeting details into a usable form.

12.2.3 Usage Cycle

We now turn our attention to the usage cycle. It begins with the access of previously stored data. Our model is presented in Figure 12.7.

1. **Define a subview.** Typically a usage process (application) will make use of only a small fraction of the data available. Thus, usage begins with a definition of the subset of data to be used. The terms used to describe the first activities of the acquisition and usage cycles are intentionally similar, as both aim at selecting a subset of

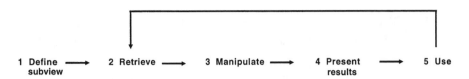

Figure 12.7   A model of the data usage cycle is illustrated in this figure.

something. But there is an important distinction: The acquisition cycle defines a view of the real world; the usage cycle defines a user's view of a data collection (for a detailed discussion of this subject, see reference [16]). Also note that for computerized database systems, the discipline of user views is utilized to promote integrity and privacy.

2.   **Retrieve.** As a rule, data are collected and stored for later use. Retrieval, understood as fetching data previously stored, is a necessary step toward that end. There is an obvious relationship between the operations of updating records (step 4 of the usage cycle) and retrieval: Conceptually, one is the reverse of the other. And both are often accomplished by the same DBMS software. Nevertheless, the following points should be kept in mind. First, storage and retrieval need not be accomplished by the same technical means. Second, even when they are, the two activities may be performed by different people and organizations. Third, a considerable period of time may elapse between the two. All can exacerbate data quality issues.

3.   **Manipulate.** Retrieved data serve as input to processing. Murdick [17] notes four principal types of processing: classification, analysis, manipulation, and synthesis. And, of course, this step may be bypassed, as data are often retrieved for the sole purpose of being presented to the user. Such is the case in the operations of a customer service center, for example. In this case, the manipulate step can be considered as an identity transformation of data into themselves.

4.   **Present results.** In this activity, results of the retrieval and manipulation are passed on to the user. It is the form of the results, rather than their content, that is of interest here. The appropriate presentation form should be determined by a number of factors, including the nature of the results (numeric, text, graphic, etc.), the medium (paper, computer screen, etc.), and the user's preference (people, applications software, and optical readers all prefer different forms, for example).

5. **Use.** Here the results are finally used. The users of data (e.g., those receiving a bill or making a business decision based on data) are the final judge of the quality of data used.

12.2.4 Checkpoints, Feedback Loops, and Data Destruction

In this section we enhance the life-cycle model by adding important quality checkpoints,[3] feedback loops, and activities that destroy data. Diagrams of the enhanced models are presented as Figures 12.8 and 12.9. These checkpoints include the following.

1. **Assessment.** The purpose of this activity is to assess the quality of values obtained. What characteristics should be checked? Obviously values should belong to their respective domains. In addition, four principal quality dimensions for data values—accuracy, currency, completeness, and consistency (to be defined in Chapter 13)—can be assessed. If the data volume is large, it may be appropriate to use sampling techniques, as discussed in Chapter 2. Specific recommendations can be found in the general statistical literature [18] or in more specialized references [19]. If data values are of acceptable quality, they are stored; otherwise, corrective activities are undertaken.

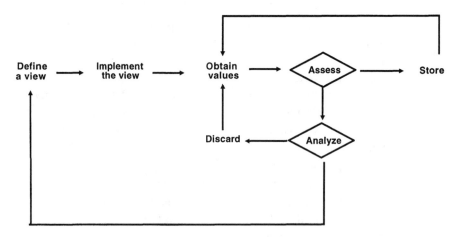

Figure 12.8 A model of the enhanced acquisition cycle is shown here.

3. Checkpoints that bear only on the previous activity are not included.

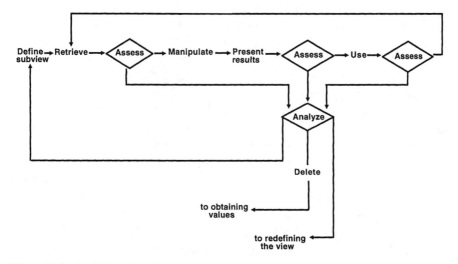

Figure 12.9 A model of the enhanced usage cycle is shown here.

2. **Analysis.** Reasons underlying failed assessments are investigated. Depending on the reasons discovered, the process may continue—either by adjusting the faulty values, discarding and replacing them, or redefining the view.

3. **Adjust.** In some cases, unsatisfactory data can be repaired or patched.

4. **Discard.** If a faulty data value cannot be corrected, it should be discarded.

To enhance the usage cycle, three assessments have been added: after the retrieve, present results, and use activities. These assessments are conceptually similar to one another, although they assess different things: The first checks data to be used as input to the "manipulate" activity, the second looks at data in light of manipulation and presentation, and the third looks at data after use.

As with the acquisition cycle, assessment is followed by *analysis* and, when appropriate, by *delete*. Both are self-explanatory.

12.2.5 Discussion

Six aspects of the life-cycle model are noteworthy. First, the model is general. It applies to simple situations, such as a person's calendar, to complex situations, such as development and use of a telephone directory, and to even more complex situations, such as the large information systems used by corporations. Thus, it provides a good foundation for data quality.

Second, the model clearly distinguishes data acquisition and usage. This separation is not theoretical hairsplitting. Rather, it reflects the concern that arises when data are created by one person or organization and used by another [20]. This concern motivates, in part, the need for data policy. The model balances these two phases of the data life cycle. This distinguishes this model from those of Ahituv [21] and Murdick [17]. Those models pay much more attention to usage. This model also highlights the critical roles that acquisition plays on data quality. It directly contradicts Highsmith's assertion that "data quality concerns can be seen to primarily impact data usage [22]." Similarly, it negates Davis and Olson's assertion that "if the data are received from an external source, the organization cannot impose its own quality control standards [23]." Indeed, those responsible for acquisition are suppliers to users, and the customer-supplier model of Chapter 7 overlays the life-cycle model.

Third, the model of data acquisition enumerates four separate activities. While this is important because it provides a more complete listing, it is indispensable for data quality. Quality characteristics of a view are distinct from those of data values (see Chapter 13) and permit us to properly focus on quality improvement.

Fourth, the model is expressed in terms of cycles, reflecting the repetitive and dynamic nature of data and information chains in the real world. Recognizing this dynamic is critical if long-term improvements are to be made. It also highlights the futility of attempts to make improvements through inspection and rework.

Fifth, none of the activities presented here includes death as a final activity. This is because data are not consumed with use. Data can, in principle at least, be immortal. Thus, the term "life cycle" is not quite appropriate. Of course, most data are eventually destroyed or retired—not always intentionally. But many data are maintained long after they have outlived their usefulness—an observation that may be worth some consideration to enterprises swamped with data.

Finally, data can be viewed as any other product. Product life cycles generally include activities such as requirements specification, development, testing, installation, maintenance, and retirement. These activities have counterparts in the life-cycle model. Requirements specification corresponds to view definition, development to view implementation and obtaining values, testing to assessment, and so forth. Life-cycle management is well known in data processing for hardware, software, and data systems [24–26]. As data continue to be bought and sold like products, one may expect interest in such models to increase. In addition, of course, our application of process management to information chains clearly resembles the application of process management to manufacturing processes.

12.3   Data Defined

12.3.1   Preliminaries

Having discussed a model of the data life cycle, we are still left with the question: Just what are data? In this section, we discuss several definitions of "data." Our main goal is to develop a definition that complements the life-cycle model and is useful for improving data quality. In particular, we seek an approach that meets two sets of criteria—first, a definition that meets Linguistic Criteria; second, one that provides the necessary foundations for improving data quality (Usefulness Criteria) [4].

Our Linguistic Criteria are as follows.

- Clear and simple: The approach selected should lead to a clear and simple definition of data (of course any good definition is clear and simple).

- Not mention "information": The approach should not make use of the concept of information to avoid circular definitions.

- Agree with common usage: The definition should agree with everyday uses of the term "data," not create a new definition for a commonly used term.

Our Usefulness Criteria are as follows.

- Comprehensiveness: The definition should include both conceptual and representational facets of data, as both are important to users and for data quality.

- Widely applicable: The approach should apply to a wide range of cases, especially those involving computerized databases, since such data are of greatest importance in quality improvement.

- Quality dimensions: The approach should suggest practical dimensions of data quality.

12.3.2   Competing Definitions

Most authors have avoided defining data or use the term, perhaps informally, as a synonym for the word "information." This approach is unacceptable. Dozens of other definitions have been proposed. They generally involve one or a combination of the following approaches.

- Data as a set of facts;
- Data as the result of measurement;
- Data as raw material for information;
- Data as symbols;
- Data as surrogates for real-world objects and concepts;
- Data as a representable triple (entity, attribute, value).

12.3.3   A Set of Facts

Some authors [27, 28] follow the Latin origins of the term by defining "data" as a set of facts. Although these writers do not define "fact," a fact is usually understood to be something that has been or can be verified [29], the way the world actually is. Facts are the standard for judging truth. There is no question that data are collected and used with the hope that they accurately represent reality. However, as a standard for truth, a fact cannot be false. This implies that false data cannot exist. But of course they certainly seem to.

A second drawback with this definition is that it implies that all sets of facts are data. A purely factual newspaper account would thus be considered data. It seems more reasonable that such an account contain data, rather than be data.

Third, this definition says nothing about representational aspects of data.

12.3.4   The Result of Measurement

A second approach defines data by indicating how they are obtained—for example, Davis and Rush [30] propose: "The simplest way of defining data is to say that it is the result of measurement or observation." Yovits [31] combines etymology with this approach: "Data are facts or are believed to be facts that result from the observation of physical phenomena." Measurement and observation are indeed two important sources of data (there is no need to restrict attention to physical phenomena, though). However, there are many other ways to obtain data—for example, a person's name, Social Security number, phone number, and so on were assigned; they were not the result of measurement or observation. The way data are obtained is of great importance, especially to data quality. But it does not follow that the means of obtaining data define what data are.

12.3.5   Raw Material for Information

Many specialists define data as "the raw material from which information is developed" [32]. In other words, data are the raw input to a process whose output is "refined" information. This definition has intuitive appeal. Isn't the purpose of statistics to extract meaningful information from data [33]? But it has severe limitations. First, we noted that data should not be defined using the concept of information. Second, what about data that are never used? Are they still data? Third, there is no clear demarcation between data and information. And, finally, this approach fails to consider representational aspects of data.

12.3.6 Surrogates for Real-World Objects

A fourth alternative is exemplified by the definition of Burch [34]: "Data are language, mathematical, and other symbolic surrogates, which are agreed to represent people, objects, events, and concepts . . . The sound of a train whistle and a customer order are two examples of data." The strength of this approach is the stress on representational aspects of data. But its principal weakness is that it reduces them to the representational level of symbols. But data can clearly be represented in many different ways, which is impossible if data are nothing but symbols. Even proponents of the "data are symbols" school [35] agree that "it is common to consider data as items that can be talked about without necessarily considering details of their stored format." Clear separation of conceptual and representational aspects of data, called the *data-independence objective* [36], was a major breakthrough in data modeling.

From the usefulness perspective, it does not seem relevant to consider the sound of a train whistle as a datum, even if the sound may be informative and symbolic. Further, a customer order per se, with no context provided, is better considered as an entity or relationship about which we may have data.

12.3.7 Representable Triples

This example brings us to the approach developed by the database research community, with roots as far back as Mealy [6]. Though our interest in data usually concerns real-world objects (be they physical or abstract) or relationships among them, we work with an abstract *view* or *model*. This view or model is created in the first step in the data life cycle. A view yields *entities*, which serve as models of their real-world counterparts. In the classical database approach, an entity is an element of an *entity class* (also called a type) and is defined by a set of *attributes*—for example, an entity class EMPLOYEE can be defined by attributes such as Employee-Number, Name, Date-of-Birth, Address, Dependents, and so forth. Each attribute has a *domain* of permissible values. There are no a priori restrictions on the domain: The values may be other entities (e.g., departments), sets of entities (e.g., a list of dependents), measurements, and so forth. When the values are measurements, units of measure must be included. Finally, to accommodate situations where an attribute does not apply, a null value may be contained in the domain—for example, `Spouse's Name` does not apply if `Marital Status` takes on the value "single."

Following the same logic, another special element can signify an unknown or illegitimate value. Within this approach, Tsichritzis and Lochovsky [37] define a *datum* (or *data item*) as a triple *<e,a,v>*, where the value *v* is selected from the domain of attribute *a* for the entity *e*. *Data* are then defined as any collection of data items.

This definition meets several of our criteria. It recognizes that any data are the result of a model and allows us to separate quality dimensions of the view from quality dimensions of data values. By emphasizing that a data model defines entity classes, it reflects the repetitive nature of most data, consistent with the concept of cycles in the life-cycle model. Finally, the definition imposes a certain amount of discipline on data. However, the definition does not recognize the representational aspects of data, as the Usefulness Criteria demand. To correct this deficiency, we define a *data representation* to be a set of rules for recording triples on some medium, and we define a *data recording* (or *record*) to be a physical instance standing for a set of data items according to the data representation. The value portion is represented via a *format* and the recording via a *symbol*. As an example, an attribute `Date` can be represented by the American format *mm/dd/yy*, the European format *dd/mm/yy*, or other formats.

Figures 12.10 and 12.11 summarize the most important features of this approach.

12.3.8   Discussion

Table 12.1 summarizes whether the definitions presented here meet the criteria presented for good definition. The definition of data as triples *<e,a,v>*, along

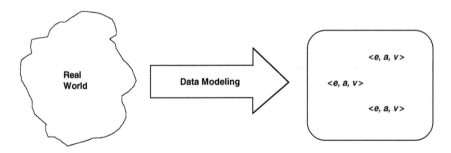

Figure 12.10   Data are the result of modeling.

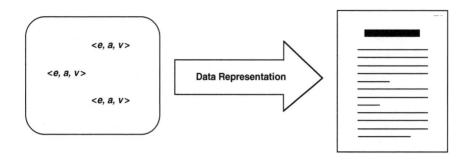

Figure 12.11   This illustrates the data representation approach.

with definitions of data representation and data recording, meets these criteria. Note that this approach does not confuse data with the facts that they model. Nor does it impose any requirements on how data are obtained. It avoids mention of the term "information." This approach separates data from its representation, so the same data may be represented in many ways, data represented in a prescribed manner may be recorded many times, and data can exist

	Linguistic Criteria			Usefulness Criteria		
	Clear & simple	No mention of information	Consistent with common usage	Includes conceptual and representation facets	Wide applicability	Suggests quality dimensions
Facts	P	P	F	F	F	F
Obtained by certain means	F	P	F	F	P	F
Raw material for information	F	F	P	F	P	F
Symbols	P	P	F	F	P	F
\<Entity, Attribute, Value\>	P	P	P	F	P	P
Representable triples	P	P	P	P	P	P

P = Pass; F = Fail

Table 12.1   This table summarizes the assessment of whether the competing approaches to defining data satisfy our criteria for a good definition [4].

without being represented or recorded. A particularly attractive feature is that it leads naturally to three sets of quality issues: Those related to the quality of the model or view, those related to the quality of data values, and those related to the quality of data representation and recording. Therefore, we accept these definitions. In Chapter 13 we explore three dimensions of data quality.

How are these definitions applied in practice? Consider a simple statement: That girl is pretty. Is this statement data or not? The answer depends on the circumstances under which the statement was made. As an offhand remark, the statement is not data. However, if GIRL is a well-defined entity class, "that girl" is a well-defined entity, and Prettiness is a well-defined attribute with a predefined domain of possible values (even if "pretty" and "not pretty" are the only possible values), then the statement is data.

The example illustrates the critical role played by the domain. It is usually easy to imagine or construct well-defined entity classes and attributes, and entities exist, at least implicitly. A well-defined domain is usually a bit more difficult.

In practice, most interesting data are:

- Collected purposely;
- Stored on some medium;
- Repetitive in nature, with several entities and attributes.

These criteria are not equivalent to our definitions. A coin collection meets these criteria. But they are easy to apply and, in the proper context, fairly reliable. For instance, if the statement "That girl is pretty" is not to be stored, it is unlikely that the statement corresponds to data.

12.4   Management Properties of Data

We have noted throughout that a management science for data has not yet been developed. This situation stands in stark contrast to other resources, such as financial resources, human resources, plant and equipment, raw materials, and energy, for which both management theory and practice are well developed. As yet, we are in no position to fully define such a theory. However, a start can be made by comparing pertinent properties of data to other assets. In the following sections, we'll consider 14 properties of data that are different from most traditional resources, and we will note important implications for data quality [5].

12.4.1 How Data Differ From Other Resources

Consumability. Unlike other resources, neither data per se nor data records are consumed with use.

Context Dependency. Data have no meaning independent of context. In contrast, other resources exist in and of themselves.

Copyability. Data are unlike other resources in the degree to which they can be copied. One can create an identical data record for a fraction of the cost of the original. You simply can't do this with other resources.

Cost to Obtain and Store. Acquiring and storing most resources is expensive. Not so with data. The cost of data storage in particular has decreased exponentially for several decades, and there is no letup in sight. And while progress is not as dramatic, the cost of obtaining new data is relatively low. In many cases, data are obtained essentially for free, because obtaining them is bound up with the process of manufacturing a product, serving a customer, and so forth.

Depreciability. Depreciation is "a decrease or loss in value because of wear, age, or other cause" [29]. Buildings (but not the land), most equipment, and raw materials depreciate. Energy does not. Many factors impact the appreciation or depreciation of financial and human resources, although in most cases, either appreciation or depreciation is relatively slow. As for data, as discussed in Section 12.2, they can be immortal. And their value does not diminish with use, but the utility of most data deteriorates rapidly in time. On the other hand, the value of some data increases dramatically with time.

Fragility. Fragility refers to how easily a resource can inadvertently be lost or destroyed in routine use. Most traditional resources are not especially fragile, although there are many counterexamples. The fragility of data records depends on the recording medium and the amount of data stored. Paper records are occasionally accidentally destroyed, but they are more apt to be lost. Data stored in computers are much more fragile.

Fungibility. Fungibility means that one unit of a resource can easily be exchanged for another, assuming another unit is available. Money, raw materials, and energy are quite fungible, as are human labor and plants and equipment, albeit to lesser degrees. But data "units" are inherently unique. You simply cannot substitute one person's `Date-of-Birth` for another's.

Lag Time. There is an inherent lag in updating a database from the time a data value changes. Thus, for example, when a subscriber to a magazine moves, he or she typically does not inform the magazine of a new address until after the move. So subscriber databases will always be out-of-date, at least for a portion of subscribers and at least for a time. The lag time can be reduced, but it cannot be eliminated. There is no corresponding property for other resources.

Shareability. By shareability, we mean the possibility that two or more users may simultaneously use the same unit of the resource. Traditional resources are not shareable. But data are—in two ways: First, a given collection may have multiple recordings, each of which can be used by a separate user. Second, database management systems allow nearly simultaneous, multiuser access.

Supply. The supply of traditional resources is, for most practical purposes, limited. There are exceptions, of course. New sources of energy may be found and a new wave of workers, trained in some specialty, may graduate. But, even when the supply can be increased, it is still limited. While the supply of relevant, easily obtained data is not infinite, data are usually much easier to obtain (and cheaper, as previously noted).[4] Each new customer order, for example, enriches and renews a marketing database—and for free! New data are created at astonishing rates. So few organizations claim they are "data poor."

Tangibility. Perhaps the most obvious difference between data and other resources is data's *intangibility.* While data recordings can be seen and touched, data themselves are intangible.

Transportability. Data are also unlike any other resource in the degree, ease, and speed with which they can be transported over long distances. It can be argued that the transportability, as much as anything else, ushered in the Information Age.

Valuation. Valuation refers to the expression of the resource's value in monetary terms. For all traditional resources, market economies or standard accounting practices make valuation easy. Unfortunately, this is not the case for data. Although some data are for sale (historical performance of financial markets, many customer lists, etc.), most are not. Nor are standard accounting practices applicable. At the same time, enterprises could not survive without their data, so data clearly have value. Valuation has proven to be a knotty problem from both practical and theoretical viewpoints. In fact, more than two decades of research are yet to produce clear results [38, 39].

Versatility. Versatility means that a resource can be used for a variety of purposes. Money is the most versatile resource. Certain raw materials used in specialized manufacturing processes are the least versatile. Data occupy a unique middle position. Data collected and used for one purpose are often used in other applications. Data-driven (i.e., target) marketing [40, 41] is one such example. But some alternate uses of data are illegitimate. Data about a person's age, for example, cannot be used in a hiring decision.

---

4.   This is not to say that the most relevant, up-to-date, and properly formatted data are always readily available. But one can usually get his or her hands on some relevant data.

12.4.2 Implications for Data Quality

In this section we consider some of the most important implications of the ways that data differ from other resources for data quality. First, we have noted many times that the high rates of data creation ensure that the most commonly applied technique for improvement, error detection and correction, doesn't work very well. Process-focused methods are required.

Second, due to the nonfungibility and relatively low versatility of data, an enterprise's main concern is more often obtaining the most relevant data, rather than some optimal amount. This leads the enterprise to keep more data than it needs, increasing redundancy and making management more difficult.

Third, since data are not tangible, they have no physical properties. In contrast, all other resources have physical properties, as do manufactured products. Many physical properties can be objectively measured, and quality improvement activities can be directed at changing physical properties to improve customer satisfaction. It would be nice if the same principle held for data. But all the important quality attributes must be abstract and so are difficult to measure. You simply can't tell by direct examination whether data are correct or not.

Fourth, that which is "out of sight, is often out of mind." So there seems to be a tendency to pay less attention to data, particularly given the other compelling, and highly visible, problems facing the enterprise. For data quality, the failure to develop clear methods of valuation is especially disappointing. It is much easier to spur management action when there are clear monetary costs or benefits.

A number of properties help create difficult political situations (see Chapter 4 and [42]). Since data are relatively inexpensive to obtain and store, copy, and transport, organizations within an enterprise often acquire, store, and manage their own. This immediately raises issues of ownership—issues that are among the most brutal in many enterprises. It also makes any kind of centralized planning for data and standards difficult to establish and enforce.

These properties, together with fragility, also exacerbate issues related to data redundancy. They encourage the enterprise to maintain more data than it needs. While data are shareable, in many enterprises this is the exception rather than the rule. Nonfungibility of data poses special problems. The manager of other resources may guard against many situations by maintaining a larger supply. But this action is meaningless for data. Maintaining an extra copy (i.e., a backup) can help, but it is time-consuming and expensive. Data redundancy can sometimes help infer a correct value—but, as we have noted throughout, it too carries a high cost.

Data's copyability has other positive and negative consequences. On the one hand, it helps mitigate the fragility of data and allows users to work with data in environments of their own choice (e.g., it helps make the office at home feasible). And allowing any person (or organization) who wants a copy to have one may mitigate battles over data ownership. On the other hand, synchronization is difficult enough in database environments—keeping disparate copies current when data values change is impossible, expensive, or both. Properties of data have profound consequences for security, privacy, and confidentiality as well [43], but we'll not consider them here.

12.5   A Model of an Enterprise's Data Resource

So far, this chapter has dealt with a single datum and individual collections of data. We can also consider data from the enterprise perspective. Most enterprises of more than a few people possess many data collections. These collections often overlap, feed one another, and interact in subtle ways. In addition, a single information chain may populate several databases, just as downstream applications may access data from several databases. In large enterprises the situation is of stunning complexity. Figure 12.12 is an attempt to capture some important features. The "Enterprise Data Resource Model" features three databases, interconnected by four information chains that create data values (left) and use the data (right). The figure also depicts data that are common to more than one database. While the figure is too simplistic to capture the complexity in a large enterprise, a number of important features are illustrated even on a picture as simple as this one. In particular:

- There are unique data needed by a downstream application.
- Some (common) data are developed by one chain and fed into all databases.
- Some common data are developed by separate chains.
- Some applications depend on data from multiple databases.

The figure does not illustrate it, but there are probably data that are purposely collected, yet never used.

This model complements earlier perspectives in which only a single database is considered. It does a much better job capturing the root cause of data redundancy and the related problem of data inconsistency. Indeed, most enter-

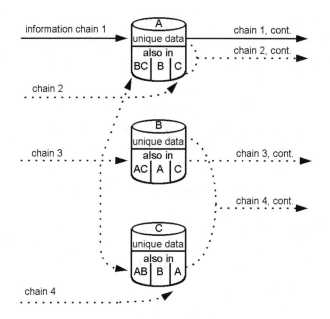

Figure 12.12   The enterprise data resource model is shown.

prises would do well to keep an inventory of their data assets, including information chains and databases. This point was previously noted in Chapter 3.

12.6   Information

If defining and understanding data is difficult, defining and understanding *information* is a hornet's nest.[5] The purposes of this section are to briefly describe the main approaches that have been developed, specify the one that has been used herein (albeit implicitly), and describe the principal difficulty in developing a solid definition. We cover the latter subject because, if there is interest in data quality, one can expect similar interest in *information quality*. But without solid foundations, extension of the techniques to manage data quality presented herein may carry some risk.

In defining data, we sought a definition that embraced common uses of the term. And, fortunately, we were able to find a definition that did so. But the word "information" is in common usage in virtually all facets of everyday life and many

---

5.   The reader can safely skip this section without losing the main flow of ideas.

sciences, and the variations in meaning are considerable. Indeed, the concept of information embraces deep philosophical considerations [44–47].

The following concepts of information are in more or less common use in one field or another.

- The Information Management School. Information are processed data.

- The Infological School. "Information is any kind of knowledge or message that can be used to make possible a decision or action [48]."

- The Information Theory School [49, 50]. Information is the removal or lessening of uncertainty. Almost equivalently, it is the nonredundant part of a message.

- The Statistical School [33]. Information is the relevant part or a summary of data from a statistical experiment. Information is usually measured with respect to a defined parameter of interest.

- The Thermodynamics School. Information is the inverse of entropy.

- Everyday Use. Information is the part of a message that informs.

Each of these concepts tends to emphasize either a static or a dynamic aspect of data. As with data, it seems that coupling of these two aspects will be necessary to develop a good understanding. Tricker [51] has a similar idea about the complexity of information and pursues a slightly different direction, defining "levels of information," including "basic data," "information as a message," "information in use," and "valuable information."

A consistent thread, which depends on a somewhat more primitive concept than data, runs through most of the approaches to defining information. This concept is "signals." Data are signals, as are newspaper articles, the sound of a train whistle, and other messages from the real world. A signal is slightly more general than a message, because the concept of a message implies that it was actively created. A signal can also stem from an inanimate object. As a matter of practice, it is not possible to isolate a single signal. An observer must be introduced, and he or she is simply incapable of considering a single signal. Rather, an observer considers a collection of signals. If nothing else, this collection includes the observer's past experiences and forms the context in which the signal in question is interpreted.

Collections of signals necessarily contain redundancies, but it is possible, conceptually at least, to isolate a nonredundant part. This nonredundant part is, by definition, "informative" and the content is "information." These definitions do not require that there be a unique nonredundant part. They also imply that any superset of the nonredundant part is informative.

This approach is not without logical traps, however. Most critical is the role of the observer. On the one hand, the information in a collection of signals is independent of the observer. But any two observers have had different experiences. Thus, their collections of signals are inherently different. This leads to the conclusion that imprecision in the definition of information and in actual information content is inherent. Any dynamic model of the "information life cycle," since it must include the observer, would be horribly complex. This suggests that the inherent imprecision in information is even greater.

It is insightful to restrict attention to data and consider where information appears in the data life cycle. Applying the reasoning of the preceding paragraphs to the model presented in Section 12.2, we conclude that the core of the acquisition cycle is data and the core of the usage cycle is information. As has been pointed out, whether one is in the acquisition or usage cycle depends upon point of view. Many processes use source "data" as information and also create "information," which is later stored as data in a database. However, once a point of view is fixed, no conflict should arise.

12.7 Summary

This chapter has examined data from many perspectives. Data, it seems, are complex enough that no single perspective yields all the needed foundations for improving data quality. The first approach examined data's life cycle. Indeed, data are incredibly dynamic, being defined and created, stored and manipulated, accessed and used at incredible rates. The life-cycle model features two high-level activities: acquisition and usage. Two steps of acquisition, creating a data model and obtaining values, are the most important steps for data quality. And we have shown that sustainable improvements result from applying techniques of process management to the information chains that create data.

The static approach presupposes a view, and a datum is defined as a triple consisting of an entity, attribute, and value. Data representation is defined as rules for recording data. Thus, data exist on both conceptual and representational levels.

Properties of data as a resource, especially ways that data are distinct from other resources, were presented. And a number of implications for data quality management were presented. Another perspective is provided by the enterprise data resource model, which is concerned with the major databases and information chains of an enterprise. Finally, a number of issues underlying the definition of "information" were reviewed. In addition to being useful for data quality, these perspectives can form the beginnings of a management science for data and information.

REFERENCES

[1]   Fox, C. J., A. V. Levitin, and T. C. Redman, "The Notion of Data and Its Quality Dimensions," *Information Processing and Management*, Vol. 30, No. 1, January 1994, pp. 9–19.

[2]   Levitin, A. V., and T. C. Redman, "A Model of the Data (Life) Cycles with Applications to Quality," *Information and Software Technology*, Vol. 35, No. 4, April 1993, pp. 217–223.

[3]   *Data Quality Foundations,* AT&T, Select Code 500-490, 1992.

[4]   Fox, C. J., A. V. Levitin, and T. C. Redman, "Data and Data Quality," *Encyclopedia of Library and Information Science*, Vol. 57, Supplement 20, 1996, pp. 100–122.

[5]   Levitin, A. V., and T. C. Redman, "Data vs. Traditional Resources: Properties and Management," submitted to *Communications of the ACM*.

[6]   Mealy, G., "Another Look at Data," *Proc. AFIPS 1967 Fall Joint Computer Conference*, Vol. 31, Washington, DC, 1967, pp. 525–534.

[7]   Kent, W., *Data and Reality,* Amsterdam: North-Holland, 1978.

[8]   Steel, T. B., and R. A. Meersman (eds.), *Data Semantics (DS-1)*, *Proc. IFIP WG2.6 Working Conference on Data Semantics*, Hasselt, Belgium, January 7–11, 1985, Amsterdam: North-Holland, 1986.

[9]   Meersman, R. A., and A. C. Sernadas (eds.), *Data and Knowledge (DS-2)*, *Proc. Second IFIP 2.6 Conference on Data Semantics*, Albufeira, Portugal, November 3–7, 1986, Amsterdam: North-Holland, 1988.

[10]   Taylor, D. A., *Object-Oriented Information Systems: Planning and Implementation,* New York: John Wiley & Sons, 1992.

[11]   Orfali, R., D. Harkey, and J. Edwards, *The Essental Distributed Objects Survival Guide,* New York: John Wiley & Sons, 1996.

[12]   Brodie, M. L., J. Mylopolous, and J. W. Schmidt, *On Conceptual Modeling: Perspectives from Artificial Intelligence, Databases, and Programming Languages,* New York: Springer-Verlag, 1984.

[13] Brodie, M. L., and J. Mylopoulos (eds.), *On Knowledge Based Management Systems,* NewYork: Springer-Verlag, 1986.

[14] Kent, W., "A Simple Guide to Five Normal Forms in Relational Database Theory," *Communications of the ACM,* Vol. 26, No. 2, 1983, pp. 120–149.

[15] Fidel, R., and M. Crandall, "Fitting Reality into a Database Mold: Rules for Data Collection," *Information Systems,* Vol. 14, No.2, 1989, pp. 141–149.

[16] Langefors, B., "Infological Models and Information User Views," *Information Systems,* Vol. 5, No. 1, 1980, pp. 17–32.

[17] Murdick, R. G., *MIS Concepts and Design,* Englewood Cliffs, NJ: Prentice Hall, 1986.

[18] Chaudhuri, A., and H. Stenger, *Survey Sampling,* New York: Marcel Dekker, 1992.

[19] Guy, D. M., and D. R. Carmichael, *Audit Sampling: An Introduction to Statistical Sampling in Auditing,* 2d ed., New York: John Wiley & Sons, 1986.

[20] Te'eni, D., " Data Feeding/Data Consuming: Problems and Solutions," *Journal of Information Systems Management,* Vol. 7, No. 2, 1990, pp. 23–32.

[21] Ahituv, H., "A Metamodel of Information Flow: A Tool to Support Information Systems Theory," *Communications of the ACM,* Vol. 30, No. 9, September 1987, pp. 781–791.

[22] Highsmith, J., "Synchronizing Data with Reality," *Datamation,* Vol. 27, No. 12, November 1981, pp. 187—193.

[23] Davis, G. B., and M. H. Olson, *Management Information Systems: Concpetual Foundations, Structure, and Development,* 2d ed., New York: McGraw-Hill, 1985.

[24] Hammer, C., "Life Cycle Management," *Information Management,* Vol. 4, 1981, pp. 71–80.

[25] Schach, S., *Software Engineering,* Homewood, IL: Askin Associates/Irwin, 1990.

[26] Wang, R. Y., and H. B. Kon, "Towards Total Data Quality Management," in R. Y. Wang (ed.), *Information Technology in Action: Trends and Perspectives,* Englewood Cliffs, NJ: Prentice Hall, 1993.

[27] Blumenthal, S. C., *Management Information Sysems,* Englewood Cliffs, NJ: Prentice Hall, 1969.

[28] Fry, J. P., and E. H. Sibley, "Evolution of Database Management Systems," *ACM Computing Surveys,* Vol. 8, No. 1, 1976, pp. 7–42.

[29] *The American Heritage Dictionary,* 2d ed., Boston: Houghton Mifflin, 1982.

[30] Davis, C. H., and J. E. Rush, *Guide to Information Science*, Westport, CT: Freenwood Press, 1979.

[31] Yovits, M. C., " Information and Data," in A. Ralston (ed.), *Encyclopedia of Computer Science and Engineering*, 2d ed., New York: Van Nostrand Reinhold, 1981.

[32] Dorn, P. H., "Business Information in the Eighties," *Business Information Systems, INFOTECH State of the Art Report*, Series 9, No. 7, 1981, pp. 245–260.

[33] Basu, D., "Statistical Information and Likelihood," in D. Basu and J. K. Ghosh (eds.), *Statistical Information and Likelihood: A Collection of Critical Essays*, New York: Springer-Verlag, 1988.

[34] Burch, J. G., *Information Systems: Theory and Practice*, 3rd ed., New York: John Wiley & Sons, 1983.

[35] Langefors, B., and K. Samuelson, *Information and Data in Systems*, New York: Petrocelli/Charter, 1976.

[36] Codd, E. F., "Relational Database: A Practical Foundation for Productivity," *Communications of the ACM*, Vol. 25, No. 2, 1982, pp. 109–117.

[37] Tsichritzis, D. C., and F. H. Lochovsky, *Data Models*, Englewood Cliffs, NJ: Prentice Hall, 1982.

[38] Brinberg, H., "Information Economics: Valuing Information," *Information Management Review*, Vol. 4, No. 3, 1989, pp. 59–63.

[39] Repo, A., "Economics of Information," *Review of Information Science and Technology*, Vol. 22, 1987, pp. 239–247.

[40] Goodhue, D. L., J. A. Quillard, and J. F. Rochart, "Managing the Data Resource: A Contingency Perspective," *MIS Quarterly*, Vol. 12, No. 2, June 1988.

[41] Sabberwal, R., and W. R. King, "Toward a Theory of Strategic Use of Information Resources," *Information & Management*, Vol. 20, 1991, p. 191–212.

[42] Davenport, T. H., R. G. Eccles, and L. Prusak, "Information Politics," *Sloan Management Review*, Vol. 33, Fall 1992, p. 53–65.

[43] Violino, B., "Tempting Fate," *InformationWeek*, October 4, 1993, pp. 42–52.

[44] Fox, C., W. Frakes, and P. Gandel, "Foundational Issues in Knowledge-based Information Systems," *The Canadian Journal for Information Science*, Vol. 13, No. 3, 1988, pp. 90–102.

[45] Teskey, F. N., "User Models and World Models for Data, Information, and Knowledge," *Information Processing and Management*, Vol. 25, No. 1, 1989, pp. 7–14.

[46] Thiess, H., "On Terminology," in A. Debons (ed.), *Information Science in Action: System Design*, Vol. 1, The Hague: Martinus Nijhoff Publishers, 1983.

[47] Wiederhold, G., "Knowledge Versus Data," in M. L. Brodie and J. Mylopoulos (eds.), *On Knowledge Based Management Systems*, New York: Springer-Verlag, 1986, pp. 77–82.

[48] Langefors, B., *Theoretical Analysis of Information Systems*, 4th ed., Philadelphia: Auerbach Publishers, 1973.

[49] Ash, R., *Information Theory*, New York: Wiley-Interscience, 1965.

[50] Pierce, J. R., *Signals: The Telephone and Beyond*, San Francisco: W. H. Freeman, 1981.

[51] Tricker, R. I., *Effective Information Management*, New York: Van Nostrand Reinhold, 1982.

Chapter **13**

Dimensions of Data Quality

"Knowledge and human power are synonymous."
—Francis Bacon

13.1 Introduction

This chapter focuses on dimensions of data quality.[1] Data were defined in Section 12.3 as consisting of two abstract parts: a conceptual model and data values. In addition, data representation and recording are necessary if the data are to be stored and/or used. Thus, we consider dimensions associated with these three aspects of data. These quality dimensions map quite easily in quality dimensions associated with the "define a view," "obtain values," and "present results" activities of the life-cycle model.[2]

---

1. Anany Levitin [1–3] has done much of the work to define the dimensions of data quality presented here. Christopher Fox and Errol Caby [4] have also contributed greatly.

2. See [5–7] for alternative approaches.

Users may have other important data-related requirements, such as privacy, security, optimal redundancy, and efficient use of the storage media. Such concerns may be associated with other activities in the life-cycle model, but they are not considered here. Many issues not addressed here are well covered in management information systems and database literature. Instead, our focus is on dimensions associated with the data per se, rather than details of their storage, how they are secured, and so forth.

The following three sections focus on quality dimensions associated with a conceptual view, data values, and data representation and recording. Then some subtleties involving data consistency are discussed in greater detail.

13.2   Quality Dimensions of a Conceptual View

It is important to recognize that most data users are only vaguely aware of most aspects of a conceptual view. Their usual desire is to use data in their application without giving the conceptual view much thought and without worrying that they may be making incorrect assumptions about the data. Despite (and maybe due to) its near invisibility to users, a high-quality conceptual view is of great importance. At the individual data-item level, the importance of the conceptual view is that it provides the context in which the data item is to be interpreted. At the application level, the conceptual view is the model of the real world captured in the data. Thus, the view determines the ultimate utility of the data, assuming that the data are accurate and presented in an appropriate manner. This invisibility of the view also implies that most users and potential users are unlikely to evaluate the quality of the view explicitly. Rather, they evaluate it implicitly in terms of its ability to support their applications.

We begin with a list of 15 characteristics of an "ideal" view (perhaps the reader can add some characteristics of his or her own). Almost all characteristics are subjective. This list will be followed with a short discussion of each characteristic, grouped into six dimensions: content, scope, level of detail, composition, consistency, and reaction to change. The reader will immediately note that the 15 characteristics are not independent of one another. In fact, many appear to be in direct conflict. We conclude this section with a discussion focusing on the relationships among and between them.

For the user's perspective, 15 characteristics of an "ideal" view are:

1. The view should provide data needed by the application (relevance).

2. Data values should be easily obtainable (obtainability).

3. Each term in the definition of the view should be clearly defined (clarity of definition).

4. Each needed data item should be included (comprehensiveness).

5. No unneeded data items should be included (essentialness).

6. The attributes should be defined at the right level of detail to support applications (attribute granularity).

7. The domains of possible values should be just large enough to support applications (domain precision).

8. Each item in the view should have a "natural" counterpart in the real world (naturalness).

9. The view should make identification of individual entities easy (occurrence identifiability).

10. Entity types should be defined to minimize the occurrence of unnecessary attributes (homogeneity).

11. Redundancy should be kept to a minimum (minimum redundancy).

12. The view should be clear and unambiguous and consistent (semantic consistency).

13. Entity types and attributes should have the same basic structure wherever possible (structural consistency).

14. The view should be wide enough so that it does not require change every time applications change (robustness).

15. When necessary, the view can be easily changed (flexibility).

We now proceed with a discussion of the six dimensions and the characteristics associated with each.

13.2.1 Content

The content dimension encompasses three considerations: *relevance of data*, *obtainability of values*, and *clarity of definition*.

Relevance is a user-driven or application-related concern. An important user concern is that of data be relevant. It is not easy for users to be precise about how data will really be used, and there are other issues associated with requirements.

A second relevance issue often arises as a result of the first—the use of existing data as surrogates for desired and/or unobtainable data. Thus, for example, a new application may require data almost like the data in an existing database. A frequent occurrence is that the new application requires data of greater precision than the existing data.

The use of surrogates can become quite elaborate. Loebl [8] cites several examples in which the Energy Information Agency used various energy data surrogates. Data on changes in consumption were used as indicators of conservation, data on changes in supply as changes in consumption, and so forth. The use of surrogates is justified when good empirical models relate the data of interest to the data used. But in the absence of such models, the use of surrogates is dangerous.

Obtainability of values is often an important concern. Data are not free and there may be legal problems as well. For example, it is relatively simple to obtain and use a person's age for medical purposes, but not in hiring decisions. A further consideration is the ease of obtaining correct values, especially in the case of data used for various competitive purposes. The owners of the data, knowing their value to the competition, may make incorrect data readily available while correct data are kept hidden.

The use of surrogates is often justified on obtainability grounds. In many instances, the data needed are not obtainable. For example, in a marketing application, the latest data on the competitor's prices to his or her best customers may be the data that are needed. But those are the data that the competitor tries most strenuously to keep secret. Methods of obtaining these data may be expensive or illegal. A second example involves airplane crashes. Data useful in determining what led to the crash, and by implication what is needed to prevent future crashes, include readings on the airplane's instruments prior to the crash. But that data may have been destroyed in the crash. In such cases, surrogates are the only choice, other than using no data at all.

The potential use of surrogates hints at a third set of general issues surrounding the content dimension—that of clarity of definition. It is important that all components of the view, including the entities, attributes, and their domains, be clearly defined. Such definitions are needed by existing and potential data users and by data collectors. The definition should also include authoritative sources of data (if such exist) as well as rules for resolving ambiguities, borderline situations, and other issues [9].

13.2.2   Scope

Scope refers to the degree to which a view encompasses enough data to meet the needs of all applications and the amount of excess data. Ideally, a view should be broad enough to satisfy the needs of all applications and no bigger. The competing considerations are *comprehensiveness* and *essentialness*.

Comprehensiveness is affected by:

1. The number of users and the degree to which their data needs overlap;

2. The desirability of incorporating future as well as present applications into the view. Obviously, if the view only must satisfy current applications, then the scope of the view can be reduced.

At the same time, each item in the view should be essential in one respect or another. Unless there is a good reason to do so, obtaining, storing, and generating unnecessary data should be avoided. The problem is not the obvious costs associated with nonessential data. The more important point is that nonessential data may draw attention away from essential data, compromising their careful definition, creation of correct values, and so forth.

13.2.3   Level of Detail

Loosely, level of detail refers to the quantity of data to be included and how precise those data must be. More specifically, two issues are of importance: *granularity of attributes* and *precision of domains*.

Granularity refers to the number and coverage of attributes that are used to represent a single concept. To illustrate, consider an entity class PERSON and an attribute ADDRESS. In some applications it may be sufficient to define address using a single attribute: COUNTRY; while in other applications four attributes are needed: APARTMENT NUMBER (if any), STREET ADDRESS (including street and number), STATE (including zip code, if appropriate), and COUNTRY. The second set of attributes provides a more granular view. Greater granularity is only achieved with cost, as described in the following chart.

Greater Granularity	
Advantages	Disadvantages
Greater detail	Added cost in obtaining and storing values
May provide for additional consistency checks	Data may be less flexible
Wider applicability	Detail may annoy users

Precision of domain refers to the level of detail in the measurement or classification scheme that defines the domain. A short discussion of types of domains is included in the section dealing with quality characteristics of data representation. The greater the number of values in the domain, the greater the precision. For example, HEIGHT of a person, as measured in inches, provides for greater precision than height measured in feet. Similarly, a classification scheme involving 20 categories is more precise than one involving seven categories.

13.2.4 Composition

Composition refers to the internal structuring of the view. Good composition is characterized by:

- *Naturalness*—entity types, attributes, and their domains are natural. Naturalness encompasses a number of desirable characteristics, such as the use of single-fact data.
- *Identifiability*—each entity is easily and uniquely identifiable.
- *Homogeneity*—attributes are generally applicable across as many entities of a given type as possible.
- *Minimum unnecessary redundancy*—the view contains a minimum of unwanted redundancy.

Naturalness is akin to a requirement that the number of ad hoc situations be kept to a minimum. Each entity type should have a simple counterpart in the real world, and contrived entity types should be avoided. Each attribute should have a natural single-fact counterpart in the entity type, which means that each attribute should bear on a single fact about the entity.[3] There is an important distinction between composite attributes and multifact attributes. For example,

---

3.   See reference [10] for a full description of single-fact data.

NAME may consist of a first, middle, and last name and is a perfectly legitimate composite attribute. But an attribute defined by (SEX, MARITAL STATUS) is a multifact attribute and should be avoided. Tasker [10] notes that such attributes are often motivated by implementation considerations.

The domains of each attribute should provide natural ways to specify values. Unnatural domains are often employed to incorporate secondary information into an attribute.

There are many exceptions to the multifact and natural domain rules. For example, in some apartment buildings, the first digit in ROOM NUMBER reflects the floor on which the room is found. In this particular example, ROOM NUMBER can be viewed as a composite or multifact attribute. The decision to follow this method of numbering is influenced by the degree of acceptance of the ROOM NUMBER = (FLOOR/NUMBER) convention. If, for intended applications, it is accepted, then ROOM NUMBER can well be viewed as a composite attribute.

Identifiability requires that each entity be distinguishable from every other entity. This fundamental requirement is usually achieved by means of a *primary key* (see any book on database design for a general discussion of primary keys).

The third characteristic of a good view is that attributes are applicable to all entities of a given type. This homogeneity requirement does not exclude null values (see the discussion on *completeness* later in this chapter). As an example, consider an entity type EMPLOYEE and an application in which the employee's pay is of interest. Further suppose that the company employs people who are paid monthly and hourly. In one view, EMPLOYEE is structured as follows:

```
EMPLOYEE = (NAME, CLASSIFICATION, MONTHLY SALARY, HOURLY RATE)
```

Depending on the value of the first attribute, the value of either the second or third attribute "does not apply." In the second view, the entity type EMPLOYEE features two subtypes, defined as:

```
SALARIED EMPLOYEE = (NAME, MONTHLY SALARY)
HOURLY EMPLOYEE = (NAME, HOURLY RATE)
```

The second view makes use of the notions of sub- and supertypes [11, 12] to promote homogeneity.

A final consideration in composition involves keeping unwanted redundancies to a minimum. While there are many reasons to incorporate redundancy, those that are not explicitly defined as desirable (including their purpose) should be avoided. As with any data of little utility, unwanted redundancy increases cost and distracts attention from more important data.

13.2.5 View Consistency

Consistency of a view has two aspects: *semantic* and *structural consistency*. Semantic consistency refers to the consistency of the various components of the view. The definitions of related entities should resolve issues involving their relationships. For example, definitions of EMPLOYEE and DEPARTMENT should make clear whether each employee must be assigned to one and only one department, whether a department must have at least one member, and so forth.

Structural consistency refers to the consistency of attributes across entity types. For example, a person's name should have the same structure for all entity types unless there is a compelling reason otherwise.

13.2.6 Reaction to Change

Each of the quality characteristics in the five dimensions can be evaluated in terms of a given set of applications. As time passes, both changes to existing applications and new applications will require that the view evolve. The final quality dimension and last two quality characteristics of a view consider the ability of the view to accommodate change. The two important aspects are *flexibility* and *robustness*.

Four types of change should be considered.

- Addition or deletion of an entity;
- Change to a value, within the existing domain;
- Change to a value outside the domain (in effect a change in the domain);
- Addition or deletion of a new entity class or attribute.

The first two types of changes are routine and should not even require a change in the definition of the view. The last two are of concern here.

Robustness refers to the ability of the view to accommodate changes in the world and/or user requirements without changing the basic structure of the view. Flexibility refers to the capacity to change a view to accommodate new demands.

Relationships Between Quality Characteristics

When quality characteristics are independent of one another, one can work to improve one without fear of compromising others. This is usually a desirable situation. Unfortunately, these 15 quality characteristics are not independent of one another. Indeed, many are highly correlated. There are both positive and negative correlations. This section describes a number of such examples. We include examples of positive correlations, where improving one quality characteristic also improves another, and negative correlations, where improving one compromises another. The reader is cautioned that the examples selected here may not be those of greatest importance to a given view. Further, it is even possible that a pair of characteristics may be positively correlated in one view and negatively correlated in another. The essence of good design is to take advantage of positive correlations and resolve negative correlations in an acceptable manner. Examples of correlations follow.

Comprehensiveness, attribute granularity, and *domain precision,* deal with *depth* in some way—scope in terms of entity classes, granularity in terms of attributes, and precision in terms of the domains. The following example illustrates relationships among them. Consider an entity type called SALES and three potential views. In the first view, total sales are recorded each quarter and the view is defined by:

```
SALES = (1Q, 2Q, 3Q, 4Q)
```

This view features four attributes. In the second view, data are recorded monthly:

```
SALES = (JAN, FEB, MAR, APR, MAY, JUN, JUL, AUG,
SEP, OCT, NOV, DEC)
```

The second view is more granular than the first.

In the third and final view of our example, each sale is an entity, and the view is defined as:

```
SALE = (DATE, PRICE)
```

The third view is more comprehensive than either of the first two. While it is possible to compare the granularity of the second and third views by simply counting the number of attributes used to define them, such a comparison is not really meaningful. Any of the views will be more precise if the sales figures are recorded in dollars and cents than if only dollars are recorded.

Semantic consistency, clarity of definition, and *occurrence identifiability* are all simply good practice in defining the view. Semantic consistency and clarity of definition can be closely related. For example, Kent [13] describes a situation in which the term "well" refers to different entities in an oil company's databases. From the geological point of view, a well is a single hole drilled into the ground, oil or not. From the production point of view, a well refers to at least one hole, tapped into a pool of oil and covered by a piece of equipment.

Obtainable values and *naturalness* are related. The values of more natural entities and attributes tend to be more easily obtained than the values of less natural entities and attributes.

Essentialness and *homogeneity* usually make the view smaller. Their desirability is especially clear when few well-defined applications are to be supported.

Robustness and *flexibility* work together to increase the useful lifetime of a view. At first blush, these characteristics may appear to be competing. There is a temptation to equate robustness with rigidity, the opposite of flexibility. But the better way to think of robustness is that it increases the probability that a view can accommodate a change. Flexibility increases the probability and ease with which a view can be changed if a change is necessary.

We now turn our attention to potential conflicts. A good view is one that makes appropriate choices among competing desirable ends. For example, all things being equal, one prefers a domain with greater attribute granularity over one with lesser attribute granularity. This statement is naive in that all things are never equal. Thus, a good view establishes a reasonable middle ground between such tensions. Perhaps the most difficult aspect of creating a view lies in resolving tensions that impact these characteristics.

Cost to obtain values is a frequently encountered problem—the best data for a given application may be more expensive to obtain, while data less relevant or accurate can be obtained readily. A good view balances these considerations.

Utility takes into account that the most relevant data may not have a natural counterpart in the real world. For example, in trying to evaluate the likelihood that an EMPLOYEE will succeed on a potential job assignment, intelligence may be a prime factor. But intelligence is a complicated, multidimensional, and little understood characteristic with no good, natural data counterpart in the real world.

Detail affects redundancy and a number of characteristics (domain precision, attribute granularity, comprehensiveness), which are also in opposition in terms of the level of detail specified by the view. For example, the more comprehensive a view, the greater the redundancy.

13.3   Quality Dimensions of Data Values

In this section, we define the dimensions of data quality that are most pertinent to data values. These include *accuracy*, *currency*, *completeness*, and *consistency*.

Of the four dimensions, accuracy is perhaps the most fundamental, with currency, completeness, and consistency being special cases.

This section also considers the "obtain values" activity of the life-cycle model and specific processes that create data values. For the most part, the relationship between the quality of data values and processes that create them are straightforward (e.g., an accurate process is one that produces accurate values). But there are distinctions worthy of note.

13.3.1 Accuracy

Accuracy of a datum $<e,a,v>$ refers to the nearness of the value v to some value v' in the attribute domain, which is considered as the (or maybe only a) correct one for the entity e and the attribute a. In some cases, v' is referred to as the standard. If the datum's value v coincides with the correct value v', the datum is said to be *correct*.

For example, consider an entity EMPLOYEE (identified uniquely by, say, the employee number 314159) with YEAR OF BIRTH as the attribute of interest. If there is a recording of the employee's year of birth and one knows when the employee was actually born, it is easy to determine the accuracy of the value. In this and many cases, it is even possible to quantify the inaccuracy by computing the difference between the actual and recorded years of birth.

Accuracy and correctness are often far more involved than the above example suggests. One difficulty lies in knowing the correct value. Obviously, a correct value may simply be unknown or an assumed standard may be incorrect. Such is often the case with data gathered some time in the past—no corroborating evidence exists. Second, there may be more than one correct value. Some names have alternative spellings, for example. Third, and most importantly, a correct value may be undefined. This situation occurs when the attribute defines an entity (i.e., serves as a key or a part of a key). Thus, for the above example, there may be no correct value for an entity with an incorrect employee number.

It is often difficult to quantify accuracy, even when a correct value is known. Consider, for example, EMPLOYEE, SEX, DEPARTMENT NAME, and YEAR OF BIRTH as attributes. Sex is either correct or incorrect. So that one is easy. But the possible ways to quantify the accuracy of department name are many and varied. We could, for example, quantify accuracy by counting the number of correct letters or the number of correct letters in correct positions only. Knuth [14] proposed the more sophisticated soundex method. So this one is not so easy. Quantifying the accuracy of numerical attributes (quantities) such as year of birth is not always straightforward, either. It has already been noted that the absolute value of the difference between actual and recorded year of birth serves as a natural measure of accuracy. However, according to this measure, the error is the same when 1980 is recorded instead of 1989 as when 1960 is recorded instead of 1969. But employment of the first person may violate a juvenile labor law—a fact that might be worth reflecting with an appropriate accuracy metric. This example raises the possibility that measures of data accuracy, like many of the quality characteristics of a view, need to be application-specific.

To summarize, quantification of data accuracy is a nontrivial task even when it is possible. In particular, the specific form of the metric for measuring accuracy may well depend not only on the type of entity and attribute in question, but also on the application. Metrics can be summarized at the field- or record-level levels. Here we have considered values correct (accurate) or incorrect (inaccurate) and employed summary statistics of the form

$$p = \frac{\text{Number of correct values}}{\text{Number of total values}}$$

Such summary statistics obviously ignore many of the nuances noted above. Where required, more focused or precise metrics should be defined.

Accuracy, correctness, and other terms are also used to describe or quantify the accuracy of processes that create data values.

13.3.2 Completeness

Completeness refers to the degree to which values are present in a data collection. As far as an individual datum is concerned, only two situations are possible: Either a value is assigned to the attribute in question or not. In the latter case, null, a special element of an attribute's domain can be assigned as the attribute's value. Depending on whether the attribute is mandatory, optional, or inapplicable, null can mean different things.

If the attribute is mandatory, a nonnull value is expected. The null is interpreted as "value unknown," the classical interpretation of database theory, and the datum is incomplete.

Next, consider an optional attribute, RESIDENCE TELEPHONE NUMBER of an EMPLOYEE. Here, the null value can mean four different things: The employee has a telephone number that is not known, the employee has an unlisted telephone number, the employee does not have a residence telephone, and whether the employee has a telephone number is unknown. In the first case, the attribute is applicable to the entity, but its value is unknown. The datum is incomplete. In the second case, the value is known and null is a special and correct value of the attribute. In the third case, the attribute is not applicable. In the second and third cases, the data are complete, although in the third case it is somewhat odd that something that is not there is complete. Finally, in the fourth case, we have no knowledge about applicability of the attribute and hence of its completeness.

For an inapplicable attribute, the null value simply signifies an attribute's inapplicability. A good example is SPOUSE NAME for an unmarried employee. Note that the null value is the only correct one in such situations, and the datum is complete.

In total, six different situations requiring a null value have been noted. These can be collapsed in four classifications of null values [15].

1. An unknown value of an applicable attribute (and an indicator of incompleteness);

2. A nonapplicable attribute (and an indicator of completeness);

3. An attribute of unknown applicability;

4. Null as a special value of an attribute (and an indicator of completeness).

Theoretically, it would be easy to distinguish different types of null values by incorporating special elements into an attribute's domain when defining the view. But the introduction of even one null element can pose problems for standard database operations [16].

Completeness can also be a little more subtle. In particular, it is often of concern to know whether all required entities for an entity class are included in a database. We refer to completeness of the entity class as *entity completeness* and completeness of values as *attribute completeness*.

Note the subtlety entity completeness may involve. For a given entity it is trivial to observe whether a value for a specified attribute is present. But to determine whether an entity should be present, an external standard is needed. Errors of two types can be made. For example, for an ACTIVE EMPLOYEE entity class one must be concerned that all and only active employees are included. The standards needed to make such determinations are not easy to come by.

As with accuracy, the definitions given for completeness are easily applied to "create values" processes.

13.3.3 Currency and Related Dimensions

As our dynamic model of the data life cycle shows, data values change with time. In addition, a lag between the time a data value changes and its update in a database is inherent. The issue of data currency is of such importance that proponents of the so-called infological school [17] require a time indicator in the definition of a datum. Although there may be problems incorporating time into a view [18, 19] it can often be treated as an optional attribute of entities and relationships. However, time-related changes can have a special influence on data accuracy. This section discusses this influence and the related topic, process cycle time.

A datum value is *up-to-date* if it is correct in spite of a possible discrepancy caused by time-related changes to the correct value; a datum is *outdated* at time *t* if it is incorrect at *t* but was correct at some time preceding *t*. *Currency* refers to a degree to which a datum in question is up-to-date.

Consider as an example the ANNUAL SALARY of an employee. Further, suppose that salary can only change at the beginning of the calendar year. Assume also that an employee's actual salary was $38,000 in 1994, $39,000 in 1995, and is $40,000 in 1996. If at some moment during 1996 a value indicates the employee's current salary to be $40,000, it is up to date. If, on the other hand, it shows $38,000, the data value is outdated and its currency, or, more precisely, lack thereof, is two years off. Finally, if the datum indicates the salary for 1996 as $42,000, a figure that is not the actual salary in the previous years, then the datum is not outdated, but simply incorrect.

The previous example dealt with an attribute whose value is supposed to be updated periodically. The definitions also apply to attributes whose values are not required to change, such as employee's ADDRESS or NAME.

According to these definitions, being up to date and currency are special cases of correctness and accuracy, respectively. Being out of date is simply a specific type of inaccuracy—namely, time. This makes the concepts of currency inapplicable to permanent properties—for example, to attributes such as DATE OF BIRTH and BLOOD TYPE and to historical records. Some care is needed, however, in qualifying a property as permanent. While date of birth is permanent, the country of birth is not, if a specific jurisdiction is implied. A person's name can be changed as long as the person is alive, but it becomes permanent after death. Who could imagine until recently that a person's sex is changeable?

Two related terms often used in connection with information chains are "cycle time" and "timeliness." Cycle time is the time it takes a process to create data values. Timeliness is the difference between the times when the process is supposed to have created a value and when it actually has.

13.3.4 Value Consistency

Consistency, in popular usage, means that two or more things do not conflict with one another. This usage extends reasonably well to data values, although a bit of added discipline is desired. Inconsistency problems may arise when two or more collections of data overlap. One expects that values are the same for overlapping entities and attributes. When they are not, the collections are inconsistent. Attributes need not have the same definition for their data values to conflict. Inconsistency can arise with any two related data items. For example, if a person's address is given as STATE = New Jersey, and ZIP CODE = 97234, then there is a conflict.

Note that in both situations, there is redundancy in the data. In the first situation (overlapping data collections), the two data items are exactly the same and each item is wholly redundant with respect to the other. In the second example, STATE is fully implied by ZIP CODE, although ZIP CODE is not implied by STATE. In full generality, one data item or collection of data items may give some (although not complete) insight into another data item or collection of data items.

Data consistency can be a real problem. But it also provides a cost-effective way to identify data values that cannot be correct. More specifically, two or more data values are inconsistent by definition if they cannot be correct simultaneously. The example involving STATE and ZIP CODE is a good one. Thus, note the following.

If STATE and ZIP CODE are inconsistent, at least one of them is incorrect, and both may be.

If STATE and ZIP CODE are consistent, we cannot properly infer that either is correct.

Similarly, information chains are consistent if they produce consistent data values.

Later in this chapter we will be explicit and define consistency in terms of constraints. The needed definitions also apply to data representation and are introduced after a discussion of quality dimensions of representation.

13.4 Quality Dimensions of Data Representation

So far, the discussions of dimensions of data quality have related to data at the conceptual levels in terms of views and values. To be useful, data must be presented to users. For the purposes of this discussion we consider a data recording as consisting of two parts.[4]

1. Format;
2. Physical instance or multiple physical instances of the data value.

We will consider three types of data: labels, categories, and quantities. A full discussion of these major data types is given by Levitin [3]. For the purposes of this book, a definition and a few simple examples of each will suffice.

Labels are data items created primarily for the purpose of naming or identifying an entity [10]. George Bush, AT&T, Niagara Falls, and 911 are examples of labels.

Categories are data items that indicate specific categories within a classification scheme [3]. SEX, MARITAL STATUS, and INCOME BRACKET are examples of attributes with category domains.

Quantities [10] are data items that are the result of measurement in well-defined units, or counts.[5] BLOOD PRESSURE, AGE, and HEIGHT are examples of quantities.

The principal distinctions between data types concern the size and structure of their domains. Quantities have well-structured, ordered domains; category data types have fixed and small domains; label data types have large unstructured domains.

For any data type, a *format* is a mapping from the domain to a set of symbols. Let V denote the conceptual domain and S a set of symbolic representations. Then a format is a function from V to S:

$$f : V \to S$$

---

4. Levitin [3] extends the definition of data to be a quintuple $<e,a,v,f,i>$, where f is the format and i the physical instance to accommodate these two parts.

5. Sometimes numbers are used as labels. For example, SOCIAL SECURITY NUMBER is a number, but it is not the result of a measurement.

The various types of formats are defined by types of symbols making up S. These include: strings, position formats, icons, and color. *Strings* are composed of characters from some alphabet. The set S may impose some structure (called a *syntax*) on allowable combinations of letters. As an example, many computer security systems require that a password be supplied with each user identification. The set of allowed characters (i.e., the alphabet) consists of the characters on a standard keyboard. The syntax is defined by requirements such as "passwords must be at least three characters long and contain a numeral."

Positional formats make use of the positioning of characters to convey data values. Standardized tests such as the college boards make use of positional markings. For quantitative data, most graphical methods make use of positional formats (references [20, 21] are excellent examples of graphical methods).

Icons are a special class of symbols used to represent categorical data. For example, universally accepted symbols for male ($\female$) and female ($\female$)can be found throughout the world.

Finally, *color* is sometimes used to represent data. For example, the color pink often represents the female category; blue, the male.

Quality dimensions for formats include the following: appropriateness, interpretability, portability, format precision, format flexibility, ability to represent null values, and efficient usage of storage. For each physical instance of the value, the important quality dimension is representation consistency—that is, consistency with the format. Each is briefly discussed below.

13.4.1 Appropriateness

The most important quality characteristic of a format is its appropriateness. One format is more appropriate than another if it is better suited to users' needs. The appropriateness of the format depends upon two factors: user and medium used. Both are of crucial importance. The abilities of human users and computers to understand data in different formats are vastly different. For example, the human eye is not very good at interpreting some positional formats, such as bar codes, although optical scanning devices are. On the other hand, humans can assimilate much data from a graph, a format that is relatively hard for a computer to interpret. Appropriateness is related to the second quality dimension, interpretability.

13.4.2 Interpretability

A good format is one that helps the user interpret values correctly. Consider a domain consisting of three values and two candidate representations: (1, 2, 3) and (poor, good, excellent). Obviously the second format is superior because it is less likely to be misinterpreted. This point is one where the connection of data quality to the user is most clear. Data are being presented to users so they may be used properly. Formats that hinder correct interpretation may increase rework and lower downstream data quality, drastically lowering the utility of data given by such a format.

The recording medium can also play an important role in determining the interpretability of a format.

13.4.3   Portability

Good formats are portable or universal. This means that they can be applied to as wide a range of situations as possible. The male and female icons mentioned earlier are excellent for this reason. Portability is especially important in situations similar to those employing these icons—a variety of users with varying levels of skill in understanding the format. It can be expected that portability will be of increased importance as worldwide telecommunications continue to improve.

13.4.4   Format Precision

The set S should be sufficiently precise to distinguish among elements in the domain that must be distinguished by users. This dimension makes clear why icons and colors are of limited use when domains are large. But problems can and do arise for the other formats as well, because many formats are not one-to-one functions. For example, if the domain is infinite (the rational numbers, for example), then no string format of finite length can represent all possible values. The trick is to provide the precision to meet user needs.

13.4.5   Format Flexibility

Good formats, like good views, are flexible so that changes in user needs and recording medium can be accommodated.

13.4.6   Ability to Represent Null Values

Null values were discussed earlier in this chapter. Good formats provide ways to represent them. An excellent story of what can happen when null values are not adequately provided is by Celko [22]. A motorist whose LICENSE read "none" got thousands of traffic tickets intended for people whose cars did not have a license plate.

13.4.7   Efficient Usage of Recording Media

A good format uses the recording media efficiently. An icon, such as (♂) may require thousands of bytes in conventional computer storage, while (0,1) bits may require only a few. But it is important not to compromise appropriateness or interpretability for a few cents' saving of storage cost. It is often possible to address both concerns. For example, it may be better to store data values in a string format and the code to reproduce a graph rather than the graph itself. The graph can then be produced when needed.

13.4.8   Representation Consistency

Representation consistency[6] refers to whether physical instances of data are in accord with their formats. For example, an EMPLOYEE's salary cannot be represented "$AXT," as there is (or should be) no such element in S. One would often like to know whether a physical instance is the proper representation for the intended (correct) value. But in practice this is rarely possible, as the intended value is conceptual and not known. So one is left with the issue of whether the representation conflicts with S. In the following section, representation and value consistency are discussed in terms of a common foundation.

13.5   More on Data Consistency

This section considers view, value, and representation consistency from a different perspective. So far, these dimensions have been defined in terms of absence of conflict in the conceptual model, between data items, and between a format and a physical instance, respectively.

More generally, data are *consistent with respect to a set of constraints* if they satisfy all constraints in the set. The distinctions between the various types of consistency, view, value, and representation consistency lie in the nature of the constraints. For view consistency, the constraints are posed in terms of the model. As an example, a model constraint may disallow null values for a particular attribute. For value consistency, the constraints are posed in terms of the multivariate domains. For representational consistency, the constraints are

---

6.   We restrict attention here to this single dimension of quality of a physical instance of a data
     item. Other dimensions are confounded with the representing medium. As an example, a data
     item may be represented on a sheet of paper, then repeatedly photocopied. One could be
     concerned with the quality of the copies—an issue we do not pursue here.

posed in terms of membership in the set S or in terms of conformance to a format standard. The nature of representation and view constraints is straightforward. For value constraints, the situation is somewhat more interesting and the following explores the bivariate (two data items) case in some detail. We consider finite domains only. Both of these restrictions—to two dimensions and to finite domains—are easily relaxed.

Let

$$V_1 = v_{11}, v_{12}, \ldots, v_{1n}$$
$$V_2 = v_{21}, v_{22}, \ldots, v_{2m}$$

denote the domains of two attributes, d_1 and d_2, respectively. Also let $V_1 \times V_2$ denote all possible ordered pairs of the values of the two data items. In effect, $V_1 \times V_2$ is the bivariate domain for the (hypothetical) composite data item (d_1, d_2). Value consistency constraints restrict the possible values in $V_1 \times V_2$. Four cases are worthy of note (Figure 13.1).

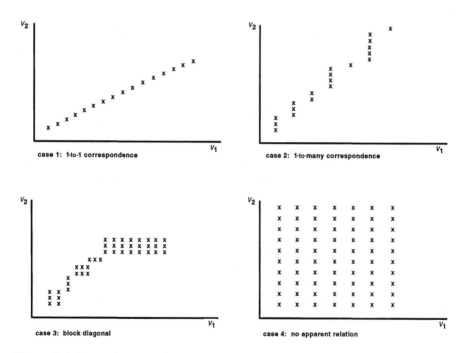

Figure 13.1 Potential correspondences between attribute domains for wo data items, d_1 and d_2. In each case, the domain of d_1 is on the x-axis, of d_2 on the y-axis, and the marked regions indicate the domain $V_1 \times V_2$ of the composite data item (d_1, d_2).

Case 1. One-to-one correspondence. In this case one, and only one, value in V_2 is permitted for each element of V_1. This case occurs when the two data items are the same and should match. It also occurs with scale and/or unit changes (HEIGHT measured in English and metric units, respectively). In this case, $m = n$.

Case 2. One-to-many correspondence. In this case several values in V_2 are permitted for each element of V_1. The situation is graphically illustrated in Figure 13.1 (case 2). An example of this case is the correspondence between STATE and ZIP CODE. Each state may have several zip codes, but each zip code implies one, and only one, state.

Case 3. Block diagonal correspondence. This is a more general case of case 2 in which the domains may be arranged as

$$V_1 = V_{11}, V_{12}, \ldots, V_{1k}$$
$$V_2 = V_{21}, V_{22}, \ldots, V_{2k}$$

and the permitted domain of (d_1, d_2) is $(V_{11} \times V_{21}, V_{12} \times V_{22}, \ldots, V_{1k} \times V_{2k})$. ZIP CODE and AREA CODE exhibit such a relationship.

Case 4. Unrestricted correspondences. In this case, any value of V_2 is permitted for any value of V_1 (Figure 13.1 [case 4]). This is not to imply that the data items d_1 and d_2 are independent of one another. For example, adult males tend to be taller than adult females. But in principle at least, constraints that always hold do not exist.

This last example suggests an extension of consistency into a probabilistic framework. In particular, one might infer that for an individual whose height = 76 inches, sex = male with high probability (though less than one). The interested reader should see reference [23].

The importance of consistency in terms of constraints is that automated checking of constraints is feasible. Individual instances of automated constraints are called "edits." (Edits can also be used to determine checking representational consistency.) Naus [24] provides suggestions for creating good sets of edits. Edits are often built into modern database management systems. In the DBMS literature, consistency often is termed "data integrity." Good references include [25–27]. Edits are often applied either at the tail end of an information chain or as soon in the life cycle model as practical.

While edits are useful, they also pose a trap. In particular:

- If an edit is failed, a constraint is not satisfied, and at least one data value is not accurate.

- If an edit is passed, it is *not* proper to assume that data values are correct.

This second point is often ignored. Passing edits may lead to a false sense that the data are correct. But edits *cannot* ensure that the data are correct. Representational constraints only guarantee that formats are met. Even value constraints for which one-to-one correspondences exist do not ensure accuracy, because both values may be wrong. The problem is minimized when d_1 and d_2 were created independently of one another, but caution should be exercised. Often, particularly with historical data, a single, incorrect source may have been used to create both d_1 and d_2.

One final point regarding value consistency: As noted, consistency is made possible by redundancy in data. Either a LOGIN or a PASSWORD is usually sufficient to identify a computer user. If the two codes are consistent, the computer system has strong evidence that the user is legitimate (i.e., that the data are accurate). This suggests that redundancy in data can be designed into information chains. Error-detecting and error-correcting codes have been successful in communications applications. These ideas have not yet been developed for general use.

13.6 Summary

This chapter has explored dimensions of data quality. It is surprising that something as simple as a data item can have so many quality aspects—27 were discussed. These 27 relate to the conceptual view, to data values, and to data representation and correspond to three activities of the data life-cycle model. They are summarized in Table 13.1.

One is tempted to state that the most important quality dimension is data accuracy. After all, accurate data are fundamental to all its uses and accuracy ensures consistency and other dimensions. But the concept is simplistic. Data do not exist independent of context and are of little practical use without representation. Nevertheless, accuracy is the most important of the quality dimensions associated with data values.

There has been a great deal of discussion about data consistency. Consistency is important because it is comparatively easy to check. In particular, consistency can be posed in terms of constraints that can often be programmed and run automatically. Consistency bears on accuracy and is at the heart of data tracking, as discussed in Chapter 11. But data consistency is *not* data quality and caution is urged.

The Conceptual View			
Content	relevance	obtainability	clarity of definition
Scope	comprehensiveness	essentialness	
Level of Detail	attribute granularity	precision of domains	
Composition	naturalness	identifiability	
	homogeneity	minimum unnecessary redundancy	
View Consistency	semantic consistency	structural consistency	
Reaction to Change	robustness	flexibility	

Values	
accuracy	completeness (entities and attributes)
consistency	currency/cycle time

Representation		
Formats	appropriateness	format precision	efficient use of storage
	interpretability	format flexibility	
	portability	ability to represent null values	
Physical Instances	representation consistency		

Table 13.1   A Summary of 27 Data Quality Dimensions

REFERENCES

[1]   Fox, C. J., A. V. Levitin, and T. C. Redman, "The Notion of Data and Its Quality Dimensions," *Information Processing and Management*, Vol. 30, No. 1, January 1994, pp. 9–19.

[2]   Levitin, A. V., and T. C. Redman, "Quality Dimensions of a Conceptual View," *Information Processing and Management*, Vol. 31, No. 1, January 1995, pp. 81–88.

[3]   Levitin, A. V., "Formats for Data Representation: A Taxonomy and Quality Dimensions," unpublished report.

[4]   Caby, E. C., "A Framework for Data Consistency," unpublished report.

[5]   Wang, R. Y., and D. M. Strong, "Beyond Accuracy: What Data Quality Means to Consumers," *Journal of Management Information Systems*, Vol. 4, 1996, pp. 5–34.

[6]   Marchand, D., "Managing Information Quality," in I. Wormell (ed.), *Information Quality Definitions and Dimensions*, London: Taylor Graham, 1990.

[7]   Nayer, M., "A Framework for Achieving Information Integrity," in V. Rajaraman and V. Mandke (eds.), *Information Integrity Issues and Approaches*, New Delhi: Information Integrity Foundation, 1996.

[8]   Loebl, A. S., "Accuracy and Relevance and the Quality of Data," in G. E. Liepins and V. R. R. Uppuluri (eds.), *Data Quality Control: Theory and Pragmatics*, New York: Marcel Dekker, 1990, pp. 105–143.

[9]   Fidel, R., *Database Design for Information Retrieval: A Conceptual Approach*, New York: John Wiley & Sons, 1987.

[10]   Tasker, D., *Fourth Generation Data: A Guide to Data Analysis for New and Old Systems*, Englewood Cliffs, NJ: Prentice Hall, 1989.

[11]   Smith, J. M., and D. C. Smith, "Database Abstractions: Aggregation and Generalization," *ACM Transactions on Database Systems*, Vol. 2, No. 2, 1977, pp. 105–133.

[12]   Elmasri, R., and S. B. Navathe, *Fundamentals of Database Systems*, Redwood City, CA: Benjamin Cummings, 1989.

[13]   Kent, W., *Data and Reality*, Amsterdam: North-Holland, 1978.

[14]   Knuth, D., *The Art of Computer Programming, Vol. 3*, Reading, MA: Addison-Wesley, 1973.

[15]   Lee, R. M., "Logic, Semantics, and Data Modeling: An Ontology," in R. A. Meersman and A. C. Sernadas (eds.), *Data and Knowledge (DS-2A)*, Amsterdam: North-Holland, 1988.

[16]   Imielinski, T., and W. Lipski, "Incomplete Information in Relational Databases," *Journal of the ACM*, Vol. 31, No. 4, 1984, pp. 761–791.

[17]   Langefors, B., and B. Sundgren, *Information Systems Architecture*, New York: Petrocelli/Charter, 1975.

[18]   Bolour, A., "The Role of Time in Information Processing: A Survey," *ACM SIGMOD Record*, Vol. 12, No. 3, 1982, pp. 27–50.

[19] Jardine, D. A., and A. Matzov, "Ontology and Properties of Time in Information Systems," in R. A. Meersman and A. C. Sernadas (eds.), *Data and Knowledge (DS-2A)*, Amsterdam: North-Holland, 1988.

[20] Tufte, E. R., *The Visual Display of Quantitative Information*, Cheshire, CT: Graphics Press, 1983.

[21] Tufte, E. R., *Envisioning Information*, Cheshire, CT: Graphics Press, 1989.

[22] Celko, J., "Make or Brake Your System," *Data Programming and Design*, No. 3, 1989, pp. 19–20.

[23] Sarndal, C. E., "Methods for Estimating the Precision of Survey Estimates When Imputation Has Been Used," *Proc. Symposium 90: Measurement and Improvement of Data Quality*, Ottawa, Canada, October 29–31, 1990, pp. 337–347.

[24] Naus, J. I., *Data Quality Control and Editing*, New York: Marcel Dekker, 1975.

[25] Brodie, M. L., "Specification and Verification of Database Semantic Integrity," Ph.D. diss., University of Toronto, 1978.

[26] Date, C. J., *An Introduction to Database Systems, Vol. 2*, 3rd ed., Reading, MA: Addison-Wesley, 1983.

[27] Tsichritzis, D. C., and F. H. Lochovsky, *Data Models*, Englewood Cliffs, NJ: Prentice Hall, 1982.

Part IV: Summary

Chapter **14**

Summary: Roles and Responsibilities

"The truth shall set you free."
— John 8:32

14.1 Introduction

The first three parts of this book have been directed at various audiences within an enterprise. Part I was aimed at the enterprise's leaders—those self-selected few who take the responsibility to motivate the enterprise and make things happen. Part II was aimed at process owners. In enterprises that already support process management, these people are already named and here we propose that their responsibilities should explicitly include data. Process management has not yet penetrated many enterprises, so these people will have new and unfamiliar roles. Part III was aimed at information professionals, including those whose job responsibilities involve data, data management, database design and management, data networking, or computers (such as those in the Chief Information Office), and those who depend on data to add value to their enterprises.

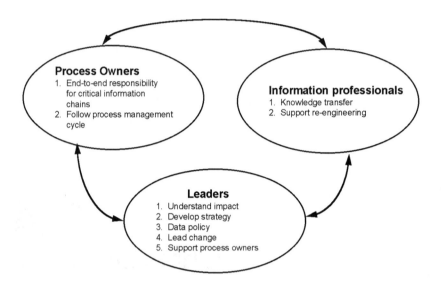

Figure 14.1 Three groups—leaders, process owners, and information professionals—have important contributions to make to an overall data quality program.

Each audience (leaders, process owners, and information professionals) must make important contributions to the enterprise's overall data quality program. In this concluding chapter we will summarize the main points in terms of the roles each group plays within the enterprise. Figure 14.1 summarizes the complementary roles played by each group.

14.2 Roles for Leaders

We begin with the roles played by leaders. Hopefully, at least some leaders will be members of senior management, such as the Chief Information Officer, the Chief Quality Officer, and the Chief Financial Officer. While much can be accomplished without senior leadership, experience confirms that programs move further and faster with such support. The principal roles for leaders are as follows.

<u>1.</u>   Understanding the impact of poor data on the enterprise. We cited any number of such impacts in Chapter 1, including lowered customer satisfaction, increased expense, inability to benefit from advanced technologies such as data warehouses, and so forth. While all may harm the enterprise, some will be more important based on

the enterprise's business purposes and strategies. Leaders must make the connection between the enterprise's most important directions and data—specifically the need for improved data quality.

2. Developing an overall strategy for addressing the enterprise's data quality issues. Leaders have two specific responsibilities in this regard.

    - They must rally improvement efforts around the data most important to the entire enterprise.
    - They must properly integrate database clean-ups and process improvements. Data clean-ups are effective on data that turn over slowly, but relatively little important data fall into this category. Improvements to information chains are needed for long-term sustainable gains, especially data that are created at high rates. Most of the enterprise's critical data fall into this category. In most enterprises, some data require one approach, some data the other, and some data require both.

3. Developing and deploying a data policy. In many enterprises, management responsibilities for data throughout their lifetimes are not clearly delineated. The data policy has to sort through the options and align the enterprise accordingly. We favor policies that recognize separate responsibilities of data creators, those who process and store data, and users in line organizations. A few functions, such as keeping track of the data assets and managing redundancy, are reserved for centralized staff organizations.

4. Leading change. Implementing the strategies, policies, and methods described here do not come easily in any enterprise. Leaders make it happen. Difficult though it may be, enterprises and organizations must (obviously) change to survive, and the change process can be managed. Leaders can start small and build upon success to extend their impact. At each step, they can ensure that four elements of successful change are in place: a sense of urgency; clear, shared vision; capacity to change; and actionable first steps. Ultimately, they wish to create an enterprise that embraces Deming's Fourteen Points, focused on data and information. These points are summarized in Figure 14.2.

Dr. W. E. Deming's Fourteen Points for Quality Management, Adapted for Data

1. Recognize the importance of data and information to the enterprise's objectives and create constancy of purpose in improving them and their use.

2. Adopt the new philosophy. The enterprise can no longer live with currently acceptable levels of data quality and the decreased customer satisfaction, expense, and delays it causes.

3. Cease dependence on error detection. Eliminate the need for error detection by building accuracy and other quality attributes into processes that create data and information.

4. End the practice of awarding business on the basis of price. In particular, require that associated data and information be of high quality. Encourage suppliers to provide statistical evidence and eliminate those who will not.

5. Constantly improve the systems by which data and information are produced and used to create value for customers, the enterprise, and its stakeholders.

6. Institute job training. Help individuals and organizations understand how their actions impact data and others downstream. Teach them how to solve problems they can solve on their own and bring those they cannot solve to the attention of others.

7. Teach and institute leadership for supervisors of workers who produce data. Managers of organizations that produce data must become responsible for quality, not simply numeric production. The entire enterprise's productivity will improve with improved data.

8. Drive out fear, so people can focus their efforts on the good of the enterprise.

9. Break down barriers between organizations. In particular, ensure the free flow of high-quality data and information across organizational boundaries.

10. Eliminate slogans and numerical goals that seek improved productivity or quality without providing the means. Don't simply expect improved data—show how this can be achieved.

11. Eliminate production quotas and management by objective. They lower data quality and harm the enterprise as a result. Instead, learn how to manage and improve processes that create and use data and information.

12. Remove barriers that stand between data producers and their right to pride in their work.

13. Institute training on data, information, their roles in the enterprise, and how they may be continuously improved.

14. Create a structure in top management that recognizes the importance of data and information and their relationship to the rest of the business. Develop and implement a plan to put everyone's talents toward the transformation.

Figure 14.2   These are Deming's Fourteen Points, adapted for data.

5. Supporting process owners. Owners of the most important data-creating information chains have the most difficult jobs. The first few owners have especially difficult times. Leaders need to recruit process owners from among the enterprise's best, and help them succeed.

14.3   Roles for Process Owners

Information chains[1] are the large, cross-functional portions of day-to-day activities that create, store, and use data and information. "Billing" is a good example. In some enterprises, "billing" is interpreted as the "Billing Department"—the organization responsible for making sense of the half-completed forms, confused and inconsistent department records systems, and phone calls explaining corrections, as well as producing an invoice and collecting the money. In others, "billing" is interpreted as the "Billing System"—the large, antiquated mainframe computer that requires a battery of clerks to feed, an army of programmers and data processors to operate, and a huge budget to maintain (and still doesn't accommodate new products and services very quickly). Neither of these interpretations is wrong, of course. But here the focus is on the end-to-end "Billing Information Chain," which may begin with the receipt of a customer order, include a credit check, continue through production and delivery, and result in an invoice and payment credit. Experience confirms that high-quality billing is achieved through horizontal management of this end-to-end chain.

Process owners are ultimately responsible for this horizontal management, and process management is the formal approach for doing so. Process management can be contrasted with the more familiar hierarchical management, in which most of the management activity is up and down the organization chart. In process management, most of the managing is done from left to right, in the direction of customers. Process management does not obviate the need for hierarchical management, rather it helps ensure management in all directions (sometimes called 360-degree management).

Formally, process management has seven steps, although it is best described as a cycle with tight interactions between steps. The cycle is shown in Figure 14.3. The first step involves establishing management responsibilities. As noted

---

1. The term "process" is established in much of quality management to mean a "set of interrelated work activities." We use the term "information chain" to describe the data and information portions of a very large, cross-functional process or processes.

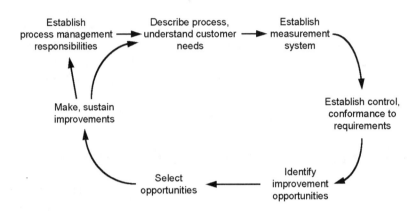

Figure 14.3   The process management cycle is shown here.

above, these responsibilities are embodied in the process owner. A good working definition of the process owner is "the person who has end-to-end responsibility for the results of the information chain and has the authority to change it."

The next step is to understand what customers want and what the information chain does. The concept that customers are the ultimate judges of quality is fundamental, so knowing what they want is essential. Similarly, the details of how the information chain operates dictate whether those needs will be met. Finally, customer requirements need to be turned into specifications for the internal steps of the chain and for suppliers to the chain. Most customer requirements are stated in vague, subjective terms, such as "I want the bill to be right and delivered on time." At a high level, "right" and "on time" need to be defined and at lower levels turned into actionable, objective specifications. Thus, "on time" may mean "the bill must arrive at the customer's Accounting Department by the third business day of the calendar month." And specifications ensuring this happens may include:

- Data for all items shipped to customers by month's end must be properly input into the system by close of business on the first business day.

- Charges for all items must be properly applied by noon of the second business day.

- Invoices for customers requiring third business day billing (such as the one above) must be printed, put in envelopes, addressed, and arrive at Shipping by 3:00 P.M. on the second business day.

- Our overnight shipper (a supplier) must deliver by 10:00 A.M. the next (third) day.

A number of tools, such as quality function deployment, flowcharting, and the Functions of Information Processing (FIP) approach, are available to help the process owner.

The third step in process management is to establish a measurement system. Measurement systems connect customer needs and the technical details of the information chain on the one hand, and the management actions on the other. Managers act best when clear, objective, and prescriptive measurement summaries of the most important customer requirements and process specifications are at their disposal. Good measurement systems provide these summaries in a cost-effective manner. In most cases, in-process measurements of data accuracy and process cycle time are needed, and the data-tracking technique is the method of choice for making needed measurements. The steps of data tracking are summarized in Figure 14.4.

The control chart is perhaps the single most important management summary provided by the measurement system, and establishing statistical control and checking conformance to user requirements is step 4 of the process management cycle. Figures 14.5 and 14.6 illustrate the control chart and appropriate management actions. As Figure 14.5 depicts, performance levels are plotted in time. Then a Center Line, upper control limit, lower control limit, and (usually) a customer requirement line are added. Statistical control is indicated when all points lie within the control limits, and the customer requirement is met when the upper control limit is below the requirement's line. (Depending on the nature of the customer requirements and plot details, it may be that the requirement is met when the lower control limit exceeds the requirement's line.)

Step	How to implement
1. Sample/label	Randomly sample records entering information chain and tag them
2. Track	Write out each record as it exits each process/subprocess
3. Identify errors, calculate cycle time	Examine tracked records to determine errors. Calculate cycle time within and between processes.
4. Summarize	Analyze data top-down to determine where errors occur, plot control charts, etc.
5. Take appropiate action	Return to process management cycle, steps 4 or 5.

Figure 14.4 Steps of data tracking are summarized in this figure.

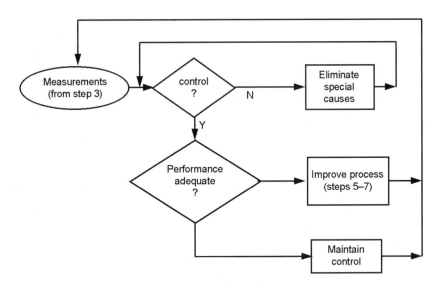

Figure 14.5 This flowchart gives the appropriate actions for the process owner to take based on the stability of the process and conformance to requirements.

A state of statistical control is the foundation on which improvement is based. The final three steps of the process management cycle focus on making improvements and sustaining gains. Based on comparing actual performance to customer requirements, the process owner identifies improvement opportuni-

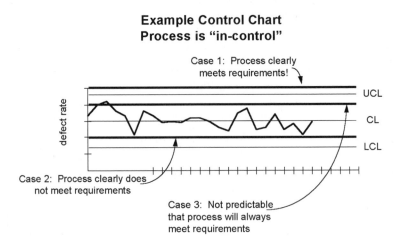

Figure 14.6 This process is in-control—whether its performance is adequate depends on customer requirements.

ties, selects a few, and pursues the selected improvement projects. Most improvements, once they are understood, are simple and straightforward. Perhaps the biggest impediments to change are organizational politics and people's fear of change.

14.4   Roles for Information Professionals

Information professionals are those people with data and information management responsibilities within their enterprises. Many report to Chief Information Offices, Information Resources Divisions, Chief Finance Offices, and the like, and some report to almost every other organization in the enterprise. Information professionals must be responsible for gathering and disseminating the enterprise's knowledge about data and information: their life cycle, their properties as assets to the enterprise, their quality dimensions, and so forth. Information professionals may have other roles assigned by policy, such as maintaining the inventory of data and information assets, managing redundancy, and promulgating data standards.

We urge information professionals to consider static (definition) and dynamic (life cycle) as complementary approaches to understanding what data are.

Figure 14.7 presents a model of data's life cycle. It stems from the simple observation that new data come into existence, new values are created and old ones replaced, data are stored in or on a variety of media, and data are used in seemingly incongruous applications—all at enormous rates. For data quality, the most important activities of the life-cycle model are:

- Define a view, in which entity classes, attributes, and domains are defined.
- Obtain values, in which values for specific entities are determined.
- Present results, in which data, perhaps manipulated by intervening steps, are presented to users.

In the static approach, we define data and data representation as triples and quintuples, respectively:

$$\text{data} = \text{<entity, attribute, value>}$$
$$\text{data representation} = \text{<entity, attribute, value, representation rule, symbol>}$$

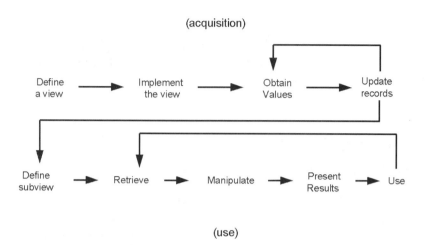

(acquisition)

(use)

Figure 14.7   The data life-cycle model is shown in this figure.

In these definitions, the value is selected from a well-defined domain of possible values.

Taken together, these approaches suggest that important dimensions of data quality fall into three major categories: those associated with the conceptual view, those associated with data values, and those associated with representation. Specific dimensions are presented in Table 14.1.

Information professionals must help their enterprises realize just how different data are from most other assets and the impacts these differences engender. There are at least a dozen differences of major consequence. Four examples suffice for this concluding chapter. First, compared to other assets, data are created at enormous rates. This means that error detection and correction won't work well and process-focused methods are needed. Second, data are not tangible, so they don't have physical properties like other assets. So you can't tell by direct examination whether a data value is correct. And data are elusive, so the enterprise may pay less attention to data than other, more readily visible, assets. Third, data are relatively inexpensive to obtain, store, copy, and transport. So ownership can always be contested. As a result, the politics associated with data and information can be brutal and debilitate an enterprise.

Finally, information professionals play important roles in process re-engineering and the design of new processes. Throughout this book, often in examples, we have noted a number of principles of good design, which we summarize here.

Conceptual View			
Scope	comprehensiveness	essentialness	
Level of Detail	attribute granularity	precision of domains	
Composition	naturalness	identifiability	
	homogeneity	simplicity	
Content	relevance	obtainability	clarity of definition
View Consistency	semantic consistency	structural consistency	
Reaction to Change	robustness	flexibility	

Values			
	accuracy	completeness (entities and attributes)	
	consistency	currency/cycle time	

Representation			
Formats	appropriateness	format precision	efficient use of storage
	correct interpretation	format flexibility	
	portability	ability to represent null values	
Physical Instances	representation consistency		

Table 14.1 Dimensions of Data Quality

14.4.1 Design Principle: Process Management

Principles: As early as possible in design, arrange for the start-up management of the process/information chain. Determine who the process owner will be and involve him or her in design decisions.

Rationale/Benefits: The single most important factor in an information chain's performance, the quality of data it creates, their use, and the ability to evolve the process to meet changing customer needs, is its active and concerted management. The sooner in design this is recognized, the more likely that process management will be in place when the process is activated. These principles are an extension of the process owner's responsibility to ensure that the voice of the customer is heard throughout the information chain. Here design is considered as nothing more than an early step.

These principles can also be explained from the point of view of design. The customer for the design project is (or should be) the process owner. Without such a person, the design manager has no customer to satisfy and it is ludicrous to expect him or her to meet the customer's needs if he or she cannot consult with the customer.

14.4.2   Design Principle: Measurement Systems

Principles: Embed the measurement system in the information chain. Specifically, plan the measurements and build the measurement device and protocol into the design. Data-analytic capabilities should also be planned, although they need not be incorporated into the design.

Rationale/Benefits: If the first principle is to establish process management, the second is to give the process owner the tools needed to do the job. It is almost always less expensive to build measurements into a new information chain than it is to add them later. Data tracking in particular may often be incorporated into the overall design and built into the new information systems that support it. At the very least, edits should be part of the design. Measurement of failed edit rates should also be included.

14.4.3   Design Principle: Data Architecture

Principles: Extend data architecture to recognize information chains and the data life cycle, including sources of data, connection to other data stores, other legitimate uses of the data, the enterprise's data inventory, and management accountabilities for data.

Rationale/Benefits: Data architects typically design databases. They determine the most critical data entities and attributes and organize the data within databases. In other words, data architecture does a good job embracing the static aspects of data. Data architecture should also embrace dynamic aspects.

14.4.4   Design Principle: Cycle Time

Principle: When designing an information chain in which speed (cycle time) is of importance (as is almost always the case), concentrate first on minimizing queue and transmit times.

Rationale/Benefits: Queue and transmit times often dominate overall cycle time. Keeping them to a minimum thus provides the greatest reduction in overall cycle time. These are often the easiest to reduce because they don't directly impact most people's jobs. Finally, experience suggests that errors often hide in queues. Reducing queue time forces them out of hiding, where they must be addressed. The end result is improved quality—especially accuracy.

14.4.5   Design Principle: Data Values

Principle: Create data values as few times as possible (once is best).

Rationale/Benefits: There is little to be gained by creating a data value more than once. Either the values agree, in which case multiple creations have added unnecessary expense, or they don't agree, in which case the data are inconsistent. Inconsistencies often go unnoticed until they cause rework or other problems. In any event, a great deal of non-value-added effort is required to find inconsistencies and correct them. It is usually better to concentrate on creating correct data values at the outset. This point applies not just to individual information chains, but to the entire enterprise.

14.4.6   Design Principle: Redundancy in Data Storage

Principles: Store (a given collection of) data in as few databases as possible. Equivalently, minimize unneeded redundancy. If multiple storage is needed, link storage mechanisms to minimize redundancy.

Rationale/Benefits: Considerations similar to data creation apply to data storage. When loss of data is not a concern, it is best to store data in only one database. Multiple storage makes it difficult to maintain consistency, especially when data change. Previous comments about the impact of inconsistency apply. Unfortunately, database failures do sometimes occur, so it is often a good idea to maintain a second or a back-up copy. The principles expressed here do not argue against planned, designed backup or careful design for a small amount of redundancy. But in some enterprises, as many as a dozen copies are kept. This number can and should be reduced.

14.4.7   Design Principle: Computerization

Principles: Put data in machine-readable form as early in the information chain as possible. Employ automated data collection whenever possible. Test data collection devices and procedures and keep all equipment in working order.

Rationale/Benefits: Computers, bar-code scanners, and the like improve data accuracy because they are better than people at certain activities such as reading and inputing data. And data entry jobs are often tedious and unrewarding. Further, putting original data directly into a computer at the start of the information chain saves time and expense later. However, there may be a tendency to assume that the computerized data collection is perfect, when, in fact, it is not.

14.4.8   Design Principle: Data Transformations and Transcription

Principles: Avoid data format changes within the information chain. Use computers, not people, to make format changes. Similarly, design information chains to minimize data transcription.

Rationale/Benefits: Transformation and transcription do not improve data accuracy. They do, however, provide opportunities for errors, add expense, and increase complexity. Information chains employ transformations because without them, a subsequent process within the chain may be unable to use the data at all. But such transformations can be minimized with good design. Similarly, the number of transcriptions can be minimized by putting data into machine-readable form as early as possible. These principles do not extend to data presentation. Data should be presented in ways best suited to their various users and justify various formats.

14.4.9   Design Principle: Value Creation

Principles: When data are being obtained for the first time, it is best to obtain them just before the time they are first needed. Subsequently, capture changes to data values as soon as possible after they change.

Rationale/Benefits: These principles stem from the observation that new data are created and existing data values change so rapidly. For data not already obtained, there is not much sense in obtaining them far ahead of time. The likelihood of the values changing is simply too great. But once a set of data has been obtained and stored, it is best to keep up with the changes.

14.4.10   Design Principle: Data Destruction

Principle: Discontinue gathering and storing data that are no longer useful.

Rationale/Benefits: As customer needs evolve, certain data may outlive their usefulness. But the enterprise will continue to gather and store them. This is expensive and takes attention from more important data. So plan for periodic review of data needs. When data are no longer useful, they need not be destroyed, simply moved to secondary storage.

14.4.11   Design Principle: Editing

Principles: Place edits as near as possible (logically and physically) to data creation and/or modification. Use edits as input criteria to a database, as opposed to exit criteria from a database to an application. Provide mechanisms to measure failed edit rates. Finally, put mechanisms in place to ensure that edits are not bypassed.

Rationale/Benefits: These principles help use edits to maximum benefit. It is often easier to apply edits downstream, but it is more difficult to make corrections. Edits, like other quality checks, are far more effective when they are close to what they are checking.

As noted in principles concerning measurement, the failed edit rates help process owners make improvements.

Finally, there may a temptation to bypass edit routines. Obviously edits can't provide value when they are bypassed and this temptation should be avoided.

14.4.12   Design Principle: Coding

Principles: Employ codes that are easy for data creators and users to understand. Avoid long, numeric, meaningless coding conventions in favor of short, meaningful words or abbreviations. If both letters and numbers must be used in codes, don't mix them—group the letters together and the numbers together.

Rationale/Benefits: These principles aim at improving information chains by making them simpler for operators. Codes such as "high," "medium," and "low" are easier to understand than the equivalent but harder to remember codes "0," "1," and "2."

14.4.13   Design Principle: Single-Fact Data

Principle: Employ single-fact data whenever possible.

Rationale/Benefits: Single-fact data improve the quality of the conceptual view. Within an information chain, single-fact data help reduce code complexity, as noted above, and simplify operators' jobs.

14.4.14   Design Principle: Data Dictionaries

Principles: Employ extensive data dictionaries. They should provide careful definitions of entity names and relationships, domains of allowed values, and format requirements. They should extend to the entire information chain and be accessible to and readable by as many people as possible.

Rationale/Benefits: Data dictionaries are accepted as good practice in system design (even if not always followed). Their use can be easily extended to cover an information chain under design. Making them easily accessible and readable is more difficult, but no less essential.

14.5   Final Remarks—The Three Most Important Points

As a final word, we summarize the three most important features common to successful data quality programs. Here "successful" means "delivering value to the enterprise."

1. Those who succeed realize the impact of poor data on their enterprises. Their goals are to improve customer satisfaction, reduce cost, make better decisions, and the like. And they set out to improve data as the means to create business advantage, not as an end to itself.

2. Those who succeed align management responsibilities for data. Perhaps intuitively, they recognize data and information as business assets. They focus attention on creating high-quality new data and they hold creators accountable.

3. Those who succeed properly apply process management. They understand who the customers are and what they want. They measure the most important things well and they use statistical tools properly. They make improvements and they sustain those improvements.

Glossary

accuracy a measure of the degree of agreement between a data value or collection of data values and a source agreed to be correct.

associate in an information model, the function of sorting, comparing, or matching.

attribute the element of a datum that specifies a particular entity or defines a property of the entity.

clean-up (database) usually a special activity aimed at identifying and correcting errors in data values already stored (in a database).

common cause in statistical quality control, a source of variation within or internal to a process or information chain.

completeness a measure of the degree to which data values are present for required attributes.

consistency   a measure of the degree to which a set of data satisfies a set of constraints—for example, consistency may refer to two data values, which are consistent if they do not disagree.

control   also "in-control." In statistical quality control, this is a state achieved when evidence indicates the absence of a special cause of variation. Equivalently, evidence suggests that future process performance is predictable, within limits.

control chart   a graphical device for determining whether a process or information chain is in control.

currency   a measure of the degree to which data values are up to date.

customer-supplier model   a model of a process or information chain emphasizing the interfaces between suppliers, the chain, and customers.

cycle time   the time required for a process or information chain to complete an item.

data   any collection of datum. See "datum."

database   a formal, computerized collection of data.

data policy   a statement that delineates management responsibility for data and activities that touch and/or impact data and information.

data recording   a physical instance standing for a datum or data, according to a data representation.

data representation   a set of rules for recording a datum or data on a specified medium.

data tracking   an in-process technique for measuring the data accuracy, consistency, and cycle time of an information chain.

data value   the element of a datum that specifies an element of the domain assigned to the specified attribute.

datum   a triple <entity, attribute, value>.

define a view   the first step in the life-cycle model, in which the model of the real world to be captured in data is defined.

domain   a set of permitted values for an attribute.

edit　a (usually computerized) routine that verifies a constraint on a set of data.

enterprise　the highest level (organizational) structure that owns or manages the data of interest. An enterprise is typically made up of several "organizations."

entity　the element of a datum that refers to a specific individual or instance.

filter　in an information model, the function associated with creation of new (or change to existing) data or information.

flowchart　a model of a process or information chain emphasizing the sequence of work activities.

format　a specified set of rules for representing data values.

functions of information processing (FIP) chart　a formal chart that captures an information model.

impact matrix　in understanding customer requirements, a matrix that rates the relevance of customer requirements to data quality dimensions.

implement the view　the second step in the life-cycle model, in which a conceptual view is implemented.

in-control　or simply "control." In statistical quality control, this is a state achieved when evidence indicates the absence of a special cause of variation. Equivalently, evidence suggests that future process performance is predictable, within limits.

information chain　the portions of a large, cross-functional process that involve data and information. See "process."

information model　a model of a process or information chain emphasizing the movement, storage, and changes to data.

life-cycle model (data)　a model that captures the most important activities involving data: from the definition of a conceptual view, through obtaining values, storing them, presenting them to users, and to their actual use.

measurement system　an overall system for measuring process or information chain performance that links requirements, a measurement protocol, summary results, and management action.

normalization change   in data tracking, a change to data between processes where data are buffered with spaces, dashes, or other delimiters to accommodate different format specifications of those processes.

obtain values   the third step in the life-cycle model, in which data values are acquired through a variety of means.

pareto chart   in quality improvement, a bar chart in which categories on the *x*-axis are ordered by the height of bars plotted on the *y*-axis (frequency, percentage, etc.). The leftmost categories represent the greatest opportunity for improvement.

process   a set of interrelated work activities, usually characterized by specific inputs and repeated value-added steps, which produce a specific set of outputs. See "information chain"; "subprocess."

process management cycle   a set of specific, repeatable tasks for defining a process or information chain, understanding customer needs, establishing control, and making improvements.

process management team   a group assembled by the process owner to assist him or her in carrying out process management.

process owner   the person responsible for process performance. This person is assumed to have authority to make changes.

process performance matrix   in understanding customer needs, a matrix used to define detailed performance specifications on a process.

project   a defined activity for carrying out a selected improvement opportunity.

prompt   in an information model, the function that starts or ends an information chain or process and/or triggers continued processing.

queue   in an information model, the function that sets an information product aside for later processing.

redundancy   the state of having multiple copies of data.

regulate   in an information model, the function that selects among alternative processing options.

requirements   customer-derived definitions of what is expected of an information chain or process.

special cause   in statistical quality control, a source of variation external to the process.

spurious-operational change   in data tracking, a change in a data value that indicates an error somewhere in the information chain.

stable (process)   an information chain or process in a state of control. See "control."

statistical quality control (SQC) (also called statistical process control [SPC])   a technique for measuring information chain or process performance, determining whether special causes are present, and taking appropriate action.

store   in an information model, the functions that save data, usually in a database.

subprocess   an internal step of a process.

timeliness   a measure of the degree to which an information chain or process is completed within a prespecified date or time.

tracked record   in data tracking, a data record tagged during the first step of an information chain or process for further analysis.

translation matrix   in understanding customer needs, a matrix used to map subjective customer requirements into technical specifications.

translational change   in data tracking, a change in data that results from language differences between subsequent processes.

transmit   in an information model, the function that sends, delivers, or moves data.

value (data)   in a datum, the element that specifies the member of the domain assigned to the <entity, attribute> pair.

view (conceptual)   a model of the real world to be captured in data.

About the Author

Thomas C. Redman, Ph.D., is President of the Navesink Consulting Group, based in Rumson, New Jersey. Navesink helps organizations improve their data and information, thereby improving decision making, increasing customer satisfaction, and lowering cost. Prior to forming Navesink in 1995, he led data work in AT&T's Chief Information Office, where he was responsible for defining and coordinating AT&T's data program. For several years, he led the Data Quality Lab and consulting practice at AT&T Bell Labs. There he consulted with clients both inside and outside AT&T and defined the data quality research program that produced many of today's methods for improving data quality. Prior to beginning work on data quality in 1987, he worked at Bell Labs and Bell Communications Research on (telephone) network performance. He holds a Ph.D. in Statistics from Florida State University (1980) and is the author of *Data Quality: Management and Technology* (Bantam, 1992) and roughly two dozen papers. He holds one patent. Thomas Redman can be reached at Tomredman@aol.com.

Index

The Artech House Computer Science Library

ISBN: 0-89006-717-1   *Wireless: The Revolution in Personal Telecommunications,*
Ira Brodsky

ISBN: 0-89006-740-6   *X Window System User's Guide,* Uday O. Pabrai

For further information on these and other Artech House titles, contact:

Artech House
685 Canton Street
Norwood, MA 02062
617-769-9750
Fax: 617-769-6334
Telex: 951-659
email: artech@artech-house.com

Artech House
Portland House, Stag Place
London SW1E 5XA England
+44 (0) 171-973-8077
Fax: +44 (0)171-630-0166
Telex: 951-659
email: artech-uk@artech-house.com

WWW: http://www.artech-house.com